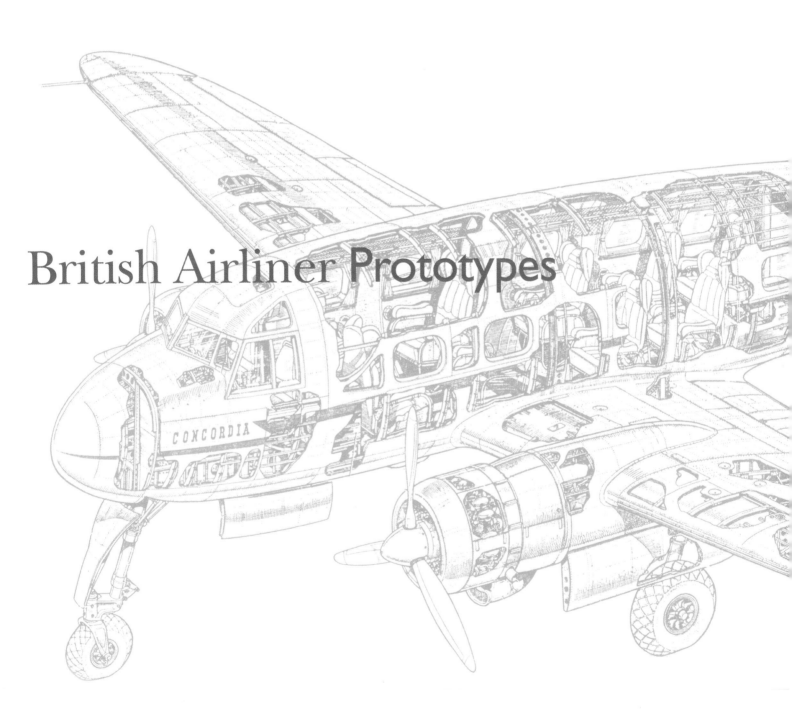

British Airliner Prototypes

British Airliner

Prototypes

since 1945

BRISTOL BRITANNIA 101

MIDLAND

An imprint of
Ian Allan Publishing

STEPHEN SKINNER

The Author - Stephen Skinner

British Airliner Prototypes since 1945 is Stephen Skinner's fifth aviation book. He has also written a large number of aviation articles and regularly reviews book for the Royal Aeronautical Society. Earlier titles include *BAC One-Eleven-the Whole Story*; *Marshall of Cambridge*; *BAe 146/RJ – Britain's Last Airliner* and *Wisley - The Story of Vickers' Own Airfield*. Stephen lives in Bishop's Stortford, Hertfordshire.

Acknowledgements

I would like to take this opportunity to thank the following for the help they have granted me in the compilation and writing of this book.

John Allam, John Battersby (Bristol Aero Collection), Peter Berry, Howard Betts, Malcolm Brazier, Brian Burrage, David Cheek (GKN), Alex Christie, Derek Ferguson, Harry Fraser-Mitchell (Handley Page Association), Mike Fielding (BAE SYSTEMS), David Gibbings, Barry Guess (BAE SYSTEMS), Ken Haynes, Mike Hooks (Aeroplane), George Jencks (Avro Heritage), David McIntosh (Hawker Archive), Mike Phipp, Brian Riddle (Librarian, RAeS), Paul Robinson, Peter Rushby, Graham Simons (GMS Enterprises), Frank Skinner, Harry Stripe, Rolando Ugolini, Ray Williams, Jack Woods, Allan Wright (Britten Norman Historians).

If there is anyone I have overlooked then the oversight is unintentional.

Special thanks

I would also like to thank my wife, Jane, for her continued support, encouragement and editorial contribution.

British Airliner Prototypes
© 2008 Stephen Skinner

ISBN (13) 978 1 85780 299 3

Produced by Chevron Publishing Limited
Project Editors: Chevron Publishing Limited
Cover and book design: Mark Nelson
© Colour profiles: Rolando Ugolini

Published by Midland Publishing
4 Watling Drive, Hinckley, LE10 3EY, England
Tel: 01455 254 490   Fax: 01455 254 495
E-mail: midlandbooks@compuserve.com

Midland Publishing is an imprint of
Ian Allan Publishing Ltd

Worldwide distribution (except North America):
Midland Counties Publications
4 Watling Drive, Hinckley, LE10 3EY, England
Telephone: 01455 254 450   Fax: 01455 233 737
E-mail: midlandbooks@compuserve.com
www.midlandcountiessuperstore.com

North American trade distribution:
Specialty Press Publishers & Wholesalers Inc.
39966 Grand Avenue, North Branch, MN 55056, USA
Tel: 651 277 1400   Fax: 651 277 1203
Toll free telephone: 800 895 4585
www.specialtypress.com

Printed in England by Ian Allan Printing Ltd
Riverdene Business Park, Molesey Road,
Hersham, Surrey, KT12 4RG

Visit the Ian Allan Publishing website at:
www.ianallanpublishing.com

MIDLAND
An imprint of
Ian Allan Publishing

CONTENTS

VICKERS VISCOUNT

FOUR ROLLS-ROYCE DART PROPELLER TURBINE ENGINES

I N this book I have identified all fixed-wing airliner prototypes built by British-owned firms intended for passenger-carrying service which were flown after 1 January 1945 from the territory of the United Kingdom of Great Britain and Northern Ireland. Helicopters have been excluded with the exception of the Fairey Rotodyne which was a compound helicopter with both fixed and rotary wings.

I have interpreted the term "airliner" to refer to a civil aircraft with two or more engines designed to carry ten or more passengers. The selection also includes the Hawker Siddeley / BAe 125 for although it is not strictly an airliner it is engaged in the carriage of passengers and the maximum capacity of most of its marks exceeds ten.

Where no aircraft were designated as prototypes, I have described the first aircraft built that served this purpose. It has been my intention to be as inclusive as possible and identify all appreciable developments of a type, for example for the Comet, all the marks including the three Comet 4 variants.

I have excluded types that were not prototypes but used as engine testbeds, such as the Vickers Nene-Viking. Similarly, aircraft used only as demonstrators, military versions of civil types, or civilianised versions of wartime types have not been included in this book.

Stephen Skinner
May 2008

What is a prototype?

IN the pioneering years of aviation a prototype was not built on a production line but possibly assembled at an experimental hangar and then, if the aircraft showed promise after testing, production would start. This was still the case to some extent after the end of the Second World War when both the Vickers Viscount and Armstrong Whitworth Apollo followed this model.

With the need to cut costs and speed up the production process in an increasingly competitive world, this approach became much less usual and there was much greater emphasis on ground testing with specialist rigs built to test various functions of the aircraft. Production would begin, the first example would fly as the prototype from the production line and soon it would be followed into the air by further examples of the type.

Sometimes firms referred to the initial aircraft as a prototype and this was owned by the manufacturer; for example the Vickers VC10 (G-ARTA). In other instances there was more than one prototype, as with the Avro 748 where there were two initial prototypes (G-APZV and G-ARAY). Handley Page went even further with the Jetstream and had four (G-ATXH-K). In contrast, with the Hawker Siddeley Trident there were no official prototypes; all the aircraft were destined for specific customers and were eventually delivered to them at the end of testing.

It is not only the prototype or prototypes that are engaged in testing as invariably some production aircraft are also used in the flight test programme. For example, following the tragic loss of the prototype BAC One-Eleven G-ASHG (see page 186), seven of the initial production aircraft played some part in testing.

Following completion of the test programme these production aircraft were refurbished and delivered to British United Airways and Braniff International.

The prototype may be kept by the manufacturer or may be brought up to production standard and enter airline service, as for instance with the first VC10, G-ARTA. Alternatively it may remain with the manufacturer and later be unceremoniously scrapped as the cost of incorporating all the modifications necessary for airline service may be prohibitive. Those British airliners that made appreciable sales, i.e. the Viscount, 748 and 146/RJ, had a number of prototypes and demonstration aircraft whose roles often overlapped. For instance, the Viscount 700 prototype G-AMAV and the Avro 748 Series 2 prototype G-ARAY were both heavily involved in development flying and were also powerful sales tools for their types.

Some prototypes stayed with firms throughout the development history of the respective aircraft and were heavily and continuously modified to test new developments. An excellent example of this process is G-ASYD, the BAC One-Eleven 400 Series development aircraft which went through very substantial metamorphoses; built initially as a 400 it was lengthened to become the 500 prototype and then reverted to its original length, though with many other changes, as the 475 prototype. It was later further refined as the one and only 670 prototype. There is a similar example with G-SSSH the BAe 146-100 and later 146-300 prototype (re-registered as G-LUXE) which after 19 years of testing and following a two year rebuild by the manufacturers, is now flying as an Atmospheric Research Aircraft.

The two Avro 748 Series 1 prototypes G-APZV and G-ARAY (nearest) in the air together on the occasion of the first flight of G-ARAY on 10 April, 1961. (Avro Heritage)

The Vickers Viscount 700 prototype G-AMAV. This aircraft had a short but busy testing and demonstrating career. (Author's collection)

What is the role of the prototype?

When the prototype is first rolled out of the hangar in what has in recent times become a media event, this is succeeded by several weeks, if not months, of ground testing of engines and systems.

Then follows the maiden flight which is normally flown with the minimum of crew in case of emergency (most prototypes have escape systems for their crew, who wear parachutes). First flights are usually carried out at light weight and mid-centre of gravity positions and provide an initial assessment of the aircraft's handling and systems.

Once the aircraft appears basically airworthy, tests are then embarked on at higher and higher weights through the centre of gravity range. These tests include stability and control, stalling and flutter, take-off and landing performance, flight with engine(s) inoperative and payload range assessment. Some of these tests, e.g. take-off and landing, may require the aircraft to be based in hot and/or high locations. All of the aircraft's

The interior of RJX85 prototype G-ORJX showing the cabin environment experienced by Flight Test Observers. Note the lack of interior furnishing, the test equipment and the rope hanging down to assist the crew to reach the right side front door in case of emergency. (BAE SYSTEMS)

A dramatic shot of G-WISC, the BAe 146-200 prototype, during trials to ensure that the engines would not ingest slush. This 146 remained with British Aerospace, later becoming G-BMYE and was scrapped at Filton, Bristol in 1995. (BAE SYSTEMS)

systems need to be tested to ensure that they continue to perform effectively in a punishing, high intensity airline environment over a sustained period. Assessments are also made of the internal and external noise of the aircraft.

In earlier times much testing was carried out in flight but post-war increasing use has been made of ground-testing and simulation. Even so, prototypes are fitted with instrumentation typically monitoring many different parameters, which has to be calibrated and engineered into the aircraft. The aircraft needs to have test equipment, to put the airframe, engines and systems through their paces and sometimes to simulate or induce failures.

Deficiencies in handling may make it necessary to adjust the prototype's shape. An obvious example of this is when a lack of directional stability indicates the need for more fin area. The Dove and Vanguard prototypes are examples of aircraft where a dorsal fin was added to counter this problem. Other examples of such additions, however, may be much less noticeable.

Prototypes generally have provision for emergency equipment, such as a stall recovery parachute at the tail, or crew escape chutes in case of dire emergency. The result is that they may be far from representative of in-service aircraft.

Certain prototypes, especially those that may be stretched to represent a later series, may be no more than aerodynamic representatives of the type. New systems will be installed on later aircraft and trials of these can only be carried out on the fully repre-sentative aircraft.

Prototypes fly very few hours in contrast to airliners in service, as modifications are made and trialled which may then impact on other aspects of the aircraft's operation. After the aircraft has entered service, trials will continue to improve performance and win sales against potential competition.

Post-war airliner development in Britain

The Brabazon Committee
In the midst of the war, in December 1942, the Brabazon Committee (named after its Chairman Lord Brabazon) first met to evaluate and advise on the types of airliner Britain would need post-war.

In the short-term, wartime bomber designs were converted in a rudimentary fashion for civilian operations. Thus the Avro Lancaster begat the Lancastrian and from the Handley Page Halifax came the Halton.

The Vickers Viking which flew in June 1945 used elements of the Wellington bomber but proved its worth and earned appreciable sales success. The Handley Page Hermes was a similar by-product of the Halifax but in this case only twenty-five entered airline service.

The Brabazon Committee continued to meet between August 1943 and November 1945 and recommended the following types:

Type	Specification	Aircraft
1	Long-range piston-engined	Bristol Brabazon
2A	Short-range piston-engined	Airspeed Ambassador
2B	Short-range turboprop	Vickers Viscount
2B	Short-range turboprop	Armstrong Whitworth Apollo
3A	Medium-range turboprop	Avro 693
3B	Medium-range piston-engined	Avro Tudor (replaced Avro 693)
4	Transatlantic turbojet	de Havilland Comet
5A	Feeder-liner piston-engined	Miles Marathon
5B	Feeder-liner piston-engined	de Havilland Dove

Unfortunately, the Committee became known for some rather spectacular failures which tended to overshadow the successful designs that were the result of its deliberations. The Vickers Viscount and de Havilland Dove proved to be very successful and made substantial sales, remaining in production until the

A view of just part of the static display at Farnborough 1949 with many types on view including the following prototypes: Comet 1 G-ALVG, Viscount 630 G-AHRF, Hermes 5 G-ALEU, Apollo G-AIYN, Marathon 2 G-AHXU and Bristol Freighter G-18-2. (BAE SYSTEMS)

G-ASGA taking off from Wisley in Surrey with a spare engine pod under the right wing and anti-spin parachute container fitted under the extreme tail. 'SGA also had an escape chute fitted to allow the crew to parachute out of the aircraft in an emergency. (BAE SYSTEMS)

The sole Bristol Brabazon G-AGPW with G-AIMF an example of the very successful Bristol Freighter. (Bristol Aero Collection)

1960s. The de Havilland Comet definitely deserved to succeed but failed due to the problem of metal fatigue, which caused a lengthy hiatus in production. The huge Bristol Brabazon and attractive Apollo were never developed beyond the prototype stage while both the Avro Tudor and the Miles Marathon entered series production but were beset by performance problems. The Airspeed Ambassador's development was delayed and its potential overtaken with the advent of the turboprop Viscount.

But for all the Brabazon Committee's deliberations, other civil aircraft were also constructed which surprisingly were outside its remit: most notably the huge Princess flying boat, constructed by Saunders-Roe, which went ahead before the realisation that the era of the flying boat had passed. Shorts also persevered with flying boats but in a more conservative fashion by developing its Sunderland into the Short Solent.

On an altogether smaller scale, Percival developed the 8-12 seat Prince which was moderately successful as a military communications aircraft, while Cunliffe-Owen flew the similar-sized Concordia which received no orders and the firm went bankrupt.

After the Brabazon Committee

Following the development of the Brabazon types, the prevailing attitudes of the 'dirigiste' wartime years continued with the Government taking the view that Britain needed a strong aviation industry and that airliners should serve with either British European Airways (BEA) or British Overseas Airways Corporation (BOAC). The Government almost invariably gave

financial assistance to the manufacturers, which was to be repaid by a levy on sales. Under these conditions the Bristol Britannia, and even later the de Havilland Trident and Vickers VC10, were born.

The Britannia flew in 1952 and should have sold well but was crippled by engine-icing problems which delayed service until 1957. The economical Vanguard turboprop came into being in 1959 in an age seduced by jets and lost the manufacturer a great deal of money. Unwisely, de Havilland shrank its three-jet Trident to suit BEA's whim which made it too small for world markets, where it was massively outsold by the Boeing 727. The VC10, a late entry into the trans-Atlantic jet market, was built for BOAC yet they virtually rejected it, which crippled its sales potential.

Britain's entries in the Dakota replacement market came first from the Scottish Aviation Twin Pioneer which should have succeeded with its phenomenal airfield performance, but did serve in quantity with the RAF. It was followed by the Handley Page Herald which won no sales in a four piston-engine form so was re-engined with twin Darts in 1958 and finally 50 were produced. In contrast its major competitor, the very successful Avro 748 flew in 1960 and 380 were built. In 1957 Aviation Traders, which was not an established aircraft manufacturer but an aircraft maintenance firm, produced the Accountant for the same market. However, as the firm lacked the wherewithal to establish production, the project soon withered.

Aircraft industry grouping 1960 - 1977

By the late 1950s the Conservative Government recognised that Britain's aircraft industry was long overdue for consolidation in order to avoid wasteful competition and to better manage resources.

To encourage the various companies to merge the Government announced its intention to only fund work for those manufacturers which had agreed to do so. As a result two major airframe manufacturers were formed, British Aircraft Corporation (BAC) and Hawker Siddeley Aviation (HSA). Handley Page failed to join either of the groups while Shorts in Belfast was a special case as it was a nationalised concern. Two major aero-engine manufacturers, Bristol Siddeley and Rolls-Royce, emerged and all UK helicopter work was centralised under Westland. As a result the remarkable Fairey Rotodyne which had the potential to revolutionise city centre to city centre travel with its vertical take off and high speed cruise, passed to Westland but then fell victim to Government cuts.

BAC came into being in January 1960 when the Boards of Vickers-Armstrongs, English Electric and Bristol Aircraft agreed to set up a joint company. In May, 1960 the first act of the new Corporation was to buy the aircraft interests of the Hunting Group. The first project of this grouping was the BAC One-Eleven, a jet Viscount replacement which at the time of its first flight in August 1963 had received 60 orders and its future looked bright. However, although very profitable to BAC, development was too slow and the One-Eleven was massively outsold by the Douglas DC-9 and Boeing 737.

Hawker Siddeley Aviation had existed as a loose grouping since 1935 when Hawker took control of Avro and Armstrong Whitworth. In 1959, Folland Aircraft was acquired, followed by de Havilland Aircraft Company and Blackburn Aircraft in 1960. Prior to the full incorporation of de Havilland into Hawker Siddeley, work started in 1960 on the 125 executive jet replacement for the Dove, which flew in 1962 and soon became very successful.

In 1963 Shorts had flown a small utilitarian design, the Skyvan, which sold well to both civil and military markets. The Skyvan was substantially lengthened to become the SD 330 airliner, which was further developed as the SD 360. The total number of Skyvans and 330 / 360 derivatives built was a surprising 454, exceeding the Viscount's 444.

Seemingly left out in the cold by the Government, Handley Page realised it could only develop a smaller type and set to work on a 19-seater turboprop airliner, the Jetstream. Handley Page ran into financial difficulties and collapsed before the Jetstream had made its mark. Fortunately the airliner was taken on by Scottish Aviation for production for the RAF and this led to its later relaunch as the Jetstream 31 under the nationalised British Aerospace.

One other manufacturer which had none of the pedigree of these other great names was Britten-Norman. It flew the 10-seater STOL Islander in 1965, which proved an immediate success and was later developed into the Trislander. Although the firm has been through many changes of ownership it remains in existence.

Through collaboration with France, supersonics seemed to offer the industry a great future. When Concorde flew in 1969 it proved a technical triumph;

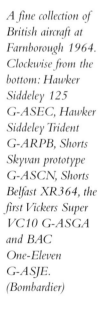

A fine collection of British aircraft at Farnborough 1964. Clockwise from the bottom: Hawker Siddeley 125 G-ASEC, Hawker Siddeley Trident G-ARPB, Shorts Skyvan prototype G-ASCN, Shorts Belfast XR364, the first Vickers Super VC10 G-ASGA and BAC One-Eleven G-ASJE. (Bombardier)

of both models were determinant on the exceedingly volatile American market and in 1997 BAe ceased production of both aircraft.

The Avro 748, which achieved 380 sales, had been a stalwart of Hawker Siddeley and was superseded by the BAe ATP in 1986. However when BAe entered a marketing consortium for regional aircraft with Aérospatiale of France and Alenia of Italy in 1995, production ceased after only 65 had been manufactured.

By the late 1990s the only remaining British airliner in production was the Avro RJ, a development of the BAe 146 which had carved out a useful niche for itself because of its quietness and ability to operate into restricted airports. BAe decided on a further revamp of this airliner as the Avro RJX, but after two prototype RJXs had flown and the test programme had progressed well, the manufacturer decided in November 2001 to totally withdraw from civil airliner manufacturing.

For a time it appeared that BAE SYSTEMS (as BAe had become in 1999) would continue to maintain its profitable 20 per cent investment in Airbus, which involved the manufacture of wings for all Airbus models – but in 2006 even that was sold off to EADS, the owners of Airbus.

In the 21st century there appears to be no immediate likelihood of any more British-built airliners and no more prototypes.

Noses of British types at Filton in 1982. From the back: Vickers VC10 K2, ZA141 (formerly BOAC's G-ARVG), BAC One-Eleven prototype 475 G-ASYD, Hawker Siddeley 125 G-AVPE and Concorde pre-production prototype G-BBDG. (BAE SYSTEMS)

but it became a commercial failure, for only 20 were built – including three British and three French prototypes.

Although collaboration worked with Concorde, in April 1969 the Government decided to withdraw from the European Airbus project at a time when the UK held the same 37.5 per cent stake in the programme as France. Fortunately Hawker Siddeley remained in the programme on a private basis and, after a series of complex negotiations, British Aerospace rejoined the programme in 1978 with a smaller 20 per cent share. Shortly after the original Airbus decision, in December 1970 the Government also decided not to support the BAC Three-Eleven, a 245-seat wide-body twin jet airliner, which spelt the end of independent large airliner development by the British Aircraft industry.

British Aerospace

The short-lived nationalisation of the aircraft industry from 1977 to 1981 created British Aerospace (BAe), which incorporated BAC, HSA and Scottish Aviation. The new conglomerate examined the available civil projects and revived both the Jetstream and the BAe 146, originally a cancelled Hawker Siddeley project.

The 125 executive jet underwent considerable development and weathered the vagaries of a volatile market. However, in 1993 BAe sold the 125 programme to Raytheon in the United States, which has continued to refine and develop the aircraft and under whom strong sales have continued to be achieved.

The Jetstream 31 proved successful and was substantially developed by British Aerospace, at Prestwick in Scotland, as the Jetstream 41. However the sales

Two prototypes at BAe Woodford, Cheshire. BAe 146-300 G-LUXE and (nearer) Jetstream 41 G-GCJL fitted with a dummy Satcom antenna and search radome for trials for the Hong Kong Government Flying Service Jetstreams. (Derek Ferguson)

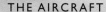

Avro Tudor

The Tudor 1 prototype G-AGPF first flew without markings from Manchester Ringway, the site of Avro's Experimental Department during the war years, on 14 June 1945. 'GPF had only a short life and was used mainly for trials but did serve in the Berlin Airlift in 1948-49. Following the decision to curtail the Tudor programme it was scrapped at Woodford in 1950. (Avro Heritage)

BY late autumn 1943 it was evident to the Brabazon Committee that a 'stop-gap' airliner would be needed for trans-Atlantic routes until the projected Bristol Brabazon, Comet and Avro 693 (later cancelled) were available. A specification was accordingly issued to Avro in March 1944 calling for an airliner capable of carrying 12 passengers in liner-style luxury over 4,000 miles. Initial designs were based on the Lincoln bomber incorporating a new pressurised fuselage, but as the aircraft developed it became virtually a new type and schedules slipped. BOAC was heavily involved in the process of design and refinement and the many alterations it requested severely hindered production.

Tudor 1, 4 and 8

The first Tudor 1 flew in June 1945 but flight trials revealed serious aerodynamic problems: poor directional and longitudinal stability (for which a larger fin, rudder and tailplane were fitted); pre-stall wing buffeting (cured by aerodynamic refinement) and landing bounce (solved by a shortened undercarriage); and range 10 per cent below specification.

After examining the prototype aircraft in February 1946, BOAC required 343 modifications to be carried out but the Ministry of Civil Aviation judged that only 81 of these modifications were essential. The incorporation of these changes together with the other modifications necessary to reduce the aerodynamic problems played havoc with the production process.

In May 1947 BOAC rejected the Tudor on the grounds that it was incapable of operating a trans-Atlantic service. Production of the Tudor 1 ceased and it was decided that of those completed three should

become freighters, four should be converted into Tudor 4s with fuselages lengthened by six feet, while the remaining two Tudor 1s became VIP Ministerial transports as Tudor 3s (although these later became freighters). All the other Tudor 1s still being built were to be completed as Tudor 4s and six were delivered to the nationalised British South American Airways (BSAA).

The BSAA fleet of Tudors began to operate satisfactorily but within the space of twelve months, between January 1948 and January 1949, two Tudors were lost in the 'Bermuda Triangle'. Neither of these two accidents was ever explained and following this the Ministry of Civil Aviation relegated the Tudor to freight duties and the entire Tudor fleet was stripped of furnishing and pressurisation.

During the 1948-49 Berlin Airlift the aircraft at last had the opportunity to confound some of its critics and the seven Tudors employed achieved a remarkable record for load-carrying reliability, but at the cessation of the Airlift they were withdrawn from service and stored.

In September 1953 the Ministry of Civil Aviation agreed to the purchase of the remaining redundant Tudor 1s, 3s and 4s by Aviation Traders and these were extensively modified. Most were reconverted to a passenger configuration, with some remaining in use until 1959.

The world's first four-engined jet airliner

The second prototype Tudor 1 G-AGST underwent a major metamorphosis to become Britain's first four jet transport. During this process it was lengthened to Tudor 4 dimensions and its piston Rolls-Royce Merlins

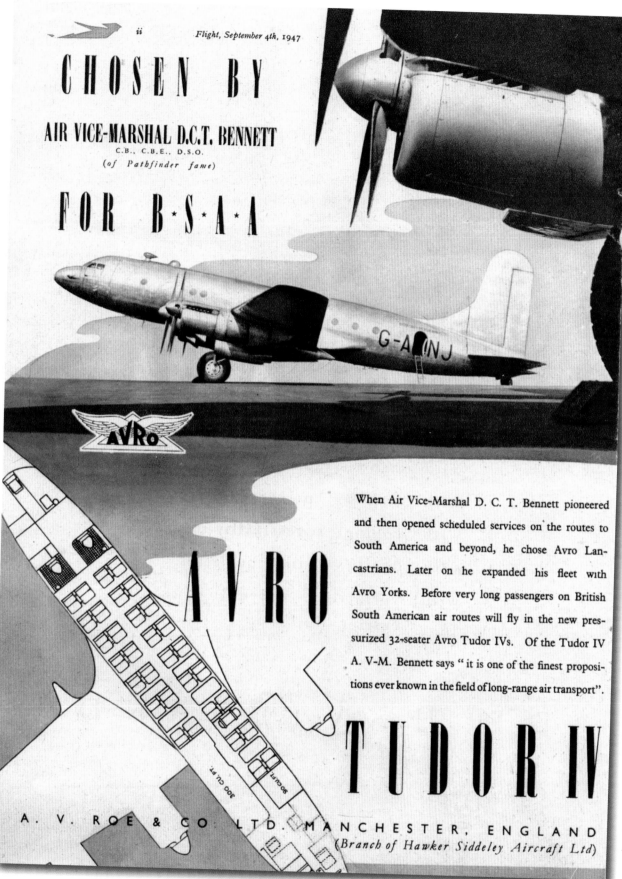

An advertisement from February 1947 depicting the first Tudor 4 G-AHNJ with a recommendation from BSAA's General Manager Air-Vice Marshall Bennett. (Flight)

were replaced by 5,000 lb thrust Nene turbojets in twin nacelles under a new wing. This jet Tudor development proved a useful tool but emphasised the need for tricycle undercarriages on jet aircraft as the tailwheel layout resulted in damage to taxiways and runways.

Building on this experience, six redundant Tudor 2 fuselages were utilised in a similar configuration to the Tudor 8 but fitted with a tricycle landing gear to produce the Avro Ashton which were to be employed as engine, navigational and bombing test beds.

The second Tudor 1 prototype flew as a conventional piston-engined aircraft on 19 June 1946. However it was substantially reconfigured and flew on 6 September 1948 as VX195 with a fuselage of Tudor 4 dimensions and new wings with four 5,000 lb Rolls-Royce Nene jets in paired nacelles. (Avro Heritage)

Advertisement for the Tudor 2. (Mike Phipp)

Tudor 2, 5, 6 and 7

While the Tudor 1 was intended as a long-distance transport, the Tudor 2 was designed to carry a larger load of up to 60 passengers over shorter distances, suitable for Empire routes with frequent refuelling stages. The Tudor 2 fuselage was 1 ft wider and 26 ft longer but all other features were common to the Tudor 1. Two prototypes were ordered in August 1944 followed by a contract for 30 production machines, soon increased to 85, then decreased to 50 and reduced in 1948 to only 18. The prototype G-AGSU flew in March 1946 but was found to suffer most of the aerodynamic troubles encountered by the Mark 1. After four months of trials it was clear that performance was below the desired figures and the weight much greater.

In an attempt to rectify performance shortfalls, the first production machine was fitted with Bristol Hercules engines providing 1,750 hp and replacing the Rolls-Royce Merlins. This was designated as a Tudor 7. Following tests it was determined that the Mk. 7 performance was no better than the Mk. 2 and production plans were cancelled. As a result of these shortcomings, BOAC cancelled its order and the aircraft originally allotted to it were transferred to BSAA. To meet BSAA requirements the Tudor 2s were fitted out as 44-seaters and redesignated as Tudor 5s. At the time of the Berlin blockade these Tudor 5s were stripped of their furnishing and used as tankers, where they carried out sterling service. The Tudor 6 designation was reserved for the Argentine airline FAMA but was never built. Like the Tudor 1 variants a number of the Tudor 2s and 5s continued to serve with charter operators until the late 1950s.

The Tudor is a sorry tale, particularly since Avro had been so successful with the Lancaster. Following the death of Roy Chadwick, the Tudor's designer, in the Tudor 2 prototype crash and its final rejection by BOAC, the Managing Director of Avro, Sir Frank Dobson, determined that development of the aircraft should end and many Tudors, both complete and incomplete, were scrapped at Woodford.

Prototypes

Avro Tudor 1 prototype 1
G-AGPF (c/n 1234)
Avro's Chief Test Pilot, Bill Thorn, made the first flight of the Tudor from Manchester Ringway (Avro's Experimental Department base 1939-46) on 14 June 1945. Although allocated the registration TT176 it flew devoid of any markings. The following four flights were flown from Ringway until relocation to Avro's nearby airfield at Woodford. The prototype was then on show at the RAE Farnborough Display on 29 October 1945 as TT176. From April 1946 it was based at A&AEE Boscombe Down for official trials by the Civil Aviation Testing Squadron (CATS) registered as TT176. Restored as G-AGPF it served in the Berlin Airlift (1948-49). Re-registered as VX192 to the Ministry of Supply, it returned to Woodford to be converted to the

prototype Tudor 4C but was scrapped in December 1950.

Avro Tudor 2 prototype 1
G-AGSU (c/n 1235)
The Tudor 2 prototype first flew at Woodford on 10 March 1946 piloted by Bill Thorn and after four months of company trials then went to the A&AEE Boscombe Down on 23 July for more tests. In September 1946 it returned to Avro for extension of the inner nacelles and the larger fin and rudder.

This prototype crashed shortly after take-off from Woodford on 23 August 1947. The aircraft climbed to 50-80 ft, whereupon the right wingtip struck the ground and the aircraft crashed into trees, coming to rest in a pond, killing four of the six on board including Roy Chadwick, Avro's Chief Designer. The cause of the crash was incorrect assembly of the aileron control circuit.

Avro Tudor 1 prototype 2
G-AGST (c/n 1249)
The second Tudor prototype made its first flight piloted by Bill Thorn on 19 June 1946. Almost immediately it returned to the factory to be modified as the sole Tudor 8 VX195 with a lengthened Tudor 4 fuselage and new wings with four 5,000 lb Rolls-Royce Nene jets in paired nacelles but still maintaining its tailwheel configuration. It flew a first flight of 69 minutes piloted by Jimmy Orrell (Bill Thorn's replacement as Chief Test Pilot) on 6 September 1948 and was delivered directly to Boscombe Down. Orrell then demonstrated it at the

Roy Chadwick, Avro's Chief Designer, tragically died when the Tudor 2 G-AGSU crashed at Woodford on 23 August 1947. He is particularly remembered for designing the Avro Lancaster bomber, its successor the Avro Lincoln and preliminary designs of the Avro Vulcan bomber. (Avro Heritage)

The Tudor 2 prototype G-AGSU first flew from Avro's Woodford airfield on 10 March 1946 piloted by Bill Thorn. (Brian Burrage)

The site of the crash of G-AGSU on 23 August 1947 just beyond Woodford airfield. The crash was caused by incorrect assembly of the aileron linkage and took the lives of four of the six on board including Avro's Chief Designer, Roy Chadwick and Chief Test Pilot, Bill Thorn. (Avro Heritage)

Tudor 4 Prototype, G-AHNJ in British South American Airways livery as 'Star Panther'. (Avro Heritage)

The sole Tudor 7 G-AGRX was an attempt to rectify performance shortfalls of the type by replacing the Rolls-Royce Merlins with Bristol Hercules engines. Unfortunately the re-engining provided little improvement. (Avro Heritage)

The second prototype Tudor 2 G-AGRY operated by Airflight and photographed at Gatow, Berlin during the 1948-49 Berlin Airlift when land connections to West Berlin through Russian-occupied East Germany were closed and West Berlin had to be supplied by air. 'GRY was converted to a tanker and flew 421 sorties during the Airlift. (Author's collection)

Farnborough Air Show on 7-9 and 11 September. Tests at A&AEE Boscombe Down indicated that a nosewheel undercarriage was required as jet blast damaged the tail and airfield surfaces. The Tudor 8 was intended as a research vehicle and on 29 August 1949, while based at Woodford, it exceeded 40,000 ft. It was broken up at Farnborough in 1951.

Avro Tudor 4 prototype
G-AHNJ (c/n 1343)
Originally intended to be a Tudor 1, G-AHNJ was altered on the production line to become the Tudor 4 prototype and made its first flight on 9 April 1947. Trials followed at Boscombe Down from 28 June 1947 with

delivery to BSAA at Langley, Buckinghamshire on 18 July 1957 as 'Star Lion'. Flight trials in the West Indies commenced on 23 July and it returned to Avro for modifications in August. It was redelivered to BSAA as 'Star Panther' and flew the first service London - Lisbon - Santa Maria on 27 November 1947. It was grounded at Heathrow from February - March 1948 following the first BSAA Tudor loss and returned to service but was grounded again in January 1949 when the type's Certificate of Airworthiness was withdrawn. Initially 'HNJ was stored at Langley, then Hurn, near Bournemouth and it was dismantled for spares at Ringway in 1953.

Avro Tudor 7 prototype
G-AGRX (c/n 1261)

The Avro Tudor 7, fitted with Bristol Hercules engines instead of Merlins, flew on 17 April 1947 captained by Bill Thorn. Its first public appearances were at the Civil Aircraft Display at Farnborough in May 1947 and at the SBAC Show at Radlett, Hertfordshire in September. Following tests at A&AEE it was delivered to the Ministry of Supply on 3 December 1948 serialled VX199. In March 1949 it joined the Telecommunications Establishment at Defford, Worcestershire for trials. It was sold to Flight Refuelling as G-AGRX at Tarrant Rushton in November 1953 but in March 1954 was sold on to Aviation Traders for spares and was scrapped at Stansted in September 1959.

Data	Tudor 1	Tudor 2	Tudor 4
Length	79 ft 6 in	105 ft 7 in	85 ft 6 in
Wingspan	120 ft 0 in	120 ft 0 in	120 ft 0 in
Height	24 ft 0 in	24 ft 3 in	24 ft 0 in
MTOW	71,000 lb	80,000 lb	80,000 lb
Cruising speed	210 mph	235 mph	210 mph
Range	3,630 mls	2,330 mls	4,000 mls
Passengers	24	60	32

Tudor 3 dimensions and weights as Tudor 1
Tudor 5 dimensions and weights as Tudor 2
Tudor 7 dimensions and weights essentially as Tudor 2

Avro Tudor 2 prototype 2
G-AGRY (c/n 1262)

'GRY first flew with Jimmy Orrell at the controls on 11 November 1947. Following the loss of G-AGSU, G-AGRY was hurriedly developed to the equivalent modification state of 'GSU and flew to Boscombe Down as VX202. To further assess performance it embarked on tropical trials in Nairobi which proved unsatisfactory. It was purchased by Airflight Ltd in September 1948 for use in the Berlin Airlift during which it flew 421 sorties, initially as a freighter but later as a tanker. It was transferred to Fairflight in July 1949 and later to Air Charter which used it on trooping flights as XF537. It was withdrawn from use in September 1954 and finally scrapped at Stansted in July 1959

Powerplant:
Tudor 1, 2, 4 & 5 – 4 x 1,740 hp Rolls-Royce Merlin 621
Tudor 7 – 4 x 1,715 hp Bristol Hercules 120

Production:
Tudor 1: 10 (including 1 converted to a Tudor 8)
Tudor 3: 2
Tudor 4: 10
Tudor 2: 4
Tudor 5: 6
Tudor 7: 1

Total built: 33 (1 at Ringway, 32 at Woodford)

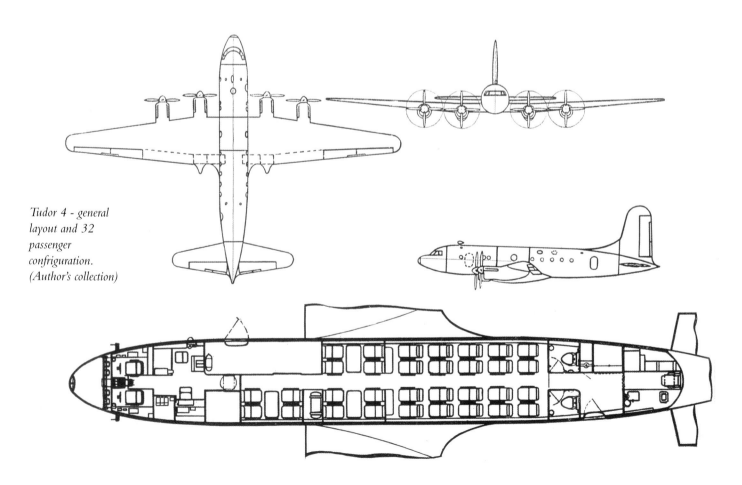

Tudor 4 - general layout and 32 passenger confriguration. (Author's collection)

Vickers Viking

'Stop-gap' design

ANTICIPATING an end to hostilities and the slump in military aircraft orders, in 1944 Vickers-Armstrongs began design work on the VC1 (Vickers Commercial 1) under the leadership of Rex Pierson, the company's Chief Designer. The Ministry of Aircraft Production, aware that the Brabazon Committee designs would not be in service until the late 1940s or later, agreed in October 1944 to the development of an interim passenger transport design which could provide a better payload than the Dakota. A contract for three prototypes was issued.

'Stop-gap' design
As a 'stop-gap' design the twin-engined short-range VC1 employed the Wellington bomber's fabric-clad geodetic wings and the Warwick's tail surfaces, but it had a new stressed-skin metal fuselage. It was powered by two Bristol Hercules engines and had a tailwheel undercarriage. Its dimensions were similar to the Dakota but it had 40 per cent more engine power.

Vickers developed the Viking (as it was now named) with great alacrity and in less than a year after the finalisation of the design, on 22 June 1945 the first prototype G-AGOK flew. This was quickly followed by the other two prototypes and all three were allocated to development flying. A Certificate of Airworthiness for the Viking was awarded on 24 April 1946. The Ministry of Aircraft Production had placed an order for 50 earlier in April and the third prototype (G-AGOM) and first production aircraft were loaned to the BOAC Development Flight at Hurn. British European Airways was established from the European Division of BOAC on 1 August 1946 and one month later operated its first Viking service with G-AHOP.

Production aircraft
The initial nineteen production aircraft (excluding the prototypes) became Viking 1A with accommodation for 21 passengers and more powerful 1,690 hp Bristol Hercules 630s than the prototypes' Hercules 130s. In the next fourteen examples, known as the Viking 1, the fabric wings outboard of the engines were replaced by metal wings and tail surfaces. All later Vikings followed suit and the fabric elements were also exchanged on most of the earlier Viking 1As. To take advantage of uprated Bristol Hercules piston engines, the Viking 1B was introduced, which was 28 in longer and could carry 24-27 passengers.

In addition to BEA's requirement, the Viking was sold extensively and ordered by Aer Lingus, the Argentine Air Force, Airwork, Central African Airways, Danish Air Lines, Hunting-Clan, Indian National Airways, Iraqi Airways, the RAF and the RAF King's Flight, South African Airways and Tradair. In their early years Vikings also flew long-range routes for Central African Airways on the London - Salisbury (Harare) services, although this included a number of overnight stops.

In 1952 BEA reconfigured its Viking 1Bs with passenger accommodation increased to 36 and higher take-off weights. However, during 1954 the last of the airline's Vikings were withdrawn as they were superseded by pressurised Ambassadors and Viscounts.

The world's first jet airliner
One Viking 1B (G-AJPH) has a remarkable claim to fame. During manufacture it was modified to receive two Rolls-Royce Nene jet engines instead of the Bristol

G-AGOK about to take off on its maiden flight from Wisley captained by Mutt Summers on 21 June 1945. Note the Vickers Warwick GR5 on the right of the photograph and a USAAF Douglas B-25 Mitchell in the background, which was adapted to take 'Highball' (bouncing bombs) for trials. (Aeroplane)

The first prototype Viking, G-AGOK, which crashed at Effingham on 23 April 1946 during single-engined handling trials and was written off. (Author's collection)

The first prototype Vickers Viking G-AGOK made its maiden flight on 22 June 1945 from Wisley. It crashed on 23 April 1946.

Hercules piston engines. With its first flight on 6 April 1948 from Wisley it became the world's first entirely jet-powered airliner. Mutt Summers made the maiden flight and on 25 July 1948 he flew it from Northolt to Villacoublay near Paris in 34 minutes 7 seconds. It was later converted to a Hercules-powered Mk. 1B and flew with Eagle Aircraft Services as G-AJPH from September 1954 until October 1961.

Conclusion

Production stopped at the end of 1947 after 166 Vikings had been manufactured. According to no less an

authority than Sir George Edwards – who became Chief Designer and Engineer of Vickers-Armstrongs Aircraft in 1948 and eventually Chairman of the British Aircraft Corporation in 1964 – Vickers lost money on the Viking as they were typically sold for £34,000 each which did not cover the cost of production. However the firm did capitalise on the design by developing it into the Valetta transport and Varsity trainer for the RAF of which 252 and 163 respectively were manufactured.

The polish on G-AGOL's fuselage, the second prototype Viking, contrasts well with its fabric-clad geodetic wings which were inherited from the Wellington. Later Vikings received conventional metal wings. The second and subsequent Vikings had larger tail fins than the first prototype. (Author's collection)

Prototypes

Vickers Viking 1A prototype 1
G-AGOK (c/n 101) Type 491

G-AGOK was built at Vickers Experimental Hangar at Foxwarren, Surrey and then transported to Wisley for final assembly. Engine runs were completed on 19 June 1945 and first flight was piloted by Mutt Summers on 22 June, with two subsequent flights on each of the two following days.

On 23 April 1946 'GOK belly-landed at nearby Effingham, fortunately without injury to the four-man crew. It had taken off from Wisley on single-engine handling trials. With the right engine shut down, the left suddenly failed and the crew were unable to restart the right one. The fuselage was returned to Wisley on 9 May, was written off on 11 May and transported to the MoD's weapons testing centre at Shoeburyness, Essex in January 1947.

Vickers Viking 1A prototype 2
G-AGOL (c/n 102) Type 495

Similarly to the first prototype 'GOL was built at Vickers Experimental Hangar at Foxwarren and then transported to Wisley for final assembly. The only major difference between 'GOK and 'GOL was greater fin area of the latter. Mutt Summers flew it at Wisley on 1 September, 1945 and it was then employed on the test programme. 'GOL was on show at the RAE Farnborough Display 29 October 1945. It was transferred to the RAE Farnborough as VX238 and then moved to RAF St Athan as 7215M in June 1955 and later scrapped.

Vickers Viking 1A prototype 3
G-AGOM (c/n 103) Type 496

First flown at Weybridge, Surrey on 19 November 1945 and loaned to the BOAC Development Unit at Hurn from 18 May 1946 until 3 June 1946. It then took military marks as VX141 and was employed by the BLEU (Blind Landing Experimental Unit) at Martlesham Heath, Suffolk and later at the RAE Bedford and broken up in March 1952.

Data	Viking Type 491 Mk. 1A	Viking Type 610 Mk. 1
Length	62ft 10 in	65ft 2 in
Wingspan	89ft 3 in	89ft 3 in
Height	19ft 7 in	19ft 7 in
MTOW	33,500 lb	34,000 lb
Cruising speed	210 mph	263 mph
Range	1,875 mls	1,700 mls
Passengers	21	24-27

Powerplant:
2 x 1,675 hp Bristol Hercules 130 (G-AGOK)
2 x 1,690 hp Bristol Hercules 634 (Viking 1B)

Production by type:
Viking 1a & 1: 48
Viking C Mk. 1 & 2: 12
Viking 1b: 113

Total built: 166 (3 at Wisley, 163 at Weybridge)

The final Viking prototype, G-AGOM, was the first to fly from Weybridge – its two predecessors had been built at Foxwarren and assembled at Wisley. 'GOM was used initially for training by BOAC at Hurn and later as VX141 was employed on blind landing trials. (Brian Burrage)

de Havilland Dove
and de Havilland Heron

de Havilland Dove

THE Dove was de Havilland's first post-war production airliner designed to conform to the Brabazon Committee's 5B specification. Constructed of metal, this low wing monoplane with a tricycle landing gear and reversible pitch braking propellers was a substantial departure from the DH Dragon Rapide it was designed to replace.

Work on the design under de Havilland's Chief Designer R. E. Bishop began in 1944, and the prototype G-AGPJ made its first flight just after the end of the war on 25 September 1945. During maker's trials a dorsal fin was added to improve directional stability and it was increased in size twice until a final satisfactory aesthetic and aerodynamic shape was achieved.

Dove developments

The development of the Dove was driven by the installation of increasingly powerful engines and correspondingly higher operating weights, yet its overall dimensions remained unchanged throughout the production run. Initial versions powered by the de Havilland 330 hp Gipsy Queen were the 7-11-seater Dove Mk. 1 and the executive 6-seater Mk. 2 which proved exceedingly popular with airlines and companies such as Vickers-Armstrongs, English Electric, David Brown, Short Brothers, Dunlop and Shell. Both the RAF and Royal Navy followed suit by ordering a military version of the Dove Mk. 4 known as the Devon. A number of foreign air forces including the Argentinian, Indian and RNZAF also operated Devons or Doves.

In 1953 the Dove Mk. 1 and 2 (many of which had been re-engined with 340 hp Gipsy Queens as Dove 1B

and 2B) were superseded by the Dove Mk. 5 airliner and Mk. 6 executive transport with twin 380 hp Gipsy Queen engines. These versions continued very successfully in production until 1960 when improved 400 hp Gipsy Queen engines led to the introduction of the final variants, the Dove Mk. 7 and Mk. 8 for the airline and executive markets. These two Marks had improved performance and also introduced the domed cockpit roof as fitted to the de Havilland Heron, a four-engined development of the Dove. The Dove saw use in many markets in the light transport role in both the civil and military field. Production continued until 1968.

After production had ceased, a number of aircraft were heavily modified by US aviation firms to further improve their performance and marketability. The Riley Aeronautics Corporation replaced the Gipsy Queens with Avco Lycoming engines and fitted a large swept tail. In 1966 this was topped by an even more substantial development when Carstedt introduced the Carstedt Jet Liner 600 fitted with 600 shp Garrett-AiResearch TPE331 turboprops and a lengthened fuselage with seating for 18 passengers.

Sales success

The de Havilland Dove, through its innovative design and ability to fill specific market needs, must be regarded as one of the successes of the Brabazon Committee. It made a large number of sales with a total of 582 aircraft constructed.

The de Havilland Dove prototype G-AGPJ being rolled out for weighing at Hatfield on 24 September 1945. Its tail fin and rudder and canopy is very reminiscent of the Mosquito. In the background are a Mosquito, two Hornets and a Dragon Rapide. (BAE SYSTEMS)

de Havilland company logo.

BAE SYSTEMS

G-AGPJ with an early development dorsal fillet, fitted to the tail fin. (BAE SYSTEMS)

The two Dove prototypes, G-AGPJ and G-AGUC at Hatfield. Both now have the production style dorsal fillet fitted. (BAE SYSTEMS)

G-AGPJ with the final fin and Test Pilot, Geoffrey Pike, who made the maiden flight, at the controls in the left-hand seat. (BAE SYSTEMS)

An evocative publicity shot of G-AGPJ. (BAE SYSTEMS)

The second and short-lived Dove prototype, G-AGUC, which flew on 17 June 1946 and was acquired by the BOAC Development Unit at Hurn but crashed on 14 August 1946. (BAE SYSTEMS)

Prototypes

de Havilland Dove 1 prototype 1
G-AGPJ (c/n 04000/P/1)

Geoffrey Pike made the first flight in the Dove at
Hatfield, Hertfordshire on 25 September 1945. After
handling trials at Farnborough the aircraft returned to
Hatfield in October to be fitted with a large dorsal fin.
This had to be increased in size and it was only in May
1946 that the final shape was decided. The aircraft was
loaned to the Ministry of Supply for type evaluation and
on 2 May 1946 was registered as WJ310. The Ministry
loaned WJ310 to Dunlop Aviation Division at Baginton,
Coventry in 1953 but it was badly damaged in 1954
when the nose leg broke off after rigorous braking trials
at nearby Honiley airfield. The aircraft left by road,
was rebuilt in 1954 and was sold to the Portuguese
Government as CR-CAC. On 14 June 1957 the Dove
prototype was reported as damaged beyond repair
at Santiago in the Cape Verde Islands.

de Havilland Dove 1 prototype 2
G-AGUC (c/n 04000/P/2)

The second prototype flew from Hatfield on 17 June
1946 and was acquired by the BOAC Development Unit

at Hurn. On 14 August 1946 it crashed at West Howe
near Hurn and was written off.

de Havilland Heron

The de Havilland Heron was an enlarged four-engined
version of the successful Dove, offering a rugged 14-17
seat airliner with Gipsy Queen 30 engines and a fixed
undercarriage for short to medium range services into
unsophisticated airfields. Like the Dove it was of all
metal construction with fabric covered control surfaces.

The prototype flew on 10 May 1950 and six months
later the type received its Certificate of Airworthiness.
Following the prototype, six Heron 1s were built at
Hatfield, followed by the prototype Heron 2 and then
production was transferred to de Havilland's Broughton
plant in Cheshire. On 14 December 1952 the Heron 2
took to the air, featuring a retractable undercarriage and
providing a 20 mph increase in cruising speed and
better fuel consumption. Of the 149 Herons built, 52
were Mk. 1s and the remainder Mk. 2s.

The first services were flown by Braathens in
Norway in August 1952. Herons rapidly spread around
the world operating in Australasia, South America, the
Middle and the Far East. They also flew with the Air

*The first Heron in
final assembly at
Hatfield in spring
1950. It flew
unpainted as
G-ALZL on
10 May 1950.
(Brian Burrage)*

The prototype de Havilland Heron 1, G-ALZL, appeared at the Farnborough Show in September 1951 in BEA colours.

The Heron 1 prototype, G-ALZL, wore many liveries and it appeared at the 1952 Farnborough Air Show in Japan Airlines colours. The Heron 1 had a fixed undercarriage but the Heron 2 benefited from a retractable landing gear. (BAE SYSTEMS)

Forces of West Germany, Ghana, Iraq, Jordan, Kuwait, Malaysia, Saudi Arabia, South Africa, Sri Lanka, the RAF (including the Queen's Flight) and the Royal Navy. Production of M.k 1 Herons ceased in April 1956 although the Mk. 2 Heron continued in production until May 1961.

In the United States, Jack Riley of the Riley Aeronautics Corporation, having re-engined and re-configured the Dove, also re-engined the Heron with 290 hp Lycomings to create the Riley Heron and, later, a turboprop-powered Riley Turbo Skyliner. In 1969 Saunders Aircraft of Manitoba carried out a far more extensive conversion by replacing the four piston engines with twin United Aircraft turboprops and altering the flight deck and cabin window shape.

The fuselage of 'LZL in 2006 at the RAAF Museum Western Australia, Bull Creek. De Havilland sold 'LZL in 1956 to Jersey Airlines and by 1973 it was flying in Western Australia. It made its last flight into Jandakot in May 1976 where it remained until January 1997, when the RAAF Association Aviation Heritage Museum of Western Australia acquired it and moved it to Bull Creek, Perth. (RAAF Museum Western Australia)

Prototypes

de Havilland Heron 1 prototype
G-ALZL (c/n 10903)

The prototype was built largely from existing components, including Dove outer wing panels, and Dove nose and tail units. On 10 May 1950 de Havilland Test Pilot, Geoffrey Pike, took the unpainted G-ALZL aloft on its first flight from Hatfield. It completed its first 100 hours flying daily demonstrations at the 1950 Farnborough Air Show. It was painted with a white fuselage top and a broad maroon cleat line. During testing the original straight tailplane was replaced with a dihedral tailplane and the cockpit roof reconfigured with a prominent bulge.

In November 1950 G-ALZL was based at Khartoum and then Nairobi for tropical trials. The following summer British European Airways trialled the Heron on its Scottish and Channel Island services in BEA colours, and it was then demonstrated at the September 1951 Farnborough Show. At the 1952 Farnborough display it appeared in Japan Air Lines' livery.

In April - May 1954 the Heron prototype was leased to Braathens and re-registered as LN-BDH. In July 1956 it was sold to Airlines (Jersey) which then sold it to Executive Air Transport in November 1962, which in turn leased it to Emerald Airways.

G-ALZL disappeared from the British register when Cimber Air of Denmark purchased it on 13 December 1966 and registered it as OY-DGS. In May 1973 it was sold to Altair of Jandakot Airport in Perth, Western Australia. Registered as VH-CJS it was chartered to WAPET (WA Petroleum) for flights from Jandakot to Barrow Island. In November 1974 the aircraft was repossessed after the bankruptcy of Altair. It was sold to Coveair in Adelaide at the beginning of 1975 but returned to Jandakot in December when it was leased by United Air Services to transport mine workers. In May 1976 the Heron flew into Jandakot on three engines, was parked and never flew again.

In January 1997 the RAAF Association Aviation Heritage Museum of Western Australia acquired the aeroplane and moved it to its museum complex in Bull Creek, Perth. Unfortunately the Museum does not have the resources to restore it and is looking for another Museum to take on this task.

de Havilland Heron 2 prototype
G-AMTS (c/n 140007)

First flown at Hatfield on 14 December 1952, it was demonstrated at Farnborough in 1953 and 1955. It was registered XL961 for Princess Margaret's tour of East Africa but reverted to DH as 'MTS on its return. The manufacturers sold it to Humber Ltd on 23 May 1960 but it crashed at Biggin Hill on 16 July 1961 with the loss of two lives.

Data	Dove 1 & 2	Dove 7 & 8	Heron 1
Length	39 ft 4 in	39 ft 4 in	48 ft 6 in
Wingspan	57 ft	57 ft	71 ft 6 in
Height	13 ft 4 in	13 ft 4 in	15 ft 7 in
MTOW	8,500 lb	8,950 lb	12,500 lbs
Cruising speed	165 mph	162 mph	163 mph
Range	1,000 mls	1,175 mls	805 mls
Passengers	8-11	8-11	14-17

Powerplant:

Dove 1 & 2 – 2 x 330 hp de Havilland Gipsy Queen 70-3
Dove 7 & 8 – 2 x 400 hp de Havilland Gipsy Queen 70
   Mk. 3
Heron 1 – 4 x 250 hp de Havilland Gipsy Queen 30

Total number of Doves built: 542 (298 at Hatfield, Hertfordshire 243 at Hawarden, Cheshire, 1 at Baginton, Coventry)

Total number of Herons built: 149 (8 at Hatfield, 141 at Hawarden)

Two views of the eighth Heron to be built, G-AMTS, the prototype Heron 2 which had the advantage of a retractable undercarriage. Following the completion of G-AMTS at Hatfield, production of the Heron was transferred to de Havilland's plant at Broughton – which thankfully still functions as an aircraft factory, as the site of all Airbus civil wing manufacture. (BAE SYSTEMS)

Bristol Freighter & Superfreighter

THE Bristol 170 Freighter / Wayfarer grew out of the need for a wartime military transport which could fly vehicles and supplies in and out of rough airstrips. In fact, although it served as an airliner and civil freighter, more than half of the initial deliveries were to the military.

Bristol's Chief Designer, Archibald Russell, conceived the Bristol 170 as a high-wing, twin-engined aircraft fitted with a fixed undercarriage well-suited to operators using small, rough airfields. The forward fuselage was fitted with clam-shell opening nose doors to provide for the loading and unloading of military trucks and hardware. To power the aircraft Bristol decided to install the tried and tested 1,670 hp Bristol Centaurus, which were built by the manufacturer's engine division.

While the requirement for a military transport was cancelled with the ending of hostilities, the Ministry of Supply still recognised the need for a rugged civil transport with 1,700 cu.ft capacity. The Ministry agreed to fund the manufacture of two prototypes and a substantial amount of the cost of production jigging, if Bristol would privately fund a further two prototypes. Thus an initial production batch of 25 was initiated at Filton, near Bristol.

Freighters and Wayfarers

The first Bristol 170 prototype G-AGPV took to the air on 2 December 1945 in the capable hands of Cyril Uwins OBE, AFC who was the firm's Chief Test Pilot for almost 30 years from 1918 until 1947. The second, third and fourth prototypes G-18-1, G-AGVC and G-AGUT joined the first in the air during 1946. Whereas the first and third prototypes were Bristol Freighter Mk. 1s with

nose freight doors and provision for freight or passengers, the other two were built as Bristol Wayfarers Mk. 2 with fixed noses and provision for airline style seating. Following evaluation at Boscombe Down the first prototype returned to Filton and was fitted with wider outer wings which increased the span to 108 ft and accordingly improved performance.

Following the manufacture of the prototypes, 44 Mk. 1s and 2s were delivered from Filton in 1946-47. Major customers included the Argentine Air Force Airwork, Australian National Airways, British American Air Services, Cie Air Transport, India National Airlines, Shell, and West African Airways Corporation.

Developments

G-AIFF flew with extended wingspan as the Mk. 11 in 1947 and in December 1947 was fitted with 1,690 hp Bristol Hercules 672s to become the prototype Mk. 21. This Mark proved a very successful combination which was in production from 1948 until 1953, and some Mk. 1s and 2s were upgraded to this configuration. One of the better known purchasers of the Mk. 21 (and later Marks) was Silver City Airways which trialled the aircraft on the Lympne - Le Touquet cross-Channel car service in 1948. With their clam-shell nose doors and strengthened floor able to accept vehicles or 4½ tons of cargo, they proved very successful in these operations.

Following the crashes of two Mk. 21s (including G-AIFF in May 1949) due to structural failure of the tail fin during an extreme-yaw single engined climb, a longer, stronger dorsal fin was specified, resulting in the Type 170 Mk. 31.

The prototype Mk. 31 – an upgraded G-AGVC – also featured Hercules 734 engines. Many earlier machines

The first Ministry of Supply owned Bristol Freighter Mk. 1 prototype G-AGPV which flew on 2 December 1945. As a freighter it had openable nose doors but, unlike later Bristol 170s, it initially had circular windows. (Brian Burrage)

Bristol

BAE SYSTEMS

33

G-AGVB – the first Bristol-owned 170 Wayfarer Mk. 2 prototype – fitted out to carry 32 passengers while on lease to Channel Island Airways in the latter part of 1946. The Channel Island Airways shield is visible on the nose. (Bristol Aero Collection)

"Bristol" Freighters on the Berlin Air-Lift

34 TONS IN ONE DAY

Conspicuous among many exceptional freighting operations carried out by "Bristol" Freighters on the Berlin Air-Lift is the impressive record of one day's work by G-AGVB. During eight to and fro journeys, this aircraft carried a total of 76,400 lbs. of mixed cargoes . . . a fine performance by a twin-engined aircraft and one which demonstrates the obvious advantages of using aircraft designed expressly for freight-carrying duties.

THE BRISTOL AEROPLANE COMPANY LIMITED ENGLAND

AGENT: N. E. HIGGS, CORRESPONDENCE, BOX NO. 1563, WELLINGTON, NEW ZEALAND.

G-AGVB was modified to a freighter configuration and operated by Silver City. It took part in the Berlin Airlift, when the Soviet Union closed road and rail links to West Berlin in 1948-49. This Bristol advertisement shows how on one day G-AGVB carried 34 tons over eight sectors. (Author's Collection)

were brought up to the Mk. 31 standard during overhaul. Besides the basic Mk. 31 Freighter, the Mk. 31E version was built to carry cars and passengers and the Mk. 31M Military Freighter was sold to many air forces.

Production ceased in March 1958, by which time the Mk. 31 had become the most successful of the Type 170 versions – in service in Britain, Australia, Burma, Canada, France, Lebanon, New Zealand, Pakistan and Spain.

The Superfreighter

A special Mk. 32 Superfreighter with 2,000 hp Hercules 734 engines was built for Silver City Airways which had the nose extended by 5 ft. This allowed the airline to offer a cross-Channel ferry service carrying 3 cars and 12 passengers or 2 cars and 23 passengers in a 73 ft 4 in long fuselage.

In total, 214 Bristol Type 170s were produced: 94 for civil operators; 116 for military service, while one was a test aircraft and three were written off prior to delivery.

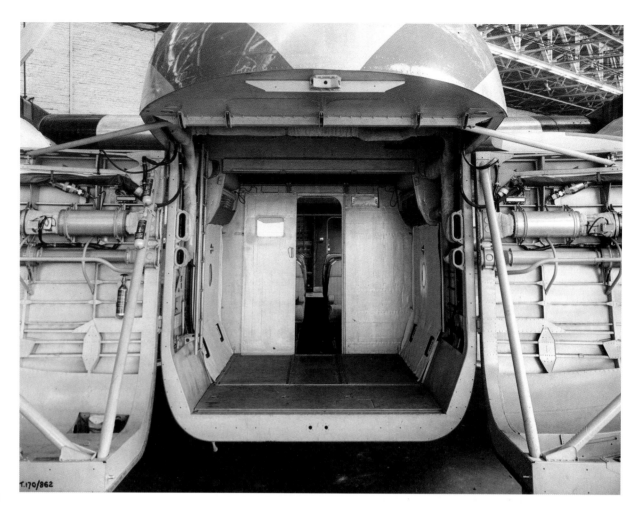

The internal layout of G-AGVB when it was employed on the Silver City Cross-Channel car ferry operations with a car deck at the front and passenger accommodation in the rear. (Author's collection)

Prototypes

37, Mark 1 prototype 1
G-AGPV (c/n 12730)

The prototype Bristol 170, the first Ministry of Supply-owned prototype, was a Freighter Mk. 1 with nose freight doors and provision for freight or passengers. The first flight took place on 2 December 1945 from Filton, piloted by CTP Cyril Uwins. Following its maiden flight the aircraft was returned to the hangars as it needed a major modification to the tailplane, which was lowered by 3 ft and its span increased by 4 ft.

From September to October 1946 it underwent official trials at A&AEE Boscombe Down registered as VR380. In 1946-47 it was converted to Wayfarer specification with square side windows and new rounded outer wingtips giving a span of 108 ft. As VR380 the prototype served until 1957, fitted with various experimental radar installations at the Telecommunications Research Establishment at Defford. It was bought by Shorts Aviation in November 1957 and two years later was sold to Skycraft Ltd and in

1960 to Air Condor. It swung on take-off at Southend and was sent by road to Hurn for repair, flying again in July 1960. G-AGPV then flew briefly with Trans-European but was scrapped at Gatwick in September 1965.

Bristol Wayfarer Mark 2 prototype 1
G-18-1 (c/n 12731)

G-18-1 first flew at Filton on 30 April 1946 and was the second Ministry of Supply prototype. This Bristol 170 was the prototype Wayfarer Mk. 2 with fixed nose and provision for airline-style seating. It soon became G-AGVB and from June to November 1946 was leased to Channel Island Airways. During 1948-49 it was converted to a Mk. 21 Freighter with nose doors and was operated at the Berlin Airlift by Silver City Airways, which at the end of the Airlift sold it to Bowmaker Ltd. It returned to use with Silver City in April 1954 and transferred to Cie Air Transport as F-BHVB. It was written off at Le Touquet on 4 November 1958.

The second Bristol-owned freighter prototype flew as G-AGVC but in 1949 became the prototype for the Mk. 31. It was exhibited in Bristol livery at the Farnborough Air Show as G18-2 in 1949 and this close-up shows the wide open nose-loading doors.
(BAE SYSTEMS)

The Mk. 21 prototype, G-AIFF, flying on one engine. It was while in a similar situation, climbing on one engine on 6 May 1949, that the fin failed and the aircraft plunged into the English Channel. (Brian Burrage)

Bristol Freighter Mark 1 prototype 2 / Mark 31 prototype
G-AGVC (c/n 12732)

G-AGVC first flew from Filton on 23 June 1946 and left on a sales tour of North and South America on 3 August. This Bristol 170 was the first Bristol-owned prototype and was a Freighter Mk. 1 with nose doors and provision for freight or passengers. It flew across the Atlantic and eventually reached Sao Paulo where it was chartered by Canadian Pacific Air Lines and LAV of Venezuela before returning to Filton in March 1948. It then inaugurated the Lympne - Le Touquet car ferry for Silver City Airways in July 1948 before joining other Bristol 170s on the Berlin Airlift.

At Filton 'GVC was converted into the Mk. 31 prototype and was exhibited at Farnborough in 1949 as G-18-2, and the following year as G-AGVC. It returned to flying with Silver City from 1952-61 and was sold to Manx Airlines, but was written off at Ronaldsway when the undercarriage collapsed on 30 June 1962.

Bristol Wayfarer Mark 2 prototype 2
G-AGUT (c/n 12733)

The second Bristol-owned prototype was a Wayfarer Mk. 2 with a fixed nose and provision for airline-style seating. It made its maiden flight on 15 September 1946 from Filton. As VR382 it served at the Telecommunications Research Establishment, Defford from September 1946 until November 1957, fitted with various experimental radar installations. It was purchased by Shorts Aviation and delivered to Blackbushe, Surrey but never flew again and was scrapped.

Bristol Freighter Mark 21 prototype
G-AIFF (c/n 12766)

G-AIFF made its first flight in 1947 as the Mk. 11 prototype and was exhibited at the SBAC Show at Radlett in September. In December 1947 it became the prototype Mk. 21, combining the wider span of the Mk. 11 with greater engine power and demonstrated in India, Pakistan and Portugal. It crashed into the English Channel 30 miles off Portland, killing all three crew on 6 May 1949 following fin failure while testing climbing performance on one engine.

Bristol Superfreighter Mark 32 prototype
G-AMWA (c/n 13073)

This aircraft – originally intended to be finished as Mk. 31 G-AMLK – was converted while on the production line to become the prototype long-nose Mk. 32 Superfreighter. It first flew with Chief Test Pilot, Bill Pegg, at the controls on 16 January 1953 and, following only 10 hours of test flying, the Certificate of Airworthiness was awarded and on 31 March 'MWA was delivered to Silver City. It crashed on Guernsey on 24 September 1963 following an engine failure during take-off and was written off.

Data	Mk. 1	Mk. 21	Superfreighter
Length	68 ft 4 in	68 ft 4 in	73 ft 4 in
Wingspan	98 ft 0 in	98 ft 0 in	108 ft 0 in
Height	21 ft 8 in	21 ft 8 in	25 ft 0 in
MTOW	36,500 lb	40,000 lb	44,000 lb
Cruising speed	163 mph	165 mph	165 mph
Range	300 mls	490 mls	490 mls
Passengers	Dependent upon layout		

Powerplant:
Mk. 1 & 2 – 2 x 1,675 hp Bristol Hercules 632
Mk. 21 – 2 x 1,690 hp Bristol Hercules 672
Mk. 31 & 32 – 2 x 1,980 hp Bristol Hercules 734

Total built: 214 (180 at Filton, 34 at Weston-super-Mare)

The first Bristol Superfreighter, G-AMWA, made its first flight on 16 January 1953 in Silver City livery. It was written off at Guernsey on 24 September 1963.

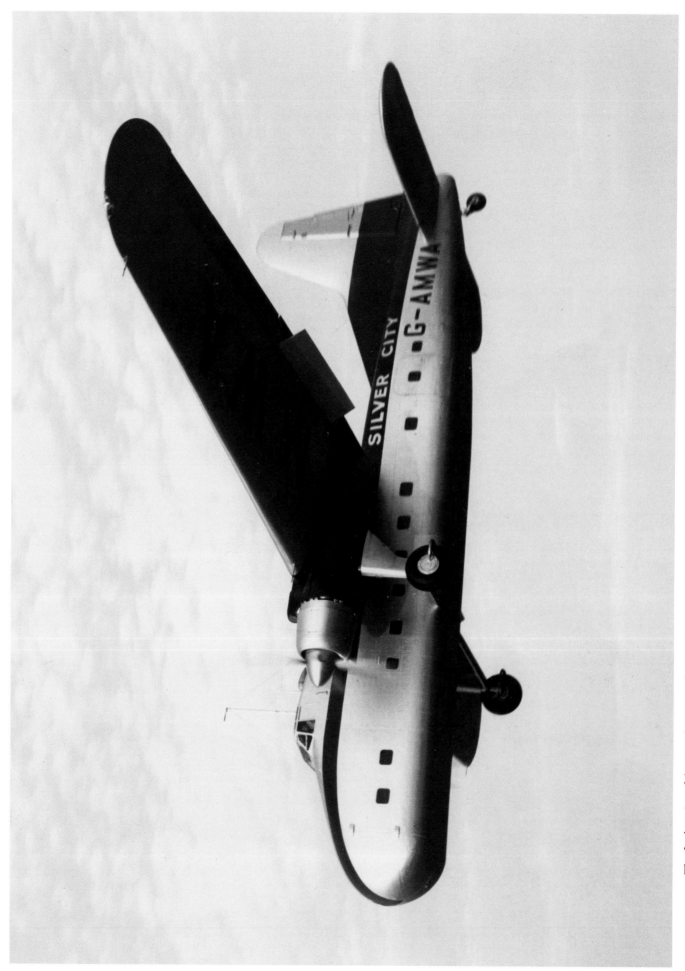

The final version of the Bristol 170 was the Superfreighter with a lengthened nose. Chief Test Pilot, Bill Pegg, took the prototype G-AMWA on its maiden flight on 16 January 1953. (Bristol Aero Collection)

Handley Page Hermes

AS the Second World War came to a close, Handley Page at Radlett in Hertfordshire began to consider constructing a new civil and military transport aircraft. The firm decided upon a design which utilised a lengthened version of the Halifax bomber's wing with a new circular fuselage and a single fin. A contract was received from the RAF to develop a military transport named the Hastings, while a civilian counterpart, to be called the Hermes and based on the same design, became an obvious companion.

The Prototype's maiden flight crash

The Handley Page Hermes had an inauspicious entry into the world when the H.P.68 Hermes 1 prototype G-AGSS crashed during its maiden flight on 2 December 1945. It had been the firm's intention to develop the civil Hermes ahead of the military version, the Hastings, but the loss of the G-AGSS led to a change of plan and work stopped on the second prototype G-AGUB. When work restarted it was decided to lengthen the aircraft by 15 ft and it was designated the H.P.74 Hermes 2 development aircraft. It finally flew on 2 September 1947. Whereas the first prototype was an empty shell, the second was fully furnished.

Some six months earlier in April 1947 the Ministry of Supply had ordered 25 examples of a further development – the Hermes 4 – for operation on BOAC's African services. (A Bristol Theseus turboprop version of the Hermes 2 which was to be called the Hermes 3 was envisaged but was not proceeded with.)

Hermes 2

Successful testing of the Hermes 2 led to the development of H.P.81 Hermes 4, the definitive production version, which primarily differed by having tricycle landing gear, more powerful Hercules engines and a fuselage which was shorter ahead of the wing and longer aft, because of BOAC's desire for a heavy forward galley. The first, G-AKFP, was flown on 5 September 1948 and was followed by 24 production aircraft. The Hermes, which received its Certificate of Airworthiness in October 1949, had the distinction of being the first post-war British design to serve with BOAC.

Hermes 4 in to BOAC service

The type entered BOAC service on 6 August 1950 with an interior layout for 40 passengers, although as many as 63 could be seated in a high-density arrangement. After only four years BOAC replaced the Hermes fleet with Canadair Argonauts as the Hermes had the tendency of flying tail-down, which increased drag, reduced speed and increased fuel consumption.

BOAC had little difficulty in disposing of the surplus aircraft, most of which were re-engined with Hercules 773 engines, which improved performance, and were redesignated as the Hermes 4A. The Hermes remained in service with a number of British operators such as Skyways, Airwork, Silver City, Air Safaris, until the early 1960s and the final service was completed by G-ALDA when it landed at Gatwick on 13 December 1964.

Hermes 5

Development did not cease with the Hermes 4 as Handley Page built two H.P.82 Hermes 5 aircraft. These were the largest and fastest turboprop airliners of the day but they were let down by the unreliable

The ill-fated Hermes 1 G-AGSS on the Radlett apron. It crashed due to control difficulties on its maiden flight on 2 December 1945, killing both crew. (Handley Page Association)

The sole Hermes 2, which was 15 ft longer than the Hermes 1, flew on 2 September 1947. It served with the Royal Radar Establishment from 1953 until 1968 and as the final Hermes flying, was scrapped in June 1969. (Handley Page Association)

THE AEROPLANE, APRIL 5, 1946

The HERMES

THESE paintings by Harold Bubb show the furnishings planned for the 34-seat version of the new Handley Page "Hermes." Powered by four Bristol Hercules engines, each developing 1,675 h.p., and having a gross weight of 75,000 lb., the "Hermes" class will be used for medium distances up to about 2,000 miles.

Top middle, the flight deck; top right, looking forward to the flight deck from the main cabin; lower left, the ladies' room and starboard side of the galley (inset, looking forward in the galley); lower right, general view of the cabin, looking aft.

Early artist's impressions of the flight deck and passenger accommodation of the Hermes. (Author's collection)

performance of 2,220 hp Bristol Theseus turboprops. Although versions of the Hermes 5 powered by other engines were considered, no further development took place and only the Hermes 4 ever saw commercial service.

Prototypes

Handley Page HP 68 Hermes 1 prototype
G-AGSS c/n HP68/1
The Hermes 1's first flight was only four months after the war's end, on 2 December 1945 with Jimmy Talbot and Ginger Wright piloting. The Hermes took off from Handley Page's airfield at Radlett at 15:40 hrs but immediately began a series of worsening pitch oscillations until it reached an almost vertical attitude and crashed at Kendals Hall not far from the airfield, killing both of the crew. The cause of the accident was believed to be elevator over-balance.

Handley Page HP 74 Hermes 2 prototype
G-AGUB c/n HP74/1
The larger Hermes 2 took to the air on 2 September 1947 and served as a development aircraft for the Hermes 4, testing the pressurisation, air-conditioning and sound-proofing of the uprated Hercules 763. It was exhibited in September 1947 at the SBAC Air Show which was held on its home airfield at Radlett. Following initial trials it returned to the factory to have its tailplane lowered and flew again on 18 January 1948. It was used for Hermes 4 and in October its Hercules 130s were replaced with Hercules 763s.

'GUB was loaned to BOAC at Hurn in May 1949 for Hermes 4 crew training, followed by 'hot and high' trials in Libya and the Sudan in August 1949.

Following storage at Radlett from early 1950 'GUB was registered as VX234 in October 1953 for radar development trials with the Royal Radar Establishment, initially based at Defford and then Pershore until June 1968. It was the final Hermes to fly and was scrapped in June 1969.

Handley Page HP 81 Hermes 4 prototype
G-AKFP c/n HP81/1
A year after G-AGUB's maiden flight the first of 25 definitive Hermes 4s, G-AKFP, made its maiden flight in the hands of CTP Squadron Leader Hedley Hazelden ('Hazel') on 5 September 1948. It made a second flight later the same day. Only two days later it flew to Farnborough to be exhibited in the annual Air Show. On its eleventh flight on 11 September 1948 it flew into low mist immediately after take-off and as a result Hazelden had to make a forced-landing at a disused airfield at Fairlop, Essex.

On 22 October while engaged in handling tests, with a newly fitted spring-loaded trim-tab on the elevator, 'KFP suffered such extreme flutter that the tail started to break up – but fortunately Hazelden landed safely. Following this incident a new tailplane was fitted. In February - March 1949 the Hermes 4 was based at Khartoum for tropical trials.

In order to expedite testing 'KFP had been built with many Hastings components and was rejected by BOAC as it was heavier than specified by the contract.

The Hermes 4 production line at Radlett. (Handley Page Association)

(This also proved a problem with other initial production Hermes.) G-AKFP completed its trials in March 1952 and its structure was lightened and its wings re-sparred. It was leased to Airwork in 1953 and bought outright in February 1957. Its life ended ignominiously on 1 September 1957 when it was landed on the wrong runway at Calcutta Dum-Dum Airport, collided with a DC-3 and was written off.

Handley Page HP 82 Hermes 5 prototype 1 G-ALEU c/n HP82/1

The first of the Bristol Theseus turboprop-powered Hermes 5s flew on 23 August 1949 and was soon on view to the public at the September 1949 SBAC Farnborough Air Show. It was then involved in testing but the unreliability of the engines was made very evident by a triple engine failure on 10 April 1951 when flying from Boscombe Down. The aircraft made a forced-landing just short of Chilbolton airfield, Hampshire and was written off.

Handley Page HP 82 Hermes 5 prototype 2 G-ALEV c/n HP82/2

Handley Page was keen to display its latest products at the Farnborough Air Show – so the first flight of the second prototype Hermes 5 took place on 26 August 1950 to enable the machine to appear at the September 1950 SBAC, where it also appeared in 1951. It differed from its sister by having double-slotted flaps installed. It took over trials originally meant for G-ALEU on Maxaret anti-skid braking.

G-ALEV was awarded a special category Certificate of Airworthiness in May 1951 for demonstration flying to Paris, but because of continuing engine problems, the demonstrations were curtailed. The surviving Hermes 5 made its final flight on 27 June 1952 and was dismantled at Farnborough in September 1953. The fuselage was eventually used for a trial installation of a Hermes freight door by Aviation Traders at Southend.

The Hermes 4 first flight crew in September: (from the left) Noel Brailsford, McPhail, McRostie, Hedley Hazelden CTP, Reginald Stafford & Jimmy Steele on 5 September 1948. (Handley Page Association)

Data	Hermes 2	Hermes 4
Length	95 ft 6 in	95 ft 10 in
Wingspan	113 ft 0 in	113 ft 0 in
Height	22 ft 6 in	30 ft 0 in
MTOW	80,000 lb	84,000 lb
Cruising speed	219 mph	280 mph
Range	2,000 mls	2,000 mls
Passengers	82	82

Powerplant:
Hermes 2 –: 4 x 1,715 hp Bristol Hercules 120
Hermes 4 – 4 x 2,100 hp Bristol Hercules 763

Production by type:
Hermes 1: 1
Hermes 2: 1
Hermes 4: 25
Hermes 5: 2

Total built: 29 at Radlett

The first Hermes 4 in Airwork livery. BOAC refused to accept G-AKFP as it was heavier than specification and eventually it was sold to Airwork. (Handley Page Association)

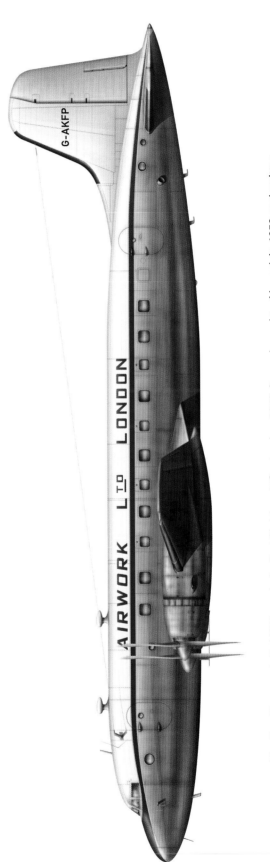

The first Hermes 4, G-AKFP, made its first flight on 5 September 1948. It was leased to Airwork in 1953 and written off when it collided with a DC-3 at Calcutta Dum-Dum Airport on 1 September 1957.

The final development of the Hermes was the Hermes 5 with Bristol Theseus turboprops. The first of two prototypes, G-ALEU, flew from Radlett on 23 August 1949. (Handley Page Association)

The Theseus turboprops were unreliable and during a flight from Boscombe Down on 10 April 1951, G-ALEU, suffered a triple engine failure and crash-landed just short of the airfield at Chilbolton, Hampshire and was written off. (Handley Page Association)

Miles/Handley Page Marathon

A NOTHER of the Brabazon Committee's Specifications, the Type 5A, was for an 18 passenger feeder-liner, which eventually became the Miles M60 Marathon and was to be the company's first metal aircraft. Miles was a manufacturer of light civil and military aircraft which between 1928 and 1948 built 47 different types of light aircraft in large quantities.

The evolution of the Marathon
Originally Miles Aircraft proposed a twin-engined, tailwheel design but it evolved into a larger, high-wing aircraft with twin finned tail, and a tricycle undercarriage powered by four de Havilland Gipsy Queen engines. Miles was contracted by the Ministry of Supply to produce three prototypes but did not have an order to start production. The first prototype flew in May 1946 followed by the second in February 1947, whereas the third machine, the M69, powered by two Armstrong Siddeley Mamba turboprop engines, only flew after the takeover of Miles by Handley Page.

Miles goes into receivership
Without a production order for the Marathon, financial difficulties had beset the firm and it entered receivership in 1947. In July 1948 Handley Page stepped in to take over production at Woodley in Berkshire and the Ministry of Supply placed an order for 50 Marathons designated as Handley Page (Reading) HPR 1 Marathons, intending that BEA should receive 20, and BOAC and its Associated Companies the remainder.

Sales problems
The Marathon was trialled by BEA for the Highlands and Islands routes but the Corporation declined to accept the aircraft as it was not able to equal the performance of the aircraft it was due to replace – the de Havilland Dragon Rapide, designed in 1933. BEA also rejected the turboprop Armstrong Siddeley Mamba-powered Marathon 2.

With no prospects of sales, Sir Frederick Handley Page agreed to close production after a total of 40 production Marathons had been manufactured, arguing that Handley Page's contract with the Ministry of Civil Aviation (which oversaw BEA and BOAC) was to manufacture the Marathon, not to sell it.

Military and civil service
With a surplus of Marathons on its hands the Ministry diverted 30 Marathons to the RAF as T.11 navigation trainers but their service was short and most were disposed of in June 1958, although a few were sold on. Other Marathons had brief careers as feeder-liners with West African Airways Corporation, Union of Burma Airways, Derby Aviation and Far Eastern Airlines of Japan. However by 1962 none remained in service.

Prototypes

Miles Marathon 1 prototype 1
U-10 / G-AGPD (c/n 6265)
With 'B' class registration U-10 the first prototype lifted off on its maiden flight from Woodley's grass runway on 19 May 1946 piloted by Ken Waller. It initially flew with three fins but the middle one was removed and then later refitted. It was exhibited at the SBAC Radlett

The first prototype Marathon 1 flew on 19 May 1946 at Woodley bearing B class markings as U-10. It was registered as G-AGPD in 1947 and crashed at Amesbury on 28 May 1948. (Brian Burrage)

G-AILH, the second prototype Marathon 1 flew on 27 February 1947 initially with only two fins. It was later converted to become the Marathon T.11 prototype for the RAF. (Mike Phipp)

1946 and 1947 Shows re-registered as G-AGPD. While flying trials from the A&AEE Boscombe Down it crashed on 28 May 1948 at Amesbury, Wiltshire.

Miles Marathon 1 prototype 2
G-AILH (c/n 6430)
The second prototype, G-AILH, flew on 27 February 1947, but only had twin fins and rudders; a central fin was added later by Handley Page. It appeared at Farnborough 1948 as the Handley Page Marathon. In October 1949 'ILH spent three months in Khartoum and Nairobi on tropical trials. Ultimately this machine, as VX229, became the prototype T11 conversion for the RAF. In October 1957 it was sold to Dan-Air and taken by road to Lasham, Hants but never flew again.

Handley Page Marathon 2 prototype
G-AHXU (c/n 6544)
Registered G-AHXU, this machine was completed by Handley Page as the HPR5 Marathon 2 powered by two Armstrong Siddeley Mamba turboprops. Hugh Kendall flew it for the first time on 21 July 1949 but encountered problems when the left undercarriage jammed in the 'up' position. By means of violent manoeuvring the pilot managed to free it and a safe landing was made.

The Mamba Marathon was exhibited at Farnborough 1949 and 1950 and loaned to the Ministry of Supply, which allotted it to de Havilland Propellers, Hatfield as VX231. It became the first turboprop aircraft to fly with reverse-pitch propellers demonstrating

backward taxiing at Farnborough 1951. Between 1953 and 1954 it flew with the ETPS (Empire Test Pilots School) at Farnborough and was then returned to Woodley where it was re-engined with two Alvis Leonides Major engines fitted in replica Handley Page HPR3 Herald nacelles. It flew in this configuration on 15 March 1955 and was used by Alvis at Baginton as a test bed until 1958 and then scrapped at Bitteswell, Leicestershire in October 1959.

Data	Marathon 1
Length	52 ft 3 in
Wingspan	65 ft
Height	14 ft
MTOW	18,250 lbs
Cruising speed	175 mph
Range	850 mls
Passengers	18

Powerplant:
4 x de Havilland Gipsy Queen 71

Production by type:
Marathon 1: 42 (including 30 Marathon T.11)
Marathon 2: 1

Total built: 43 at Woodley

Uniquely, the Marathon 2 prototype, G-AHXU, was powered by twin Armstrong Siddeley Mamba turboprops. This is a fine aerial shot of G-AHXU flying on just one of its Armstrong Siddeley Mambas. Handley Page sought unsuccessfully to interest BEA in this version of the Marathon following the airline's rejection of the Marathon 1 (Brian Burrage)

During 1954-55 the Marathon 2, now registered VX231, was grounded at Woodley for its Mambas to be replaced with Alvis Leonides Major piston engines. It first flew in this configuration on 15 March 1955 as a test bed for the Handley Page Herald, which initially flew with this powerplant. (Author's collection)

Short Solent

THE Solent was a development of the famous wartime RAF Sunderland maritime patrol and attack flying boat. During the war and after, a large number of Sunderlands converted for passenger carrying and renamed as Hythes were operated by BOAC and other airlines on world routes. To capitalise on this, Shorts developed the Hythe into the Sandringham which had even greater passenger capacity.

In August 1944 Shorts flew the Sunderland Mk. 4 which had a stronger wing, bigger tailplane and a longer fuselage as a replacement for the earlier RAF Sunderland Marks. As the changes were so substantial it was later decided to differentiate it from the Sunderland and rename it the Seaford. Although the Seaford was not adopted by the RAF, in early 1946 BOAC evaluated it and concluded that it was a better aircraft than the Sandringham.

The Ministry of Civil Aviation (MCA) then ordered twelve Seafords renamed as Solent 1s for BOAC but, following discussions between the airline and the manufacturer, this was refined into the Shorts 2 with accommodation for 34 passengers in a two deck luxury layout. The prototype flew on 11 November 1946 and a lengthy flight test programme ensued which eventually led to certification on 10 November 1947. Shortly after their entry into service in July 1948 the eight Solents already built had to be withdrawn from service for their wing floats to be reconfigured and only returned to service in October that year.

BOAC was so satisfied with its Solents that six more were converted from redundant RAF Seafords at Belfast for lease by the MCA to BOAC as Solent 3s with capacity for 39 passengers. BOAC used the Solents on the South African routes but in November 1950 the airline ceased all flying boat schedules and its Solents were put into store. Some of these were purchased by Aquila Airways to join a former RAF Seaford the airline had converted to Solent 3 configuration at Hamble.

During 1949 Shorts built four new Solent 4s at its Belfast factory with capacity for 44 passengers and delivered these to the New Zealand airline, TEAL. These final Solents had greatly increased range and were operated on routes to Australia and South Pacific Islands, the final TEAL operations continuing until September 1960.

Two of the TEAL Solent 4s returned to the UK in the mid-1950s and flew with Aquila Airways but both were written off in accidents. Aquila's three remaining Solents (all formerly with BOAC) served until the close of UK flying boat operations in September 1958 but never saw service again.

Prototype

Short Solent 2 prototype
G-AHIL c/n S.1300

The Solent prototype was built at Rochester and launched on the River Medway on 11 November 1946. It was first flown by Geoffrey Tyson CTP on 1 December. Following test flying it was delivered to BOAC on 17 June 1948 and named 'Salisbury', later 'City of Salisbury'. G-AHIL was temporarily withdrawn from service from July to October 1948. It carried out trials with new wing float configuration at Shorts, Belfast in September 1948. 'HIL was withdrawn from use on 29 September 1950.

A rather worn looking G-AHIL at mooring. The first Solent had a brief life; its maiden flight was on 1 December 1946 and after service with BOAC it was withdrawn from use on 29 September 1950. (Author's collection)

The Solent 2 production line at Rochester with G-AHIO in the foreground. These Solents were the last Shorts aircraft built at Rochester. Following their completion Shorts concentrated its activities at its Belfast factory. (Bombardier)

Data	Solent Mk. 2
Length	87 ft 8 in
Wingspan	112 ft 9 int
Height	34 ft 3¾ int
MTOW	78,000 lb
Cruising speed	244 mph
Range	1,800 mls
Passengers	34

Powerplant:
Mk. 2 – 4 x 1,690 hp Bristol Hercules 637

Production by type:
Solent 2: 12
Solent 3: 7 (all converted Seafords)
Solent 4: 4

Total built: 23 (12 at Rochester, 10 at Belfast, 1 at Hamble)

Percival Merganser and Prince

Merganser

PERCIVAL AIRCRAFT of Luton, one of the Hunting Group of companies, decided to develop a small airliner, the Merganser, at the end of the Second World War. To keep costs to a minimum it utilised components of the single-engined Percival Proctor, but with a large fuselage capable of accommodating five passengers and a crew of two, a high wing, twin de Havilland Gipsy Queen engines and a tricycle undercarriage. The Merganser proved a moderately successful aircraft but its development was crippled by the shortage of supply of suitable engines.

Prince

As a result of the experience with the solitary Merganser, Percival created the larger and heavier Percival Prince with the same configuration but more powerful Alvis Leonides engines. Through careful rearrangement of the interior, the seating capacity was increased from five to a maximum of twelve.
As is customary with most types, after a period of development, further design refinements and increased power resulted in versions with improved performance. The Prince was used by the Ministry of Aviation, by Shell which purchased eight. The Survey Prince version was bought by Hunting Air Surveys, the Tanganyikan Government, Thai Air Force and a Swiss Survey firm. The Armed Services of several countries became customers of the Prince, most notably the Royal Navy, which used 48 Sea Princes for communications and training purposes. These were similar to the civil versions except for a twin mainwheel undercarriage

and a longer nose taking the length to 46 ft. The RAF's versions were further refined and possessed not only the lengthened nose but also had the wings increased in span by 8 ft 6 in. Other military customers were Belgium, Denmark, Finland, Germany, Rhodesia, Sudan and Sweden. The military Pembroke led to the final civil version of the Prince, named the President. Only three were built and these served in executive roles with the Ministry of Aviation and the British Aircraft Corporation.

Prototypes

Percival Merganser prototype
X2 / G-AHMH (c/n AU/1)
The aircraft was completed and sent by road to Paris for display at the Paris Air Show in 1947. On return to Luton on 9 May 1947 it made an eventful maiden flight due to control problems, with L. T. Carruthers in command. Following these initial flight trials the fin area was increased, it was painted blue overall and registered G-AHMH. Displayed at the 1947 Radlett SBAC Show it was dismantled in August 1948.

Percival Prince prototype
G-23-1 / G-ALCM
The Prince prototype flew from Luton Airport as G-23-1 on 13 May 1948 piloted by Wing Commander Powell. Initial testing indicated the need for a small dorsal fin and an improved, more aerodynamic nose.
In August 1948 it was registered as G-ALCM and appeared at the Farnborough Air Show. Used for tests and demonstrations, the prototype was dismantled at Luton in July 1956.

The short-lived Percival Merganser at Luton prior to painting. It was later given the "B" registration X2 and subsequently became G-AHMH. It flew in May 1947 but was scrapped the following year. (Aeroplane)

The Prince prototype shortly after its maiden flight with "B" class registration G-23-1. (Aeroplane)

The prototype Prince was demonstrated as G-ALCM at the 1948 Farnborough Air Show. (Ed Coates Collection)

Data	Merganser	Prince 1	President
Length	40 ft 8 in	42 ft 10 in	46 ft 4 in
Wingspan	47 ft 9 in	56 ft	64 ft 6 in
Height	13 ft 9 in	16 ft 1 in	16 ft
MTOW	7,300 lb	10,659 lb	13,500 lb
Cruising speed	160 mph	180 mph	164 mph
Range	800 mls	940 mls	1,075 mls
Passengers	5	8-12	8-12

Powerplant:
Merganser: 2 x 296hp de Havilland Gipsy Queen 51
Prince 1: 2 x 520hp Alvis Leonides 501/4
President: 2 x 560hp Alvis Leonides 514

Total number of Mergansers built: 1 at Luton

Prince Production by type:
P.50 Prince 1 - 1
P.50 Prince 2 - 5
P.50 Prince 3 - 12
P.50 President - 3
P.54 Survey Prince 6
P.57 Sea Prince C1 - 3
P.57 Sea Prince T1 - 41
P.57 Sea Prince C2 - 4.

Total number of Princes and Presidents built:
75 at Luton

Cunliffe-Owen Concordia

CUNLIFFE-OWEN AIRCRAFT LTD was established at Eastleigh, Hampshire in 1935 and was heavily involved in aircraft repair throughout the Second World War. With the cessation of hostilities the firm sought to enter the civil airliner market and the COA.19 Concordia, a 10-seat medium-range transport was designed and built at Eastleigh, in 1947. This medium-range airliner was of conventional design, with twin engines, a tricycle undercarriage and capacity for ten passengers.

The prototype aircraft Y-0222 was first flown at Eastleigh in May 1947. A second aircraft G-AKBE was displayed at the 1947 SBAC Show at Radlett and made an extensive European sales tour. However, the tour was not a success as the aircraft could not compete with the many surplus DC-3s available. It was therefore concluded that there was no market for the aircraft. In May 1948 Cunliffe-Owen ceased trading and the aircraft and components were offered for sale.

Data	Concordia
Length	44 ft 10 in
Wingspan	56 ft 7 in
Height	16 ft 1 in
MTOW	12,500 lb
Cruising speed	216 mph
Range	1,200 mls
Passengers	10

Powerplant:
2 x 550 hp Alvis Leonides LE 4M

Total built: 2 at Eastleigh

The first of the two prototype Concordia bearing "B" marking as Y-0222. With bankruptcy of Cunliffe-Owen in 1948 both prototypes were scrapped. (Mike Hooks)

Prototypes

Cunliffe-Owen Concordia prototype 1
Y-0222 (c/n 1)
The first prototype flew on 19 May 1947 from Eastleigh with A. Corbin piloting.
Presumed scrapped 1948.

Cunliffe-Owen Concordia prototype 2
G-AKBE (c/n 2)
The second aircraft also flew in 1947 and appeared at the Radlett Show in September that year, following which it made an extensive European sales tour.
Presumed scrapped 1948.

The first Concordia Y-0222 on display. (Author's collection)

An artist's
impression of the
Concordia from a
Cunliffe-Owen
advertisement.
(Author's collection)

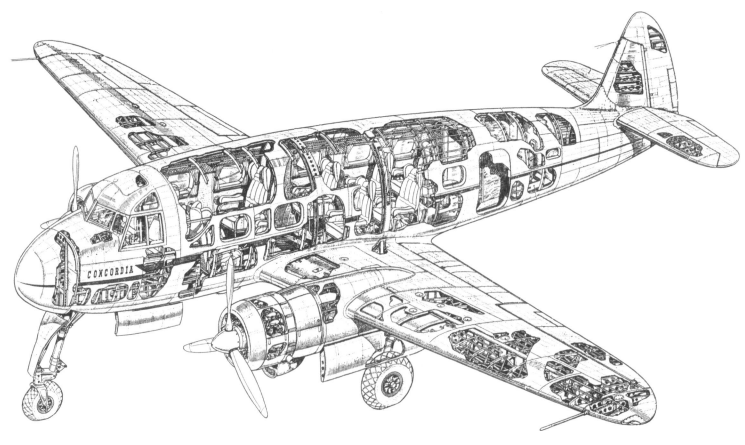

Cutaway drawing
(Author's collection)

Airspeed Ambassador

Airspeed

THE Airspeed Company was originally founded in York in 1931, but was later established in Portsmouth and at a Government-built 'shadow factory' at Christchurch, then in Hampshire. Airspeed became well known for its Oxford twin-engined trainer and the Horsa troop-carrying glider which was heavily employed during the D-Day landings in 1944.

The Ambassador project

Project design for the Airspeed AS.57 Ambassador began at Christchurch in 1943 in response to the Brabazon Committee's requirement 2A for a short/medium-haul airliner – the same requirement which led to the very successful Vickers Viscount and the far from successful Armstrong Whitworth Apollo. The project was led by Chief Designer Arthur Hagg who had previously held a similar role with de Havilland where he had designed the Comet Racer and Albatross airliner.

Flight test

The handsome Ambassador was a new experience for both the designer and Airspeed as all their previous designs had been of wooden construction.
The Ambassador, which first flew in July 1947, was a high-wing pressurised aircraft powered by twin Bristol Centaurus with a capacity for 47 passengers. Substantial delays during flight testing spoilt the airliner's chance of success as it only entered service in 1953, by which time it had been outsold by the Viscount whose turboprop Dart engines gave it a major competitive advantage. This was compounded by the takeover of Airspeed by

de Havilland in 1951 and as the parent company was over-burdened with the Comet and a number of military projects, there was no further development capacity for the Ambassador. As a result, production ceased after the construction of 23 aircraft, with the final delivery in 1953. The Christchurch factory then concentrated on de Havilland Vampire, Venom and Sea Vixen development and production until the site's closure in 1962.

Service

BEA had ordered 20 Ambassadors in September 1948 and as they entered service during 1953, Coronation year, they were branded as the Elizabethan Class with each airliner named after a famous Elizabethan. The 'Elizabethan' was marketed by BEA as the epitome of luxury travel yet with the success of the Viscount and BEA's growing reliance on the Vickers aircraft, BEA withdrew the aircraft from service in 1958.

The Ambassadors were then operated with second-tier carriers primarily in the UK and many served with Dan-Air which had the distinction of operating the last flight of the type with G-ALZO on 3 October 1971.

Prototypes

Airspeed Ambassador prototype 1
G-AGUA (c/n 61)

The first prototype, which was unpressurised, made its first flight of 45 minutes duration from Christchurch piloted by CTP George Errington on 10 July 1947. The flight was not without incident – the spring tab came off the central rudder at take-off and there were problems with electrical systems. Two months later 'GUA was demonstrated at the SBAC Display at Radlett.

G-AGUA carrying out trial hops at Christchurch on 8 July 1947. The actual first flight was on 10 July. Note that the crew door has been removed in case of the need for an emergency exit. (BAE SYSTEMS)

The second prototype Ambassador, G-AKRD (left) and the first G-AGUA outside the Airspeed factory at Christchurch. (BAE SYSTEMS)

An early advertisement extolling the virtues of the new Ambassador in service with BEA. (Author's collection)

The aircraft was involved in an unfortunate incident on 22 November 1947 when the left landing leg extended in flight and damaged the hydraulic system. Despite the loss of hydraulics the aircraft landed safely at Christchurch without flaps, on the left undercarriage leg alone as the other undercarriage legs could not be extended. Fortunately the aircraft was relatively undamaged and was soon back in the air.

G-AGUA flew airworthiness trials at the A&AEE Boscombe Down during February to March 1949. On 16 March while taxiing to dispersal at Boscombe Down the brakes failed and it collided with two Tiger Moths. As later more representative examples of the Ambassador took to the air there was less use for this aircraft and it was withdrawn from use on 12 December 1951 and broken up at Christchurch.

Airspeed Ambassador prototype 2 G-AKRD (c/n 62)

The second prototype made a 69 minute first flight on 26 August 1948 piloted by George Errington and appeared at the SBAC Display at Farnborough the following month. George Errington impressed the crowds by flying the Ambassador's whole display operating solely on the right engine.

During 1949 'KRD was painted in BEA livery (and later named 'Golden Lion'). It made demonstration flights to Aer Lingus and appeared again at the SBAC Display at Farnborough in 1949 and 1950. In the meantime on 13 March 1950, while demonstrating single-engined take-off performance at Hurn, it sank back on to the runway damaging the fuselage and a propeller. As the damage was not severe the aircraft was flown the few miles back to Christchurch for repairs.

For the remainder of its operational life G-AKRD was involved in engine/propeller testing. From 20 September 1951 it flew hollow propeller trials for de Havilland Propellers at Hatfield. Then from 15 August 1952 it was used by Bristol Engines, Filton to test Bristol Proteus turboprops which were installed in place of the Centauruses. When these trials ceased the aircraft was passed to Rolls-Royce at Hucknall and from 30 December 1955 it flew with Tyne turboprops. On 24 August 1958 it was registered as G-37-3 and appeared at the SBAC Display Farnborough in 1958. Engine tests continued and Rolls-Royce Darts replaced the Tynes in August 1961. The aircraft was re-registered G-AKRD in May 1966 and finally withdrawn from use at Hucknall in October 1969.

Airspeed Ambassador Production prototype G-ALFR (c/n 5210)

George Errington flew G-ALFR on a 73 minute maiden flight on 18 May 1950 in full BEA livery as an Elizabethan named 'Golden Hind'. Within its first year the aircraft was involved in two accidents, the first at Hurn on 12 July 1950 when the right undercarriage leg failed on landing. The second took place when it was being flown from Christchurch by Ron Clear on 13 November 1950. Operating at a forward centre of gravity, the aircraft landed heavily and the two Centauruses broke free from their mountings. 'LFR, lightened by the weight loss, bounced (now a glider!) to 40 ft before landing ahead of its engines. Nobody was injured and the aircraft was repaired and flew again before the year's end. Testing continued and from 13 August to 20 September 1951 'LFR flew on tropical trials near Khartoum, Sudan.

G-AKRD at the Farnborough Air Show in 1949 where it appeared in a spacious 36-seater layout. (BAE SYSTEMS)

A fine study of the attractive Ambassador, G-AKRD at Christchurch. (BAE SYSTEMS)

The second Ambassador prototype G-AKRD was exhibited at the 1949 Farnborough Air Show in this partial BEA livery. It later served as an engine test bed.

G-AKRD sank back on to the runway at Hurn on 13 March 1950. It was only slightly damaged and was flown back to Christchurch for repairs. (BAE SYSTEMS)

At the end of the development phase 'LFR was employed by Bristol Engines from March 1953 to August 1954 on Centaurus engine trials at Filton. Even at Filton the aircraft was not free from accident – it was damaged due to premature undercarriage retraction 13 August 1954. With the end of these trials at Bristol the aircraft was allotted to Napier Engines for Napier Eland turboprop development and appeared at Farnborough 1960 fitted with Elands. These trials finished at the end of 1960 and 'LFR was purchased by Dan-Air in March 1961, which converted it to standard Centaurus configuration. It re-entered service in January 1964, flew for three years and was scrapped in January 1968 at Lasham, Hampshire.

Data	Ambassador
Length	82 ft
Wingspan	115 ft
Height	18 ft 3 in
MTOW	52,500 lb
Cruising speed	260 mph
Range	550 mls
Passengers	47

Powerplant:
2 x 2,625 hp Bristol Centaurus 661

Total built: 23 at Christchurch

G-ALFR suffered two rather ignominious landing accidents, the first at Hurn on 12 July 1950 when the starboard undercarriage leg failed on landing. (BAE SYSTEMS)

The second landing accident for G-ALFR occurred on 13 November 1950 at Christchurch. A very heavy landing resulted in both engines breaking free from their mounts and landing far ahead of the aircraft. (BAE SYSTEMS)

G-ALFR at the SBAC Show Farnborough in 1960 as a Napier Eland engine test bed but wearing BEA livery. After these trials it was converted back to Hercules power and flew with Dan-Air until 1968. (Peter Berry)

Vickers Viscount

Starting the Rolls-Royce Darts on the unpainted Viscount 630 prototype G-AHRF at Wisley on 16 July 1948 prior to its maiden flight, piloted by Vickers CTP Mutt Summers and Jock Bryce. Note the Vickers Warwick in the background. (Author's collection)

Introduction

WHEN it entered service in 1953 the Vickers Viscount was ahead of its time – it was the world's first turboprop airliner and had no serious competitor. Airlines which adopted it found that its impact on their routes was manifold – load factors increased substantially as people wanted to travel on the fastest and most comfortable airliner available. The order book benefited accordingly and the Viscount became Britain's best-selling airliner.

The driving force at Vickers-Armstrongs behind the Viscount was Sir George Edwards who became Chief Designer in 1945 and later Managing Director, eventually retiring from the British Aircraft Corporation as Chairman in 1975. Other projects under his direction included the Viking, Valiant, Vanguard, VC10, TSR2 and Concorde. (Author's Collection)

Inception

In April 1945 the Ministry of Aircraft Production instructed Vickers to proceed with a development of the Brabazon 2B requirement. This specified a 24-seater aircraft capable of transporting a payload of 7,500 lb over a range of 700 miles, at a cruising speed of 280 mph at 20,000 feet. Vickers submitted its VC.2 Viceroy proposal powered by Rolls-Royce Dart engines in June 1945 and eventually the Ministry of Supply ordered two prototypes.

British European Airways took a close interest and at its request the design capacity was increased from 24 to 32 passengers. However, to Vickers' dismay, in 1947 BEA, which was the airliner's target customer, placed an order for 20 of the larger and rival piston-engined , Ambassadors, which had also been born as a result of the Brabazon Committee.

BEA's decision was based on caution. Turboprops were then at the cutting edge of technology and might prove unreliable, whereas pistons were a known quantity. The airline also thought that the initial 32-seat design was too small in contrast to the Ambassador's 47-seat capacity. Vickers resisted the temptation to offer the aircraft with piston engines, but did concede one change: with India's independence from Great Britain, the name was amended to 'Viscount', as 'Viceroy' was no longer appropriate.

First flight

On 16 July 1948 G-AHRF, the prototype Viscount 630, made a first flight from Vickers' test airfield at Wisley. At that stage, the Viscount's future did not appear to be very bright but fortunately in 1949 the prospect of a developed Dart 505 with 50 per cent more power gave

G-AHRF taking off on its maiden flight on 16 July 1948. The house visible beneath the tail of the aircraft is actually the Wisley control tower. (Author's collection)

G-AHRF back on the Wisley apron after the brief 20 minute flight. The crew and others then repaired to the Wisley Hut Hotel to celebrate. (Author's collection)

Vickers the opportunity to offer a stretched Viscount 700 with capacity for 40-53 passengers.

In July 1950 G-AHRF received the first Certificate of Airworthiness for a turbine airliner and operated services from London (Northolt) to Paris (Le Bourget) followed by a similar routine between London and Edinburgh. The Viscount's smoothness, speed, pressurised comfort and large windows impressed passengers accustomed to rather rudimentary Vikings and Dakotas.

A second Viscount VX217, built to G-AHRF's dimensions, was completed as a test bed with Rolls-Royce Tay jet engines and flew in March 1950. It was employed on control trials to support the Vickers Valiant test programme and later trialled the first 'fly by wire' experiments. It had a short life and was scrapped in 1960.

The Viscount 700

BEA's order for 20 Viscount 701s in August 1950 coincided with the maiden flight of the first 700 G-AMAV with its fuselage 6 ft 8 in longer, wider wingspan, modified systems and uprated Darts. This was the real Viscount prototype whereas G-AHRF was more of a 'proof of concept' vehicle.

A full Certificate of Airworthiness was received on 18 April 1953 and the first services took place that day. In September Air France joined BEA as an operator and in spring 1954, Aer Lingus introduced Viscounts.

The Viscount 630 prototype was painted in BEA livery for a tour of European capitals in March 1950 and in July operated the first scheduled turboprop passenger service between London and Paris. (Author's collection)

American orders

In the cold Canadian climate the turboprop's ability to start well in low temperatures was a compelling reason for Trans-Canada Airways (now Air Canada) to order 15 Viscount 724s (and later 36 similar 757s). This Viscount 724 incorporated a two-man cockpit, improved Dart 506 and a large number of modifications, which made the aircraft suitable for the American market. Vickers was soon rewarded for this effort when in 1954 the large US regional Capital Airlines ordered 60 – worth $67m! In the subsequent decade this order stood as the largest ever placed for a turbine airliner. Viscounts built to the Capital specification with Dart 510s became the benchmark. Designated as a 700D it became the most numerous version, with 150 manufactured in contrast to 137 of the 700 Series. More and more airlines wanted Viscounts and at the end of 1956 Vickers received the order for the 200th. Viscounts also proved suitable on long-range services – for example Central African Airways flew Viscounts on its Salisbury, Rhodesia (now Harare, Zimbabwe) - London route, and Iraqi Airways used Viscounts on its Baghdad - London services until 1965.

The stretched Viscount 800

In early 1953, before the Viscount 700 entered service, BEA ordered twelve 801s, which would have been more than 13 ft longer than the 700 with capacity for 86 passengers. Within a year this model was rethought and a new 800 was devised with a fuselage extension of 3 ft 10 in but, by moving the rear bulkhead, usable space was increased by more than 9 ft. This type, designated the 802, received the Dart 510 as did the later 700D. The maximum take-off weight (MTOW) of the 800 was the same as the 700D so what the larger version gained in capacity it forfeited in range. The 802 was best suited to shorter routes but it did have room for 71 passengers in a single class layout. BEA soon increased its order to 22 and ordered 19 similar but higher-powered 806s. A total of 68 Viscount 800s were sold to six airlines in Europe and New Zealand.

The final development – the 810

The 810 was a logical development of the V.800 which, though unaltered in size, was matched to the new Dart

525 which gave the airliner a MTOW of 72,500 lbs – 17 per cent greater than the 800. The whole airframe was strengthened so that it could transport the payload of the 800 over the range of the 700D. Continental was the first customer for the 810 with 15 aircraft and commenced services in May 1958. Lufthansa, Austrian Airlines, Pakistan International, South African Airways and other airlines also operated 810s. A total of 83 were delivered and the final customer was CAAC of China which ordered six 843s and received the last Viscount from the Hurn production line in April 1964.

Vickers' speedy development of the Viscount made the most of its potential and resulted in sales to more than 60 operators in some 40 countries with over 150 operators later receiving second-hand examples. The aircraft was also in demand with Governments in an executive role and many served in the corporate market.

Much of the credit for the Viscount's success must lie with the Dart turboprop – its reliability, compactness, ease of access and quick development were a major factor in the aircraft's success. With 438 sales the Vickers Viscount remains Britain's best-selling airliner of all time.

Prototypes

Vickers Viscount 630 prototype
G-AHRF (c/n 1)

Originally built at Vickers Experimental Hangar at Foxwarren and transferred to Wisley for assembly, the unpainted and then unpressurised prototype Viscount 630 G-AHRF made a low key 20 minute maiden flight from Vickers' test airfield at Wisley on 16 July 1948. It was piloted by Mutt Summers, Vickers' Chief Test Pilot who by the end of his career had made the first flights of 43 aircraft, including the Spitfire. His comment following the flight was "the smoothest and best I have ever flown".

Just after its first flight in September 1948 G-AHRF was exhibited at the Farnborough Air Show in Vickers livery and between October 1948 and September 1949 it bore military markings as VX211. Following 290 flying hours and 160 flights on 15 September 1949 G-AHRF received a restricted Certificate of Airworthiness

A line up of Vickers aircraft in May 1951 with, from the left, Valiant prototype WB210, Viscount 700 prototype G-AMAV, Tay Viscount VX217, Viscount 630 prototype G-AHRF, Nene Viking VX856 and a Varsity and a Valetta. (Author's collection)

The second Viscount prototype (seen here at Wisley) was originally to have been built to a similar configuration as G-AHRF and the registration G-AHRG was reserved for it. The Ministry of Supply issued a new specification for it – registered as VX217 it became the sole Rolls-Royce Tay-powered Viscount and was used for test purposes. (Author's collection)

excluding pressurisation, de-icing systems or tropical operations.

Painted in BEA livery the Viscount 630 left Northolt on 20 March 1950 on a tour of eight European capitals. One sector was even flown with two engines feathered during descent to demonstrate the engines' reliability and potential fuel economy measures at low altitudes, though this technique was later abandoned for safety reasons.

In July 1950 G-AHRF received the first unrestricted Certificate of Airworthiness for a turbine airliner and operated the first scheduled turboprop passenger service on 29 July 1950 in BEA livery from London (Northolt) to Paris (Le Bourget). These services continued for two weeks, followed by a similar route distance between London and Edinburgh from 15 - 23 August.

Prior to the passenger services in June 1950 the Viscount 630 had flown to Nairobi for tropical trials to measure its performance in high temperatures. Two years later on 27 August 1952 while carrying out similar trials in Khartoum, the starboard undercarriage leg collapsed and G-AHRF was written off. It is indicative of the number of hours that a prototype spends in the air (rather few) that it had flown only 931 hours.

Vickers Viscount 663 prototype
VX217 (c/n 2)

All except one of the Viscounts was Rolls-Royce Dart-powered – the exception was the second prototype which was built to the smaller dimensions of the first aircraft, the Viscount 630 G-AHRF. Work had slowed on this machine (originally registered G-AHRG) at Foxwarren because of the initial lack of orders but the Ministry of Supply decided to use it as a test vehicle and it was transferred to Wisley in mid-April 1949. It was assembled with two Rolls-Royce RTa1 Tay Turbojets to undertake control trials to support the Vickers Valiant test programme.

Registered as VX217 this aircraft took to the air at Wisley on 15 March 1950 piloted by Jock Bryce. Brian Trubshaw demonstrated it at Farnborough that year, after which the machine disappeared from public sight. It was involved in the first 'fly by wire' experiments with Boulton Paul at RAF Defford, which was the home of the Radar Research Flying Unit until 1957. In December 1958 it was damaged beyond repair when the main spar burnt through. With a total flying time of 110 hours 15 minutes it was scrapped at Boulton Paul's test airfield at Seighford, Staffordshire in 1960.

Vickers Viscount 700 prototype
G-AMAV (c/n 3)

Vickers had partly constructed a Viscount 640 as G-AJZW to be powered by Napier Naiads at Foxwarren but construction was suspended following BEA's order for Ambassadors. When the Ministry of Supply ordered the Viscount 700 on 24 February 1949 Vickers was able quickly to arrange assembly by utilising parts from the suspended G-AJZW.

G-AMAV was not constructed at Foxwarren. Its wings were manufactured at the Supermarine factory at Itchen, Hampshire and the fuselage at South Marston, near Swindon with final assembly at Weybridge. Fitted with Rolls-Royce Dart RDa3 Mk. 504 engines, G-AMAV's maiden flight was on 28 August 1950 from Weybridge to Wisley piloted by Mutt Summers. Painted in BEA colours it was larger than G-AHRF with a 6 ft 8 in longer fuselage, and 4 ft 9½ in wider wingspan, modified systems and uprated Darts.

The Viscount 700 prototype then embarked on the full range of test flying interspersed with regular appearances at Farnborough Air Shows and sales tours. At the 1950 Farnborough Show one of the flying passes was carried out with three engines feathered, leaving one outboard engine to maintain flight. In October 1951 'MAV left Hurn for tropical trials in

The Viscount 700 prototype G-AMAV in BEA livery named 'Endeavour' at Melbourne Essendon, homeward bound after the London - New Zealand Air Race of 1953. 'MAV was the fastest aircraft in the Transport section but owing to the race rules, a KLM DC-6 was the winner. The Viscount's range was extended for the race by the installation of fuselage fuel tanks – note the blanked-off front passenger window where the tanks were fitted. (Lindsay Wise)

G-AMAV in its final livery at Vickers Test Airfield at Wisley, Surrey. It is testing enlarged underwing 'slipper' tanks and has an area of wool-tufting around the rear of the flight deck. It was withdrawn from use in 1960 and scrapped. (BAE SYSTEMS)

The first lengthened Viscount was G-AOJA, a V.802 built for BEA. It flew from Weybridge on 27 July 1956 and was delivered to BEA on 14 February 1957. Later that year, on 23 October, G-AOJA crashed at Nutts Corner, Belfast killing all on board. (BAE SYSTEMS)

South Africa and in the following June received a full Certificate of Airworthiness. Shortly after it embarked on a sales tour of India, the first of a number of such events.

In the winter of 1952/53 G-AMAV joined two BEA Dakotas, which had been converted to Dart power, in providing BEA crews with turbine experience. Now in Vickers livery, in February 1953 Jock Bryce piloted it on the first crossing of the Atlantic by turboprop airliner to carry out cold weather trials in Canada.

London - New Zealand Air Race

In October 1953 G-AMAV was loaned to BEA, painted in its full livery with race number 23 on the fin and a banner on the nose proclaiming "London-New Zealand Air Race" and named 'Endeavour', after Captain Cook's ship.

During the race, the aircraft operated at weights of up to 65,000 lb, some 17,000 lb heavier than its design maximum. The 12,365 miles of the air race were completed in 40 hours 41 minutes flying time at an average speed of 290 mph. This included a non-stop 10 hours 16 minutes flight from Cocos Islands in the Indian Ocean to Melbourne / Essendon in Australia.

G-AMAV also set a speed record from London to Melbourne with an average speed of 293.6 mph, covered in 35 hours 47 minutes. However, owing to the rules of the race, it was a much slower Douglas DC-6 that won – but the publicity message for the Viscount was clear.

On return to Britain G-AMAV wore three liveries in 1954 – initially those of Capital Airlines, then British West Indian Airways livery at Farnborough and finally Vickers house colours which it bore (with variations) for the rest of its days. It left Blackbushe in August 1955 for a three month tour of Africa to test the higher-powered Dart 510 for the Viscount 700D. On its return it continued trials for the 800/810 Series and was fitted with RDa7 engines for Viscount 840 trials at 400 mph until its final flight on 1 April 1958, after which it was stored at Wisley. Finally its registration was cancelled when it was withdrawn from use on 11 October 1960 having flown 2,160 hours. The tail was removed and used for trial mountings of the BAC One-Eleven APU at Weybridge while the fuselage was delivered to the Fire Section at Stansted in August 1963.

Vickers Viscount 800 first production
G-AOJA (c/n 150)
G-AOJA was the first example of the larger new 800

Series of the Viscount and first flew from Weybridge on 27 July 1956. Following test flying at Wisley it was ceremonially named 'Sir Samuel White Baker' at Wisley on 27 November 1956 and delivered to BEA on 14 February 1957. On 23 October 1957 G-AOJA crashed at Nutts Corner, Belfast killing all seven on board in conditions of poor visibility.

Vickers Viscount 810 prototype
G-AOYV (c/n 316)
G-AOYV made its maiden flight from Weybridge to Wisley in Continental Airlines colours piloted by Dick Rymer on 23 December 1957. At Weybridge in 1959 it was fitted with a Vanguard fin to test its de-icing system. Following these trials it was flown to Hurn for a refit and first flew as a Viscount 827 for VASP of Brazil as PP-SRH on 2 September 1960 with delivery on 7 October. After 15 years' flying with VASP it was sold to PLUNA of Uruguay and was withdrawn from use 11 years later. In May 1990 it was derelict at Montevideo Airport.

Data	Viscount 630	Viscount 700	Viscount 800	Viscount 810
Length	74 ft 6 in	81 ft 2 in	85 ft 6 in	85 ft 8 in
Wingspan	88 ft 11 in	93 ft 8½ in	93 ft 8½ in	93 ft 8½ in
Height	26 ft 3 in	26 ft 9 in	26 ft 9 in	26 ft 9 in
MTOW	45,000 lb	63,000 lb	64,500 lb	72,500 lb
Cruising speed	300 mph	318 mph	310 mph	351 mph
Range	700 mls	970 mls	690 mls	1,275 mls
Passengers	32	40-53	53-65	56-64

The Viscount 810 prototype G-AOYV in Continental Airlines livery overflying Wisley. It made its maiden flight on 23 December 1957 and in 1959 was fitted with a Vanguard fin and water spray rig to test the Vanguard's de-icing system. At the end of its trials use in 1960 it was flown to Hurn and refurbished for sale to VASP. (BAE SYSTEMS)

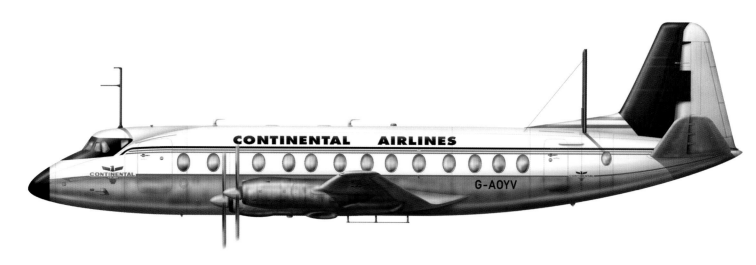

The Viscount 810 prototype, G-AOYV, which first flew on 23 December 1957, was painted in Continental Airlines livery, as it was the first customer for the 810. In 1959 'OYV was employed on Vanguard icing trials and was fitted with a mock-up of the Vanguard forward tail fin.

Powerplant:
V.630 – 4 x 1,380 ehp Rolls-Royce Dart R Da. 1
V.700 – 4 x 1,547 ehp Rolls-Royce Dart R Da. 3
V.800 – 4 x 1,740 ehp Rolls-Royce Dart R Da. 6
V.810 – 4 x 1,990 ehp Rolls-Royce Dart R.Da. 7

Production by type:
Viscount 630: 1
Viscount 663: 1
Viscount 700: 287
Viscount 800: 155

Total built: 444 (2 at Wisley, 163 at Weybridge, 279 at Hurn)

Armstrong Whitworth
Apollo

The first Apollo VX220 at Bitteswell in 1949. (Brian Burrage)

ARMSTRONG WHITWORTH produced many notable civil and military designs both before and during the Second World War. Following the cessation of hostilities and in response to the requirement outlined in the wartime Brabazon Committee's Type 2B civil transport, Armstrong Whitworth proposed the AW.55 Apollo, a short to medium-range airliner intended for operations in Europe. The specification, to which both the Apollo and the Vickers Viscount were designed, required a turboprop airliner with a capacity for 24-30 passengers and a range of 940 miles at 276 mph. In response to the company's proposal the Ministry of Supply issued it with a contract to produce two prototypes.

The Apollo had accommodation in a pressurised cabin for between 26-31 passengers seated two-abreast on either side of a central aisle. The aircraft also incorporated other modern features such as a tricycle undercarriage and reversible pitch propellers. The engine selected was the axial-flow Armstrong Siddeley Mamba, although its development was still in its infancy and prone to severe teething problems. In the prototype installation in the Apollo it should have produced 1010 hp whereas it only achieved 800 hp.

Construction began in 1948 of two flying prototypes and a fuselage for static testing. The first prototype was given the Ministry of Supply serial VX220. Bearing RAF roundels, it made its initial flight on 10 April 1949 at Baginton Airfield just nine months after the maiden flight of the Viscount.

Armstrong Whitworth had considered calling the Apollo the Achilles (and the Avon) – and the Armstrong Siddeley Mambas were to prove the Achilles' heel of the aircraft. From the beginning there were severe problems with the engines' power output, reliability and with vibration. As a result half of the flight testing of the Apollo was concentrated on the Mamba, not on the airframe.

With airframe and various engine modifications in place the prototype Apollo, re-registered G-AIYN, received a limited category Certificate of Airworthiness. Engine performance was enhanced in July 1951 when Mamba Mk. 504 engines became available, but even these had severe limitations and problems. With the continuing problems of the Apollo and evident success of the Viscount in June 1952 further development beyond the two prototypes was halted.

Prototypes

Armstrong Whitworth Apollo prototype 1
VX220 (c/n 3137)

VX220 made its first flight of 20 minutes duration from Baginton on 10 April 1949 piloted by Chief Test Pilot, Eric Franklin. After only nine hours flying the Apollo was grounded to allow for a complete engine change and soundproofing and furnishing of the cabin. Flight testing continued in August 1949 and for the 1949 Farnborough Air Show in September the Apollo, registered as G-AIYN, received a fully fitted-out cabin and basic livery. Its demonstrations at the Show were not without incident as during one take-off the left wheel brake locked and VX220 left the ground trailing a cloud of smoke. In the spring of 1950 after approximately 100 hours in the air, modifications were made to the airframe to cure the aircraft's lack of longitudinal and directional stability and poor stalling performance. The tailplane span was increased,

73

Armstrong Whitworth advertisement for the Apollo. In addition to the Apollo the Armstrong Whitworth AW.52 flying wing is also depicted. (Mike Phipp)

elevator control improved and a small dorsal fin added. On 30 October 1950 it received a Limited Certificate of Airworthiness.

On 19 August 1952 it reverted to military marks as VX220 and on 24 September 1952 was delivered to the A&AEE Boscombe Down. Following an undercarriage failure in March 1953 it was withdrawn from use for spares and was returned in December 1953 to Armstrong Whitworth Baginton where it was dismantled.

Armstrong Whitworth Apollo prototype 2 VX224 (c/n 3138)

The second prototype was allotted G-AMCH but first flew as VX224 from Baginton on 12 December 1952. Following this initial flight it did not take to the air again until 18 September 1953 by which time it had been furnished. A month later it was allotted to the A&AEE Boscombe Down for handling assessment and in March 1954 joined the aircraft at the disposal of the ETPS at

Farnborough. However it was little used and made its last flight on 14 December 1954. The fuselage was used for water tank testing at Farnborough in the 1950s, remaining there until the early 1970s.

Data	Apollo
Length	71 ft 5½ in
Wingspan	92 ft 0 in
Height	26 ft 0 in
MTOW	47,000 lb
Cruising speed	276 mph
Range	940 mls
Passengers	24-30

Powerplant:
4 ×1,140 ehp Armstrong Siddeley Mamba Mk. 504

Total built: 2 at Baginton

VX220 in the air. Following the success of the Viscount the decision was made not to proceed with the Apollo and this aircraft was withdrawn from use in March 1953 and returned to the manufacturers, where it was dismantled. (Ray Williams)

VX224, the second Apollo is seen here at the Silver Jubilee of the RAE Farnborough in 1955. It had made its last flight on 14 December 1954 and was expended in water tank trials at Farnborough. (Peter Berry)

de Havilland Comet

The world's first jet airliner, the first prototype Comet 1, flew on 27 July 1949 as G-5-1. In September it was registered as G-ALVG for its first appearance at the Farnborough Air Show. (Brian Burrage)

THE Comet was the product of de Havilland's determination to fulfil the Brabazon Committee's Type 4 specification jet-powered mail carrier. Although the design team under R.E. Bishop considered several unusual configurations they finally decided on a classic design with a moderately (20°) swept wing with four DH Ghost engines embedded in the wing roots. In September 1946 the Ministry of Supply placed an order for two prototypes and in January 1947 the MoS ordered 14 Comets on behalf of BOAC and British South American Airways.

Less than three years after the finalisation of the design, the prototype DH106 registered G-5-1 made its maiden flight on 27 July 1949 and on its anniversary a second prototype – G-ALZK – took to the air. Early indications were that the Comet met most of the design specifications. It could cruise at 490 mph at 40,000 ft and could carry 36 passengers over 2,600 miles.

The world's first jet airliner
The world's first Certificate of Airworthiness for a commercial jet passenger aircraft was granted on 22 January 1952 and on 2 May 1952 BOAC's Comet 1A G-ALYP operated the first jet airliner service from London to Johannesburg. More routes were added as the Comet with its high speeds and comfort was regarded as the acme of fashionable travel.

The developed 44-seater Comet 1A soon attracted orders from Canadian Pacific, Air France, U.A.T. (Union Aéromaritime de Transport) and the Royal Canadian Air Force. Other airlines joined the queue to place orders for Comet 2s, which were 3 ft longer, had increased range and were powered by Rolls-Royce Avons.

The even larger Comet 3 was also ordered by BOAC and Pan Am.

The accidents
The Concorde-like glamour associated with the Comet was diminished all too soon when two crashed during take-off. More seriously, on the anniversary of the first service BOAC's G-ALYV crashed into the sea en route from Colombo to Delhi. Then disaster struck in a similar manner on 10 January 1954 when G-ALYP, departing from Rome, crashed into the Mediterranean off Elba. All Comets were temporarily grounded for checks and modifications but were soon back in the air. On 8 April 1954 another Comet crashed into the sea after departing from Rome and the type's Certificate of Airworthiness was withdrawn.

A thorough investigation established that metal fatigue had caused the crashes – a subject then imperfectly understood. These events caused de Havilland major problems – orders were cancelled while the 21 completed Comet 1s and the Comet 2s coming off the production line would need substantial remanufacture to allow even limited safe use – which proved to be the case for those Comet 2s which later entered RAF service. Four of the earlier Comet 1s were also rebuilt, with heavier-gauge fuselage skins and oval windows, for the RCAF and for experimental purposes by the RAE – but the remaining Comet 1s were scrapped.

Comet 3 and 4
During the hiatus caused by the accidents, the Comet 3 G-ANLO flew and took on the mantle of ambassador for the Comet, in addition to leading the flight

de Havilland company logo.

BAE SYSTEMS

The exultant flight crew being congratulated by their de Havilland colleagues after the Comet's maiden flight. CTP John Cunningham is in the centre of the photograph. (BAE SYSTEMS)

development of the Comet 4. The Comet 3 possessed the classic look of the Comet but, enhanced by the 15 ft 5 in longer fuselage and pinion tanks on each wing, it provided a streamlined, elegant profile. The next development was the Comet 4, which, though built to the same dimensions of the Comet 3, had later Avon 524 engines. G-APDA, the first Comet 4, (there was no formal prototype), made its maiden flight on 27 April 1958 just over four years after the Comet 1s were withdrawn from service.

Back in airline service

On 29 September 1959 the Mk. 4 received a Certificate of Airworthiness and on 4 October BOAC transatlantic services began just ahead of Pan Am, which introduced transatlantic scheduled services with 707s. However, the Comets were only destined to ply the North Atlantic for two years as a refuelling stop was necessary on most westbound flights. BOAC received 19 Comet 4s and further examples were purchased by Aerolineas Argentinas and East African Airways.

The design was subsequently versioned to offer the medium-range Comet 4B with the fuselage stretched by 6 ft 6 in but the wing cropped by 7 ft and the pinion tanks deleted. As G-ANLO had flown with this wing (but not the extended fuselage) the test flying of the Comet 4B was comparatively short. BEA ordered 14 of this version and Olympic Airways had four. The final Comet, the 4C, was a combination of the longer fuselage of the 4B together with the broader span wing of the Comet 4.

Mexicana was the launch customer and among others were Kuwait Airways, Middle East Airlines, the RAF and Sudan Airways.

As the Comets were displaced by newer, more economical jets in the late 1960s and 1970s, Dan-Air snapped up a large proportion of them and at its peak had over half the Comet 4s ever built. The last commercial service was flown in 1980, although the A&AEE Boscombe Down's XS235 continued flying until 1997.

At the time of writing the longevity of this aircraft is a triumph over adversity and the Comet design continues to serve in the RAF, albeit in a much altered form as the Spey-powered RAF Nimrod MR2 and R1. The MR2s are themselves due to be superseded by the substantially developed and re-engined Nimrod MRA4 which is currently under test and due to enter service with the Air Force in 2010.

Prototypes

de Havilland Comet 1 prototype 1
G-ALVG (c/n 06001)

On 27 July 1949 the unpainted Comet registered G-5-1 made an historic first with the world's maiden flight of a jet airliner. The flight was of 31 minutes duration with de Havilland's Chief Test Pilot, John Cunningham, at the controls. On 1 September 1949 it was registered as G-ALVG and then took part in the SBAC Farnborough Air Show.

*Comet 1A three-
view drawing.
(Author's collection)*

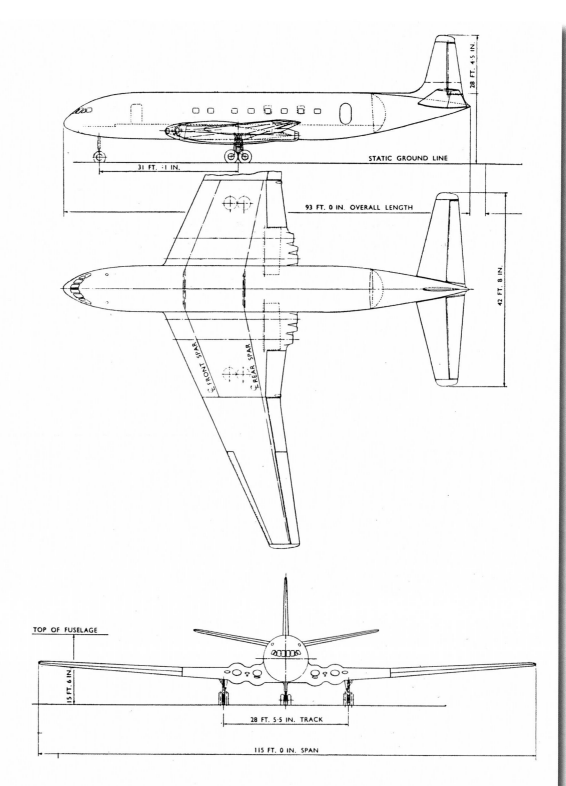

LEADING PARTICULARS

WING :

AREA	2,015 SQ. FT.
SPAN	115 FT.
ROOT CHORD	29 FT. 6 IN.
TIP CHORD	6 FT. 9 IN.
THICKNESS CHORD RATIO	11⅓ PER CENT.
SWEEP-BACK AT ¼ CHORD	20°

FUSELAGE :

LENGTH	93 FT. 0 IN. OVERALL
OUTSIDE DIAMETER	10 FT. 3 IN.
INSIDE DIAMETER	9 FT. 9 IN.

UNDERCARRIAGE :

TRACK (WITH BOGIE UNDERCARRIAGE)	28 FT. 6 IN.
WHEELBASE	32 FT. 4 IN.

TAIL UNIT :

SPAN	43 FT. 4 IN.
HEIGHT OF FIN ABOVE GROUND (STATIC)	27 FT. 10 IN.

POWER PLANTS :

FOUR D.H. GHOST DGT3 ENGINES
5,000-LB. STATIC THRUST FOR TAKE-OFF AT 10,250 R.P.M.

DE HAVILLAND COMET PASSENGER LINER D.H. 106

The original single mainwheel undercarriage had been identified as inadequate for production aircraft and from December 1949 to February 1950 trials were conducted with a four wheel bogie undercarriage, which became standard on production Comet 1s. Due to the construction of the wing this undercarriage could not be retracted on G-ALVG. Tropical trials took place at Nairobi and Khartoum in early - mid 1950 and in September 1950 'LVG returned to the Farnborough Show to make its second appearance, but now bedecked in the livery of the Comet's premier customer BOAC.

At the end of 1950 a probe was fitted to the aircraft's nose to examine the possibility of employing flight refuelling but trials proved that this was unworkable. In May 1951 Sprite booster rockets were installed in the nacelles between the engine exhausts to provide better take-off performance. Extensive tests were flown from Hatfield with the rockets and although the performance improvement was substantial, the fuel was highly volatile and would have involved serious handling and storage problems at airports. 'LVG appeared at the Paris Show in 1951 and yet again at Farnborough in 1951 and 1952. At the end of December 1952 'LVG flew with a fixed droop wing and pinion tanks to test their eventual installation on the Comet 3.

On 31 July 1953 the prototype made its final flight – from Hatfield to Farnborough where it was tested to destruction. Its registration was cancelled on 6 November 1953. The remains of the airframe were eventually broken up during the late 1950s.

de Havilland Comet 1 prototype 2
G-ALZK (c/n 06002)

The second prototype made its maiden flight with John Cunningham at the controls on 27 July 1950, the first anniversary of G-ALVG's maiden flight. 'LZK was delivered on 2 April 1951 to the BOAC Comet Unit at Hurn Airport for a 500 hours crew training and route proving programme and was returned to de Havilland at the end of the year. During May 1952 a non-retractable four wheel undercarriage was briefly fitted to test braking systems.

In April 1957 the aircraft was dismantled and taken by road to Farnborough where the fuselage was employed on aerial trials. During the early 1970s the fuselage was moved to the BAe Woodford factory for Nimrod trials and later scrapped.

de Havilland Comet 2X
G-ALYT (c/n 06006)

Although designated as a Comet 2X, this aircraft was built to Comet 1 dimensions for the Comet 2 trials, with Rolls-Royce Avon 502s replacing the DH Ghosts. 'LYT's maiden flight was from Hatfield on 16 February 1952 piloted by John Cunningham.

The Comet 2X was used to test various marks of Avon engine and thrust reversers and a water spray rig was fitted for engine-icing tests. As a result of the Comet accidents, from April 1954 the aircraft could only be flown unpressurised. G-ALYT flew its last flight (of only 12 minutes duration) from Hatfield to RAF Henlow on 28 May 1959 where John Cunningham landed it on

At the end of 1952 G-ALVG flew with a fixed droop to the leading edge and pinion tanks as tests for the Comet 3. On 31 July 1953 the first prototype made its final flight – from Hatfield to Farnborough where it was tested to destruction and scrapped in the 1950s. (BAE SYSTEMS)

The two Comet 1 prototypes in the air. The second, registered G-ALZK (below G-ALVG), flew exactly one year after the first. (BAE SYSTEMS)

The first Comet G-ALVG at Hatfield with a Mosquito night fighter in the background. Note the single mainwheel undercarriage. (BAE SYSTEMS)

The Comet 2X, G-ALYT, was actually a Comet 1 fitted with Rolls-Royce Avon engines in place of the de Havilland Ghosts and was not constructed to Comet 2 dimensions. Note the larger size of the engine intakes in contrast with those of the Comet 1. (BAE SYSTEMS)

This piece of ironmongery was fitted to spray water into the Avon intakes for de-icing trials. With the end of G-ALYT's operational use John Cunningham delivered it from Hatfield to the nearby grass airfield at RAF Henlow on 28 May 1959. (BAE SYSTEMS)

de Havilland Comet 2 first production
G-AMXA (c/n 06023)

The first Comet 2 first flew in John Cunningham's capable hands at Hatfield on 27 August 1953 in time to appear at the Farnborough Air Show the following month after which it began intensive flight trials.

It was delivered to Marshall of Cambridge in 1955 still in BOAC colours for conversion to a Comet 2R (together with former G-AMXC and 'XE) for RAF Electronic Reconnaissance duties and was re-registered XK655. Unlike most of the modified Comet 2s its fuselage was not strengthened and so it had to fly unpressurised with a total life of only 2,000 hours. On 24 March 1958 it was delivered to No. 192 Squadron which was renumbered as No. 51 Squadron in August 1958. From September 1965 to February 1967 it underwent further conversion work at Hawker Siddeley's Broughton factory.

the grass runway. It remained in use as an instructional airframe as 7610M until it was scrapped in September 1967.

G-AMXA was the first Comet 2 and flew on 27 August 1953 from Hatfield. Whereas many of the Comet 2s were rebuilt with strengthened fuselages 'MXA was not and served the RAF as an (unpressurised) electronic reconnaissance aircraft as XK655. (BAE SYSTEMS)

Following retirement on 1 August 1974 XK655 was sold to the Strathallan Collection at Perth for £4,000 including delivery flight. Unfortunately, on delivery on 21 August 1974, while at approximately 20 ft on final approach to the grass runway at the Collection, a sudden severe downdraught caught the Comet and it hit the ground hard. In so doing the starboard undercarriage broke off and the aircraft skidded some 2,000 ft along the runway. Following the accident the aircraft was repaired to static display condition. In July 1990 the Collection was closed and the Comet was scrapped, except for the nose which was displayed at the Gatwick Museum from December 1995 until August 2004, when it was removed to storage in Bedfordshire.

de Havilland Comet 3 prototype
G-ANLO (c/n 06100)

The sole Comet 3 flew on 19 July 1954 piloted by John Cunningham who demonstrated it at Farnborough in September 1954, 1955 and 1957. John Cunningham also captained it on a World Tour in December 1955. Initially engined with Rolls-Royce Avon 502s it received Avon 523s in February 1957.

In July 1956 it was rebuilt to incorporate many aspects of the Comet 4 enabling 80 per cent of the work needed for certification of that Mark to be carried out. To expedite testing of the Comet 4B it was modified to represent the aerodynamic aspects of the 4B by the reduction of its wingspan by 7 ft and the removal of wing pods. It flew in this configuration on 21 August 1958 as the Comet 3B and was exhibited at Farnborough in BEA livery the following month. Reverse thrust had already been installed on the outboard engines prior to its alteration to 3B in March 1958 to trial the 4B's configuration.

At the end of its Comet trials and after extensive modifications, 'NLO was allotted to the RAE Bedford for use by the Blind Landing Experimental Unit in June

1961 as XP915. On 19 January 1971 its tail was damaged at Bedford by a BEA Trident while preparing to take off, although this was repaired. It was finally grounded on 4 April 1972 but was still used in non-flying trials – its last activities consisted of participating in runway foam arresting trials at Bedford. On 22 August 1973 it was dismantled and the fuselage sent to Woodford for Nimrod trials where it was scrapped in the 1980s.

de Havilland Comet 4 first production
G-APDA (c/n 06401)

The first Comet 4 flew on 27 April 1958 at Hatfield and was airborne for 83 minutes piloted by John Cunningham. It embarked on the Comet 4 flight programme with tropical trials in July in Africa at Khartoum. On 12 August it flew New York to Hatfield in 6 hours 27 minutes, knocking 1 hour 17 minutes off the previous record.

September 1958 was a busy month for G-APDA with a demonstration at the Farnborough Air Show on 5 September, a visit to Hong Kong to inaugurate the new runway at Kai Tak, followed by 23,000 miles of demonstration flights in 10 days via de Havilland's Canadian factory at Downsview, then to South America and back to Hatfield via New York.

The first Comet 4 was delivered to BOAC on 2 February 1959 and was sold on 9 December 1965 to Malaysia - Singapore Airlines as 9M-AOA, later becoming 9V-BAS. Dan-Air purchased it on 19 November 1969 and it was flown back to Lasham for spares use and scrapped in September 1972.

de Havilland Comet 4B first production
G-APMA (c/n 06421)

G-APMA first flew on 27 June 1959 under the command of John Cunningham, embarking on six months of flight testing for the new mark. On 23 December 1959

Following the end of its RAF service in August 1974, XK655 (ex G-AMXA) was sold to the Strathallan Collection at Perth in Scotland. On its delivery flight into the small grass airfield it was struck by a downdraught and crashed. It was repaired for static display. (Michael Brazier)

The Comet 3 prototype G-ANLO being towed past the Farnborough Control Tower at the 1955 Air Show. (Peter Berry)

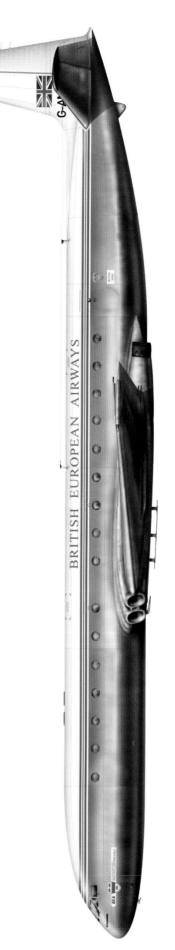

The prototype Comet 3 G-ANLO was modified in 1957 to become a Comet 3B, to trial aspects of the Comet 4B ordered by BEA and was painted in the airline's livery.

*The first three
Comets. Nearest to
the camera is the first
production Comet 1
G-ALYP and
beyond it the two
Comet 1 prototypes
G-ALVG and
G-ALZK.
(BAE SYSTEMS)*

*A beautiful, dynamic
view of the sole
Comet 3,
G-ANLO.
(BAE SYSTEMS)*

G-ANLO
in Comet 3B
configuration with
cropped wings and
thrust reversers as a
test bed for the
Comet 4B in BEA
livery. It later served
with the Blind
Landing
Experimental Unit
as XP915 and
continued in use
until 1972.
(BAE SYSTEMS)

The first Comet 4 G-APDA whose maiden flight was at Hatfield on 27 April 1958. Following delivery to BOAC
on 2 February 1959 it served with the airline for almost six years and was then sold to Malaysia - Singapore Airlines.
After four years it was purchased by Dan-Air but was only used for spares. (BAE SYSTEMS)

The first Comet 4 G-APDA outside the Hatfield Flight Shed. (BAE SYSTEMS)

Following a six-month test programme the first Comet 4B G-APMA was delivered to BEA on 23 December 1959. The 4B had a longer fuselage than the Comet 4 but a reduced wingspan. It is seen here with BEA Vickers Viscount 806 G-AOYP. (BAE SYSTEMS)

The final version of the Comet was the 4C which possessed the long-range wing and the longer fuselage of the Comet 4B. The first 4C was destined for Mexicana but initially flew as G-AOVU and after test flying it was delivered as XA-NAR. This Comet (seen here at Hatfield) still exists and is preserved at Seattle in BOAC livery (even though BOAC never operated Comet 4Cs, only Comet 4s).
(BAE SYSTEMS)

it was delivered to BEA. 'PMA conducted BEA's last Comet flight on 31 October 1971. In July 1972 it was scrapped at Heathrow although the nose was kept as a Systems Trainer until 1987.

de Havilland Comet 4C first production
G-AOVU (c/n 06424)

De Havilland Test Pilot, Pat Fillingham, made the first flight of G-AOVU in Mexicana colours at Hatfield on 31 October 1959. After 87 hours of Comet 4C certification flying, it was delivered to Mexicana as XA-NAR on 8 June 1960.

The aircraft inaugurated the 'Golden Aztec' service between Mexico City and Los Angeles on 4 July 1960 and served on Mexicana routes until 1970. It was kept in reserve for the occasional charter until 1972 when it was sold to Westernair of Albuquerque, New Mexico, which re-registered it as N888WA. It remained at Mexico City for the following two years, receiving a new livery and interior.

Redmond Air then purchased it in 1978 and ferried it to Salt Lake City where it lay parked until it was ferried to Paine Field, Everett, Washington in July 1979 where it remained. It had accumulated a total of 27,065 hours of flight time during its 20 years of service.

In 1984, ownership was transferred to the Everett Community College's Aviation Maintenance Technician School and it was painted in BOAC livery by Boeing paint shop volunteers. Unfortunately, nothing was done to protect the interior, and the aircraft was left outside

with standing water in the fuselage. However the Seattle Museum of Flight was given title to the Comet in 1994, and it was towed to the Museum's Restoration Facility in 1995 where restoration is gradually taking place.

Powerplant:
Comet 1 – 4 x 4,450 lb de Havilland Ghost 50
Comet 2 – 4 x 7,300 lb Rolls-Royce Avon Mk. 503
Comet 4 – 4 x 10,500 lb Rolls-Royce Avon Mk. 524
Comet 4C – 4 x 10,500 lb Rolls-Royce Avon Mk. 525

Production by type:
Mk. 1/1A: 21 (including 2 prototypes)
Mk. 2X: 1
Mk. 2: 15
Mk. 3: 1
Mk. 4: 27
Mk. 4B: 18
Mk. 4C: 30

Total built: 113 (72 at Hatfield, 41 at Broughton)

Data	Comet 1	Comet 2	Comet 4	Comet 4C
Length	93 ft 0 in	96 ft 1 in	111 ft 6 in	118 ft
Wingspan	115 ft	115 ft	115 ft	115 ft
Height	28 ft 4 in	28 ft 4 in	28 ft 6 in	28 ft 6 in
MTOW	107,000 lb	115,000 lb	160,000 lb	162,000 lb
Cruising speed	490 mph	490 mph	500 mph	500 mph
Range	1,750 mls	2,100 mls	3,225 mls	2,570 mls
Passengers	36-44	36-44	60-81	72-106

Bristol Brabazon

*The Brabazon
prototype
G-AGPW, being
pulled out of the
hangar, built for its
construction at
Filton. (Peter
Rushby Collection)*

THE Brabazon is synonymous with the Committee of that name which first met on 23 December 1942 under the Chairmanship of Lord Brabazon. The Brabazon Committee recommended five basic types of which the Type 1 was a long-range piston-engined intercontinental airliner, able to fly from London to New York (3,450 miles) in the most adverse conditions. Bristol bid for this contract with its Type 167 and was able to capitalise on its experience in designing a wartime 100 ton heavy bomber, even though the RAF had not selected the design for production. On 11 March 1943 it was announced that Bristol would build the Type 1. The Ministry of Supply contracted Bristol to construct two prototypes with the possibility of a later contract for ten production aircraft.

In November 1944 the design was finalised on what was to be the largest landplane then built with a 177 ft pressurised fuselage, 230 ft wingspan, powered by eight Bristol Centaurus 18-cylinder radial engines mounted in pairs inside the wing. These eight engines would drive eight paired contra-rotating propellers.

Conceived in the era when passenger flying was the domain of the elite, it was viewed in the same light as the ocean liner. BOAC considered that passengers would find a long non-stop flight almost intolerable and should therefore each be provided with 200 cu.ft for comfort, and 270 cu. ft for luxury. The Brabazon was to be a very large, heavy aircraft – weighing 290,000 lb – for only 100 passengers and 14 crew and one of the first airliners to be pressurised and air conditioned. (Today an aircraft of these dimensions might accommodate 350 passengers.)

Construction commenced at Filton in October 1945, and along with the manufacture of the aircraft, infrastructure improvements were implemented with the construction of a huge assembly building, adjoining a new 8,175 ft runway. Both remain in use to this day and were used in the construction of Concorde.

The aircraft was rolled out for engine runs in December 1948. Following extensive ground trials on 4 September 1949, Chief Test Pilot, Bill Pegg, took the Brabazon up for her first flight, viewed by many of the workforce and thousands of other spectators.

Despite the general enthusiasm, BOAC never showed any real interest in buying the Brabazon, although British European Airways considered leasing the Mk. 1. A number of problems, such as fatigue cracks appearing in propeller mountings, prevented full airworthiness certification. Airframe life was assessed at only 5,000 hours – unacceptable for an airliner.

These design problems might have been resolved, but the development of turboprops and jet engines for airliners which occurred during the Brabazon's gestation meant that passengers could travel faster and above the bad weather. The large areas dedicated to the comfort of an uneconomically small passenger load were no longer required.

In March 1952 work on the second Brabazon prototype (which was to be powered by turboprop Bristol Proteus engines) was suspended. By this time the turboprop Bristol Britannia was already under construction and it flew in August that year. Bristol saw a strong future for the Britannia and was eager to use all its resources in promoting it, while dispensing with the Brabazon. Thus in July 1953 the end of the Brabazon was announced.

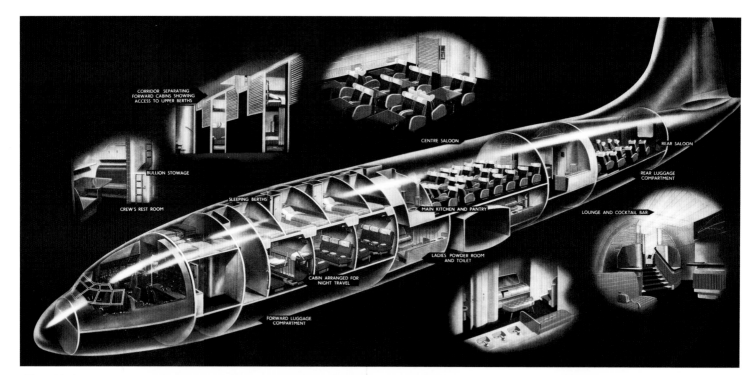

The cabin layout as depicted in a Bristol brochure. This shows the flight deck, crew rest room, bullion storage, passenger seating, sleeping berths, ladies' powder room, main kitchen and pantry, lounge and cocktail bar. (Bristol Aero Collection)

Above: Under construction in the huge Brabazon Assembly Hall. Note the nose probe and open engine access panels. (Author's collection)

The unpainted Brabazon undergoing engine runs. Alongside is an Avro Lancaster, RF131, which was used to test the Brabazon's flying control system. (Author's collection)

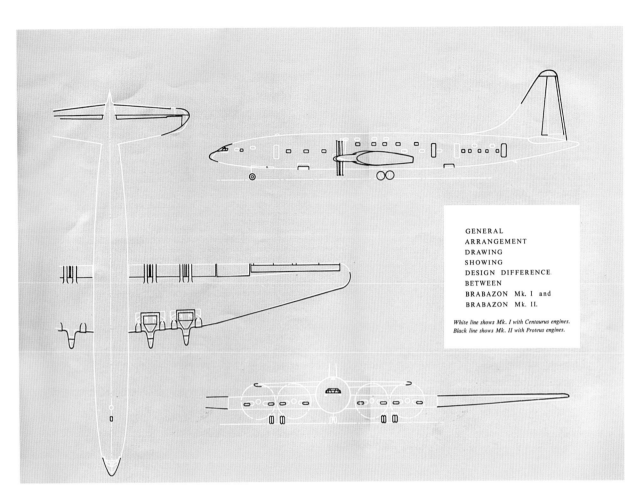

General arrangement drawing of the Brabazon 1 and the Brabazon 2, which would have been powered by Bristol Proteus engines. (Bristol Aero Collection)

GENERAL
ARRANGEMENT
DRAWING
SHOWING
DESIGN DIFFERENCE
BETWEEN
BRABAZON Mk. I and
BRABAZON Mk. II.

White line shows Mk. I with Centaurus engines.
Black line shows Mk. II with Proteus engines.

It is well evident from this photo that the Brabazon was Britain's largest aircraft. (Peter Rushby Collection)

The Brabazon coming in to land at Farnborough. It appeared at the Air Show just after its maiden flight in 1949 and in 1950 and 1951. (Bristol Aero Collection)

Prototype

Bristol Brabazon 1 prototype
G-AGPW (c/n 12759)

On 4 September 1949 the Brabazon, captained by Chief Test Pilot, Bill Pegg, with a crew of nine, lifted off after a run of only 1,200 ft for a first flight of 27 minutes. The second flight was only three days later and four days after the first flight, 'GPW made a fly past at the Farnborough Air Show. The Brabazon now set to work on its flight test programme for which it was fitted with 14 auto observer panels and recording cameras.

On 16 January 1950 a major hydraulic leak during a flight caused a problem in lowering the undercarriage. After a struggle Bill Pegg's deputy, Walter Gibb, was able to lower the gear and made a safe, though flapless, landing at Filton.

After the conclusion of the initial period of flight testing a luxury passenger cabin was installed and on June 15-16, 1950 it visited London's Heathrow Airport, making two demonstration flights. G-AGPW also appeared at the Paris Salon in June and then Farnborough again in both September 1950 and 1951.

Its last flight was only a year later on 20 September 1952 making a total of 164 flights and 382 hours over that brief three year period. Both the prototype and the incomplete second Brabazon (G-AIML c/n 12870) were broken up in October 1953.

Total time: 382 hours

Data	Brabazon 1
Length	177 ft
Wingspan	230 ft
Height	50 ft
MTOW	290,000 lb
Cruising speed	300 mph
Range	5,500 mls
Passengers	100

MEN WHO FLY THE BRABAZON

On the right is Mr. A. J. Pegg, Chief Test Pilot of the Company and Brabazon captain. Below is the flight test crew, photographed on the day of the first flight. Left to right, they are: A. Cowan *(flight test observer)*, M. W. West *(flight engineer)*, M. J. Peniston *(chief flight test observer)*, Walter Gibb *(co-pilot)*, A. J. Pegg *(pilot)*, John Sizer *(flight test observer)*, H. J. Hayman *(flight engineer)*, L. D. Atkinson *(chief flight engineer)*, K. A. Fitzgerald *(electrical engineer)*, and J. M. Cochrane *(flight test observer)*.

The first flight crew with the Chief Test Pilot, Bill Pegg, in the blazer, with his co-pilot and successor Walter Gibb on his right. (Bristol Aero Collection)

Powerplant: 8 x 2,360 hp Bristol Centaurus

Total built: 1 at Filton

G-AGPW parked outside the Brabazon hangar in February 1950. The fuselage has camera tracking markers used for measurement purposes during testing. (Author's collection)

*The mighty
contra-rotating
propellers for the
Bristol Centauruses.
The air intakes
either side of the
propellers are in the
closed position.
(Bristol Aero
Collection)*

*Lord Brabazon (left)
visits the aircraft
named after him.
This view shows
the flight test
instrumentation
in the main,
uninsulated cabin.
(Bristol Aero
Collection)*

*The Brabazon
G-AGPW and the
uncompleted second
Brabazon G-AIML
at Filton in 1953
prior to scrapping.
(Bristol Aero
Collection)*

Bristol Britannia

AS a design the Bristol Britannia had the makings of success but was hindered by the technical failings of its Bristol Proteus turboprops which severely delayed its entry into service until 1957. By then airlines were in the process of introducing jet airliners such as the Boeing 707 and Douglas DC-8 and so the market for large medium to long-range turboprops with the major carriers had much diminished.

The Britannia was devised from the Brabazon Committee's Type 3, the grandly named Medium-Range Empire requirement of the war years, refined post-hostilities to a specification for a 32-seater with a range of 1,500 miles. A number of manufacturers bid for this, including Bristol which offered its Type 175, which was selected by BOAC. The design was further refined increasing in weight and performance to accommodate 42-48 passengers. In July 1948 the Ministry of Supply awarded Bristol a contract for three prototypes all powered by Centaurus piston engines but the obvious advantages of the turbine engine stimulated its replacement by the turboprop Bristol Proteus. In November 1948 BOAC ordered 25 Bristol 175s. The initial version of the Bristol 175 was the series 100, the prototypes were 101s and the first for BOAC were 102s. (Later series followed this manner of numbering.)

Down in the Severn

The first prototype G-ALBO, now named the Britannia, flew in August 1952 but was only joined by the second prototype G-ALRX in December 1953. This aircraft crash-landed on the shore of the River Severn in February the following year, not far from Bristol, causing a severe delay to the test programme. G-ALBO

was brought up to the same standard of the second aircraft and the first three production machines destined for BOAC (G-ANBA,B,C) joined the test programme. In December 1955 the Britannia received its full Certificate of Airworthiness.

Service delays

However the Britannia did not enter passenger service until 1 February 1957 owing to severe icing problems which caused the Proteus engines to cut out when flying through tropical weather fronts. An immense amount of time, effort and money was expended to first identify and then solve the problem. The loss of earnings to BOAC and the costs were shared by the Government and the manufacturer.

The 300 and 310 Series

BOAC scaled down its original order from 25 to 15 Series 102s and considered ordering the longer 300s before refining this to 18 Series 312s which combined a longer fuselage with a greater fuel capacity. The introduction of the Series 310 stimulated interest from El Al, Canadian Pacific and Cubana which placed orders for this quiet, sophisticated, long-range transport.

Transatlantic services

The first BOAC Britannia 312 services were flown from Heathrow to New York on 19 December 1957 and on the same day El Al's 4X-AGA flew 6,100 miles non-stop from New York to Tel Aviv, then a record distance for a civil aircraft. Just prior to that Aeronaves de Mexico started operations from Mexico City to New York while in late 1958 Canadian Pacific's aircraft began 4,700 mile Vancouver - Tokyo services. The independent British

The first Britannia prototype G-ALBO, being towed past the control tower at the Farnborough Air Show in 1955, the third of its five appearances there. Unfortunately this important prototype was scrapped in 1968. (Peter Berry)

BRISTOL
Britannia

G-ALBO in Bristol livery with the Brabazon hangar in the background. In the latter part of the 1950s 'LBO was employed in Proteus and Orion engine trials. (Bristol Aero Collection)

airlines, Air Charter and Hunting-Clan also took advantage of the Bristol product as did Ghana Airways and the Argentinian airline, Transcontinental.

In the expectation of substantial further contracts in 1953 Bristol had entered into an agreement with Shorts at Belfast for the setting up of a second production line and the first Britannia from this source flew in June 1957. The Belfast line mainly concentrated on the Series 250 mixed-traffic aircraft which incorporated forward fuselage freight doors. Eventually 23 of this variant were delivered to the RAF.

Several Britannia developments were projected by Bristol but the attraction of large jetliners resulted in the end of production and therefore only 85 were produced. However Canadair signed a licence agreement with Bristol which led to the Canadair Argus, a Maritime Reconnaissance aircraft which employed the Britannia's wings and the swing-tail CL-44 freighter/airliner which used all the main structures. In Belfast, Shorts' connection with the Britannia continued after the end of production as the wing and tail surfaces were incorporated into the Shorts Belfast military freighter.

Prototypes

Bristol Britannia 100 prototype 1
G-ALBO (c/n 12873) Series 101

Bill Pegg made the maiden flight of 'LBO in BOAC livery powered by early Proteus 625s on 16 August 1952 at Filton. He found the elevator control was far too light and sensitive, giving a switchback flight path. Having decided to return to Filton, one of the bogies failed to fully rotate into the landing position when he selected the undercarriage down. The flight deck had filled with smoke and he had no option but to effect an immediate landing. Fortunately, just before touchdown the bogie rotated into the correct position. On flight 2 there were further problems when the nosewheel failed to lock down until the mainwheels touched the runway on landing. The flying control oversensitivity and undercarriage problems were easily addressed and 'LBO appeared at Farnborough 1952, 1953 and again in 1955.

Following the loss of the second prototype G-ALRX, the first prototype was modified to the higher weight of 140,000 lb and recommenced flying in March 1954.

*The second
prototype Britannia
G-ALRX making a
sprightly take-off
from Filton.
It first flew on
23 December 1953.
(Bristol Aero
Collection)*

*A fine view of
G-ALRX in flight,
though her career
was to be cut short.
(Peter Rushby
Collection)*

In May 1954, with Walter Gibb at the controls, a flap torque tube broke during stalling tests, causing the flaps on one side to retract and the aircraft half-rolled before Gibb could regain control. This required an overload of 3G to be applied which necessitated the aircraft to be temporarily grounded.

From April 1956 it was used as an engine test bed flying different marks of Proteus, sometimes with a water spray rig to simulate icing conditions. On 31 August 1956 it flew with two Proteus 755, one Proteus 705 and a Bristol Orion, the powerplant which

was due to replace the Proteus. It appeared at Farnborough 1956 and 1957 bearing Bristol livery promoting the Orion. From 1958 it was little flown and its last flight was on 30 November 1960 to RAF St Athan where it became a maintenance airframe with registration 7708M. It was broken up on 12 June 1968. G-ALBO flew 1,794 hours and made 692 flights.

Bristol Britannia 100 prototype 2
G-ALRX (c/n 12874) Series 101
The second prototype, G-ALRX took off from Filton's

The first and second prototype Britannias being assembled in the main bay of the Brabazon hangar at Filton. Beyond in the East bay the prototype Brabazon and the incomplete second aircraft are visible. (Author's collection)

Owing to a catastrophic engine fire Bill Pegg, Bristol's Chief Test Pilot, had to crash-land G-ALRX on a mudbank of the River Severn on 4 February 1954. The landing extinguished the engine fire and all 13 occupants escaped without injury. (Bristol Aero Collection)

Despite a combined effort by the Army, Air Force, Fire Brigade and local haulage contractors to drag the Britannia up the bank of the River it was covered by the rising tide and damaged beyond repair. (Bristol Aero Collection)

runway on 23 December 1953 on its maiden flight with Bill Pegg in command. On the morning of 4 February 1954, G-ALRX took off from Filton on a test flight and sales demonstration to KLM, a potential Britannia customer, which had its Chief Pilot and Vice-President (Engineering) on board. In total 13 people were on board including the Britannia's designer Dr. Archibald Russell and Dr. Stanley Hooker, Chief Engineer of the Bristol Engine Division. Seven minutes into the flight the engine temperature on engine No.3 rose and Bill Pegg requested that it be shut down. This was explained to the guests as a demonstration of how well the aircraft flew on three engines.

Bill ordered the engine to be restarted after a few minutes but the engine temperature rose again and suddenly the engine exploded, piercing the engine oil

tank, which burst into flames spreading back to the tail. The engine fire extinguishers were totally ineffectual and Bill Pegg turned towards Filton for an emergency landing with engine No.4 shut down as a precaution. To add to the drama, the crash switches were activated and engines Nos.1 and 2 automatically shut down. The two Flight Engineers, Ken Fitzgerald and Gareth Jones, quickly managed to re-light the two port engines and immediate disaster was averted.

An attempt was made to blow out the fire by diving while the Britannia was still flying over the Welsh mountains, but to no avail. With a fire that had been burning for 15 minutes engulfing the starboard wing and threatening to penetrate the fuel tanks, Filton still 14 miles away and little likelihood that the undercarriage would function, Bill elected to put 'LRX

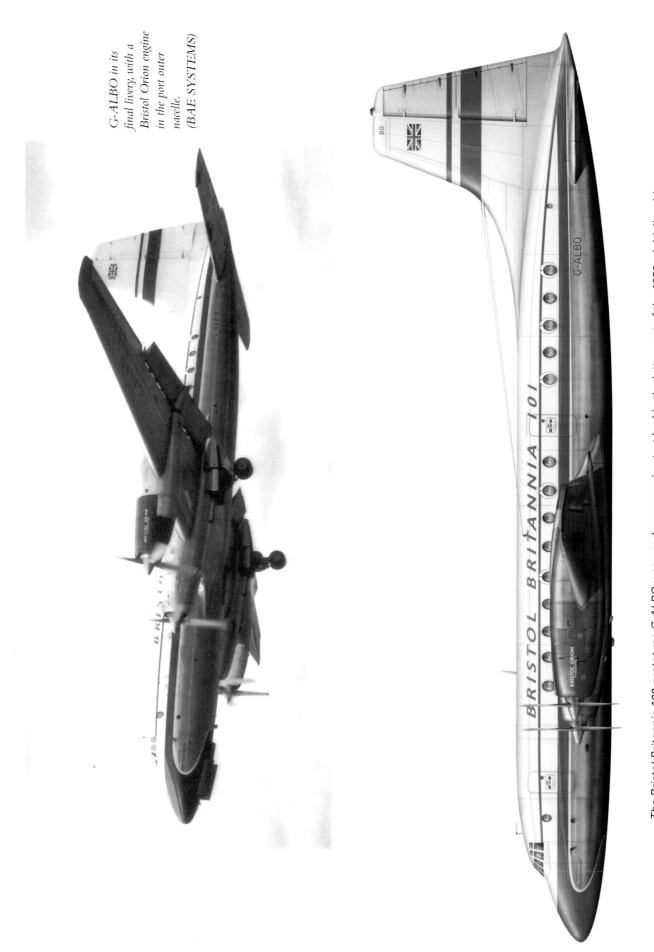

G-ALBO in its
final livery, with a
Bristol Orion engine
in the port outer
nacelle.
(BAE SYSTEMS)

The Bristol Britannia 100 prototype G-ALBO was used as an engine test bed in the latter part of the 1950s, initially with
later marks of the Bristol Proteus engine and finally with the Bristol Orion which was installed in its port outer nacelle.

Britannia quartet. From the left, the prototype G-ALBO, then the first three production aircraft; G-ANBA, 'BB, 'BC, all Britannia 102s which served with BOAC. (Author's collection)

A fine view of the prototype Britannia 300, G-ANCA, series 301. It was originally rolled out in Capital Airlines colours but the livery was speedily altered to house livery. (Bristol Aero Collection)

Britannia, G-ANCA, in its natural element, elegance personified. (Peter Rushby Collection)

down on the River Severn mudflats. As he came in to land the two port Proteus engines stopped again due to a short circuit but again the Flight Engineers restarted the engines, allowing Pegg to make a controlled (flaps and wheels-up) belly-landing on the mudflats near Littleton-on-Severn. The aircraft slid parallel to the shore for 400 yards, sending plumes of mud in the air and stopped facing out from the shore, with one engine ripped from the nacelle, but with little other damage. The mud and water put out the flames and the shaken crew and passengers evacuated the aircraft.

Although only 150 yards from the shore, the aircraft could not be pulled from the mud before the tide came in and it was 48 hours before an attempt could be made to recover it. The Britannia was a write-off as not only had salt water covered the fuselage, damaging the airframe and any equipment, but efforts to pull the aircraft to the shore had put extreme stress on the fuselage.

From its first flight 43 days earlier, G-ALRX had flown only 51 hours in 24 flights. The fuselage was returned to Filton, and served as a crew trainer for many years. Cut down to just the forward fuselage, it was used by the Aeromedical and Safety School at Boscombe Down. It was acquired by the Britannia Aircraft Preservation Trust and joined the Bristol Aero Collection store at Barnwell in December 1995, moving to Kemble the following year.

Bristol Britannia 300 prototype
G-ANCA (c/n 12917) Series 301
Originally built for BOAC, after the Corporation's decision to convert its 300s to 312s the Ministry of Supply purchased it. This aircraft initially appeared in Capital Airlines colours but these were quickly versioned into Bristol livery. It made its first flight on 31 July 1956 and was exhibited at the 1957 Farnborough Air Show. On 6 November 1957 the Britannia was returning to Filton after a 1 hour 40 minutes test flight. It entered the Filton circuit but at 1,500 ft the right wing suddenly dropped and the aircraft went into a very steeply banked right-hand turn. The Britannia briefly recovered but banked steeply again and struck the ground in a wood near Downend where all of the 15 crew were killed. The cause of the accident was unclear but may have been the result of a malfunctioning autopilot.

Bristol Britannia 310 prototype
G-AOVA (c/n 13207) Series 311
First flown by Walter Gibb, on 31 December 1956 in Bristol colours. From 29 January to 10 March 1957 it was based at Winnipeg for cold weather trials. In August and November - December that year it was then based in the Far East for trials. Originally destined to be the first Series 312 for BOAC, the Corporation chose not to accept it following its arduous test flying experiences and a further aircraft was built for the airline to replace it.

'OVA was redesignated as a Series 319 and was delivered to Ghana Airways as 'Osagyefo' on 11 November 1960. 'OVA was returned to Bristol Aircraft on 31 December 1963 and sold to British Eagle as 'Justice' in April 1964. In March 1969 it was sold to CCT Leasing and it flew with British Caledonian as 'Country of Fife' until the end of 1969, when it flew to Baginton. It was broken up for spares in July 1971.

Powerplant:
Britannia 102 – 4 x 3,870 ehp Bristol Proteus 705
Britannia 312 – 4 x 4,120 ehp Bristol Proteus 755/761

Production by type:
Britannia 100: 17 (including 2 x 101 prototypes and 15 x 102)
Britannia 252: 23
Britannia 300: 8 (including 1 prototype)
Britannia 310: 37 (including 1 prototype)

Total built: 85 (55 at Filton, 30 at Belfast)

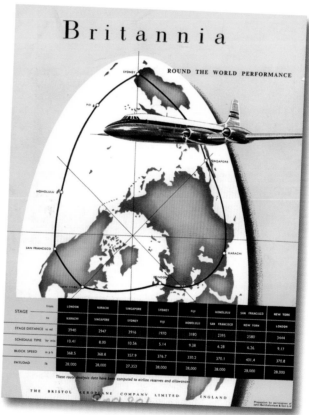

The Britannia 311 G-AOVA flew on 31 December 1956 and this photograph shows it at Winnipeg where it carried out cold weather trials from 29 January to 10 March 1957. Though strictly a 311 its titling frequently referred to it as a Series 312. (Bristol Aero Collection)

An early piece of advertising extolling the aircraft's ability as a long distance round the world airliner. (Author's collection)

Data	Series 100	Series 300	Series 310
Length	114 ft	124 ft 3 in	124 ft 3 in
Wingspan	142 ft 3 in	142 ft 3 in	142 ft 3 in
Height	36 ft 8 in	36 ft 8 in	36 ft 8 in
MTOW	155,000 lb	185,000 lb	180,000 lb
Cruising speed	335 mph	357 mph	355 mph
Range	2,740 mls	3,496 mls	4,100 mls
Passengers	90	114	114

G-AOVA was originally destined for BOAC as part of its order for 312s, but at the end of its trials it was refurbished and delivered to Ghana Airways. Later it flew with British Eagle and finally British Caledonian. (Author's collection)

The nose of the second prototype Britannia 101 G-ALRX which crash-landed on the banks of the River Severn on 4 February 1954. It is now preserved at the British Aero Collection at Kemble, Glos. (British Aero Collection)

Saunders-Roe Princess

THE development of Britain's largest flying boat started at the end of 1944 – a 140 ton transatlantic machine with luxurious, pressurised accommodation for 105 passengers and 15 crew on twin decks with a range of 5,500 miles at a cruising speed of 360 mph. In 1946, following project proposals to the Ministry of Supply, Saunders-Roe (Saro) was in receipt of a contract to build three SR45 Princess flying boats for BOAC. Even then the airline was lukewarm about the Princess and two years later serious consideration was given to cancellation.

The choice of powerplant proved troublesome for Saro as piston engines were deemed to have insufficient power and turboprops were still a very new form of traction, subject to many problems. Eventually Saro decided to fit the Bristol Proteus turboprop which was also under development for the Bristol Brabazon. Owing to the size of the Princess ten engines were necessary and were arranged in six nacelles with four coupled pairs inboard and two singles outboard. However the Proteus was beset by problems and failed to achieve its promised specification, adversely affecting the performance of the Princess.

Saunders-Roe had originally expected to deliver the flying boat to BOAC in March 1951 but delays, almost entirely attributed to the engine, meant that the first fully-functioning coupled Proteus was only received at the end of August 1951. The very size of the machine was a challenge to the manufacturer and the fitting of the outer wings and upper vertical fin plus some of the final assembly had to take place outside the hangars.

The maiden flight of a Princess

G-ALUN flew on 22 August 1952 yet even before the type's first flight it was evident that there was no longer a commercial market for flying boats. BOAC was planning to introduce Comets on its major international routes and the flying boat era had passed. Meanwhile the cost of the project had risen from the original contract price of £2.8m to £10.8m and engine costs by tenfold to almost £5m. Accordingly in the spring of 1951 the Ministry of Supply ordered Saro to suspend production of the second and third machines (and it was never restarted). In 1954 the Ministry also ended the contract on the prototype and it never flew again.

The end

There were various schemes to utilise the aircraft but as there was no likelihood that more than three aircraft would ever be built, and with the recognition that a new powerplant was needed fully to exploit the aircraft's potential, no future could be found for the Princess. G-ALUN was cocooned in 1954 while the two incomplete Princesses, G-ALUO and G-ALUP had already been cocooned in 1952 and towed across the Solent to Calshot. They were all broken up in 1967.

Prototype

Saro SR 45 Princess prototype
G-ALUN (c/n SR.901)

G-ALUN was launched shortly after midnight on 22 August 1952 and embarked on taxiing trials during the late morning. Saro's Chief Test Pilot Geoffrey Tyson, co-pilot John Booth and a crew of nine taxied the mighty Princess for more than half an hour in the Solent. As the sea conditions and visibility were ideal Tyson decided to attempt a maiden flight and the

G-ALUN on Saunders-Roe's slipway at Cowes on 19 August 1952. It was launched just after midnight. This view clearly illustrates the ten Bristol Proteus engine installation with four coupled pairs and singles outboard. Note the tail of the Saro A.1 jet flying boat fighter G-12-1, bottom left. (GKN plc)

THE "BRISTOL" COUPLED PROTEUS ENGINE FOR THE "BRISTOL" BRABAZON II. AND SAUNDERS ROE "PRINCESS" FLYING BOAT

The Bristol Coupled Proteus as designed for the Saro Princess and the Brabazon 2. The Coupled Proteus flew in the Princess but never in the Brabazon 2, which was scrapped before completion. (Bristol Aero Collection)

The Princess taking off. Take-off run was approximately 2,880 ft. (GKN plc)

The twelve-strong first flight crew: (back row from left) Stratton, Ingle, Worner, Tyson (Chief Test Pilot), Booth, Welford, New, Jones; (front row from left) Palmer, Mabey, Walker, Wraith. (GKN plc)

An ocean liner or a flying machine? The Princess taxiing on the Solent. (GKN plc)

*A view of the
Princess in its later
livery cruising over
the Isle of Wight.
(author's collection)*

G-ALUN, again in its later airline style colour scheme. (GKN plc)

Princess took to the air at 12:13 hrs, landing half an hour later.

It flew unpainted in bare metal finish and on its fifth flight appeared at the Farnborough Air Show on 2 September 1952. Unfortunately it did not appear three days later owing to a Proteus engine failure (the prototype suffered three engine failures during its short flying life). G-ALUN engaged in its flight test programme appearing again at the following year's Farnborough Show (its last public appearance) in an 'airline' style blue, yellow and white livery.

Between its first flight and its last on 27 May 1954 the Princess flew a total of 46 test flights and 97 flying hours before the Ministry of Supply contract was terminated. Most of the manufacturer's trials were completed and it was successfully assessed at the Marine Aircraft Evaluation Establishment at Felixstowe.

As the future of the project was so uncertain the Princess was cocooned and stored at Cowes in 1954. In May 1966 it was towed across the River Medina to be de-cocooned for possible use by Aero-Spacelines but as corrosion had set in the aircraft was towed to Southampton on 12 April 1967 and was gradually broken up on the River Itchen.

Total time: 97 hours

Data	Princess
Length	148 ft
Wingspan	219ft 6 in
Height	55ft 9 in
MTOW	330,000 lb
Cruising speed	360 mph
Range	5,270 mls
Passengers	105

Powerplant:
Princess – 10 x 3,780 ehp Bristol Proteus

Total built: 1 at Cowes, Isle of Wight

The only Princess to fly, G-ALUN was cocooned at the Saro factory at Cowes in 1954 and it remained in this state until 1966 when it was de-cocooned. The following year it was scrapped at Southampton. (Lindsay Wise)

Scottish Aviation Twin Pioneer

Twin Pioneer prototype G-ANTP in company livery. (BAE SYSTEMS)

THE Twin Pioneer was developed from the smaller, single-engined Prestwick Pioneer designed to an RAF requirement for a single-engined communications aircraft able to make extremely short take-off and landing runs.

The need for a larger aircraft with similar performance became apparent and Scottish Aviation set to work on a twin-engined aircraft which became the 16-passenger Twin Pioneer. To provide the necessary short take-off and landing characteristics, the Twin Pioneer was fitted with the same high lift devices as the Prestwick Pioneer. Scottish Aviation not only envisaged utilitarian roles for the Twin Pioneer but city centre to city centre passenger operation facilitated by the aircraft's dynamic STOL performance. During the 1957 Paris Air Show, Twin Pioneers regularly flew from the Paris Heliport near the Eiffel Tower to Le Bourget in order to demonstrate the aircraft's capabilities in this respect.

The prototype Twin Pioneer, registered G-ANTP, first flew at Prestwick Airport on 25 June 1955 and received British Certification in September 1956. Three pre-production aircraft were built for trials, sales and demonstrations. By the time production ceased in 1962, 87 Twin Pioneers had been built, finding their way into civilian and military service and operating in most continents of the world.

The Royal Air Force ordered 39 aircraft, built between 1958 and 1959, for use in Aden and the Far East to act mainly as light transports, while the Royal Malaysian Air Force received 15. Scottish Aviation used 10, which were eventually sold on, while 23 were sold directly to civil operators. An early delivery for civil use was to KLM De Kroonduif NV of New Guinea which received three. Two were delivered to the Kuwait Oil Company and some of

the first sales were as survey aircraft, to Rio Tinto and the Austrian and Swiss government survey departments. Civilian aircraft operated in many other countries - including Australia, Austria, Borneo, Cambodia, Canada, Indonesia, Iran, Iraq, Kuwait, Morocco, Nepal, Nigeria, the Philippines, Sierra Leone and Vietnam.

Although the Twin Pioneer's performance was well up to specification and far greater sales were envisaged, the two crashes due to fatigue failure early in the aircraft's life affected potential customer confidence.

In the end the availability of far cheaper second-hand aircraft and the development of runways, curtailed greater sales.

Prototypes

G-ANTP (c/n 501)

The prototype first flew in Scottish Aviation livery piloted by Noel Capper at Prestwick Airport on 25 June 1955 and was displayed at the 1955 SBAC Farnborough Air Show where it stunned spectators with landing runs of only 180 ft. Originally fitted with Alvis Leonides 503 radial engines, in November 1958 it was converted to a Series 3 with the installation of Alvis Leonides 531 engines. The prototype was written off after stalling on take-off at Jorhat, India on 10 March 1960.

Pre-production 1
G-AOEN (c/n 502)

The second Twin Pioneer flew on 28 April 1956 and was demonstrated at the 1956 Farnborough Show in KLM De Kroonduif colours. 'OEN was then despatched on a

G-ANTP waiting to take off at the 1955 Farnborough Air Show. Its superlative airfield performance impressed the crowds. (Author's Collection)

The first pre-production Twin Pioneer G-AOEN demonstrating at Salisbury, Rhodesia (now Harare, Zimbabwe) in 1959. (Brian Robbins)

Second pre-production aircraft G-AOEO was briefly trialled by Swissair in January – March 1957 on services into airfields with restricted runways. It is here pictured having landed on a frozen lake at St. Moritz. (Ed Coates Collection)

demonstration tour of North and South America, during which it crossed the Andes three times. It remained in the Americas for three years, only returning to Prestwick in May 1959. In July it departed on a sales tour of Africa. Unfortunately, on 12 December 1959 while flying over the Zambezi River demonstrating its single engine performance, the aircraft lost height and force- landed on an island in the river. Following impact, the Twin Pioneer slid along on soft ground and the main gear and both wings became detached. Fortunately there were no fatalities. The aircraft was a write-off.

Pre-production 2
G-AOEO (c/n 503)
G-AOEO was first flown on 26 August 1956 just in time to appear at the September Farnborough 1956 Show in Swissair colours. Swissair only used the Twin Pioneer for a very short period of time, from January - March 1957. The aircraft was used to fly into high altitude airports in Switzerland with short runways, such as Davos, Zermatt, St. Moritz and La-Chaux-de-Fonds. On 7 December 1957, while engaged on an African sales tour, 'OEO crashed near Tripoli. When it was

discovered, the outer panel of the left-hand wing was found 1,200 yds from the main wreckage. The cause of the crash was metal fatigue. Amongst the 6 killed was Group Captain McIntyre, co-founder of the firm.

Pre-production 3
G-AOEP (c/n 504)
First flown on 27 December 1956 'OEP embarked on a demonstration tour of Australasia and the Far East. On returning it was delivered to Rio Tinto on 1 May 1957. It was registered as VH-BHJ to Consolidated Zinc in July 1957 and transferred to Australian Iron & Steel in November 1959. It was written off following a hurricane at Cockatoo Island, Western Australia on 23 December 1960.

Data	Twin Pioneer Prototype
Length	45 ft 3 in
Wingspan	76 ft 6 in
Height	12 ft 3 in
MTOW	13,500 lb
Cruising speed	174 mph
Range	620 mls
Passengers	16

Powerplant:
Prototype: 2× 540 hp Alvis Leonides 503
Series 2: 2 x 600hp Pratt & Whitney Wasp R-1340
Series 3: 2× 640 hp Alvis Leonides 531

Production by type:
Twin Pioneer 1: 31
Twin Pioneer 2: 5
Twin Pioneer 3: 12
Twin Pioneer CC1: 32 (RAF)
Twin Pioneer CC2:7 (RAF)

Total built: 87 at Prestwick

Handley Page Herald

THE HPR3 Herald originated as a product of Handley Page's Reading plant at Woodley Airfield which had been taken over from the bankrupt Miles Aircraft in June 1948. (Designs from Woodley were designated HPR for Handley Page (Reading)). The concept was a Douglas DC-3 replacement which could serve in rugged environments throughout the world, able to fly out of unsophisticated airstrips but transporting a viable payload. The designers chose a high-winged single tail configuration powered by four Alvis Leonides piston engines. These were chosen as the manufacturer considered that in the early 1950s many of the targeted operators were still wary of turboprops.

Maiden flight

The first prototype registered G-AODE made its first flight on 25 August 1955. The Herald had amassed a respectable number of provisional orders, 29 in all prior to its first flight. But the prospect of further orders soon evaporated as airlines became accustomed to reliable turboprop airliners such as the Viscount, which was already in service, and the new Fokker Friendship (a similar design to the Herald though powered by Rolls-Royce Dart turboprops) which had flown only three months after the piston Herald.

Pistons exchanged for turbines

A second piston-engined prototype G-AODF flew in 1956 but Handley Page soon decided to convert the two prototypes to twin Rolls-Royce Dart power and extended the forward fuselage by 20 in in the process. G-AODE flew now as the HPR7 Herald with Darts on 11 March 1958 but en route to the 1958 Farnborough

Air Show on 30 August, one of its Darts caught fire and the aircraft crash-landed and was written off.

Fortunately G-AODF's conversion was nearly completed and it took over flight testing following its maiden flight on 17 December 1958. Only a small amount of development flying was needed before it could set forth on demonstration tours.

The initial Herald 100 could accommodate 44 passengers but wisely it was decided that following the fourth production machine the aircraft would be lengthened forward of the wing by 3ft 6in to become the Herald 200, providing accommodation room for 50 passengers. To expedite flight testing G-AODF was modified to the 200 standard and was re-registered G-ARTC.

In early 1962 trials took place at RAF Martlesham Heath for the contract for a new military transport. The contract was won by Hawker Siddeley with a version of the 748. Apparently the Herald would have won the contract if Handley Page had obeyed the Government's demands and joined one of the two large British Airframe companies, the British Aircraft Corporation or Hawker Siddeley.

Stiff competition for sales

The Herald did not achieve great sales and annual production never exceeded double figures – in 1963 the Fokker Friendship had 240 orders while the Herald had only made 35 sales. The Herald's generous fuselage had a detrimental effect on sales as it was wider than both the 748 and the Friendship and was therefore slower and had less range.

Heralds were generally operated in small numbers by second-tier carriers and in their later years were

Herald prototype G-AODE powered by Alvis Leonides piston engines at the 1955 SBAC Show at Farnborough. The Scottish Aviation Twin Pioneer prototype G-ANTP is behind.
(Peter Berry)

G-AODE landing at the Farnborough Air Show in 1955. It is in the colours of Queensland Airlines livery. (Brian Burrage)

The two herald prototypes both Leonides engines at Woodley (Handley Page Association)

increasingly sought after as freighters for which their low sill height and double loading doors made them very suitable.

As the Herald only proved moderately successful, production ceased in August 1968 following the sale of only 48 aircraft, while both the Fokker Friendship and Avro 748 sold substantially more.

Prototypes

Handley Page Herald prototype 1
G-AODE (c/n 147)

G-AODE was built at Woodley, Berkshire and then transported to Handley Page's main plant at Radlett, Hertfordshire on 2 August 1955. It made its first flight in

G-AODE following its short-lived conversion to Rolls-Royce Dart power. (Author's collection)

Queensland Airlines livery on 25 August 1955 piloted by Chief Test Pilot, Hedley Hazelden. This aircraft was both unpressurised and unfurnished. It was converted from four Alvis Leonides engines to a twin Dart configuration and flew from Woodley, Berkshire on 11 March 1958 in house colours flying 50 hours on trials in the first five weeks. After initial trials a dorsal fillet was fitted to the vertical tail.

While making its 187th flight on 30 August 1958 from Woodley to the Farnborough Air Show, the Herald formated at 6,000 ft with Victor bomber XA930 for a photo session with an RAF Hastings. During this photo session the right Dart engine suddenly caught fire over Dunsfold. As this conflagration could not be extinguished Hazelden, who was piloting, realised a forced-landing was imperative. During descent the tailplane was badly burned by the flames, causing severe elevator control problems and the burning engine then fell out of the nacelle. Having identified a field to land in Hazelden then spotted high tension cables crossing it but he realised he had no alternative and so forced the Herald down and slid under the cables at 140 knots. On landing in the field near Godalming, Surrey the Herald hit a tree trunk which

tore open the fuselage, providing an escape route through which all nine on board escaped unhurt. The aircraft burnt out and was a write-off.

Handley Page Herald prototype 2 G-AODF (c/n 148)

The second prototype (which was pressurised) made its first flight with Alvis Leonides from Woodley on 14 August 1956, but just over two years later was converted to Darts and flew with these from Woodley on 17 December 1958, piloted by Hazelden. 'ODF was then employed in a sales role in BEA livery and between April and December 1959 made three sales tours visiting 44 countries, including an appearance at Farnborough. It returned to Woodley in the winter of 1960 for conversion to the longer 200 Series prototype and first flew on 8 April 1961 piloted by John Allam. In August it was re-registered as G-ARTC and appeared at the Farnborough Show the following month in Maritime Central Airways livery. In November 1961 'RTC left on a sales tour of Southern Europe, the Near East and East Africa. In competition against the Avro 748 it carried out take-off, landing and taxiing trials on rough ground at Martlesham Heath in February 1962

G-AODE burning in a field near Godalming, Surrey on 30 August 1958. En route to the 1958 SBAC Show the newly-converted turboprop Dart Herald, G-AODE was engaged in a photo session with a Victor when the right Dart exploded necessitating an emergency landing. (Author's collection)

Right: Sir Frederick Handley Page (1885 - 1962) presenting Squadron Leader Hedley Hazelden with a gold watch to commemorate his outstanding airmanship in safely landing the burning Herald. He was also awarded the Queen's Commendation. (Author's collection)

Below: Between April and December 1959 Dart Herald 100 prototype G-AODF made three sales tours resplendent in BEA livery, visiting 44 countries including an appearance at the SBAC Show at Farnborough. (Peter Berry)

Recognition of Outstanding Feat of Airmanship

Sir Frederick Handley Page has presented Squadron Leader H. G. Hazelden, Handley Page's chief test pilot, with a gold watch to mark his recent outstanding feat of airmanship when he crash-landed a Dart Herald prototype without injury to any of the eight passengers aboard or anyone on the ground.

An uncontrollable fire had developed at 6,000 feet following upon the serious failure of the aircraft's starboard Dart propjet engine.

All occupants of the aircraft were present at the ceremony. They received a photograph each of the Dart Herald taken in the air just before its engine failed; all had signed these pictures, which they are keeping as mementoes of the occasion. Photo: Sport & General

G-AODF was modified in the winter of 1960-61 to become the longer Herald 200 prototype and was re-registered as G-ARTC and painted in Maritime Central colours for the 1961 Farnborough SBAC Show. It was withdrawn from use in 1962 and scrapped at Radlett in 1969. (HPA)

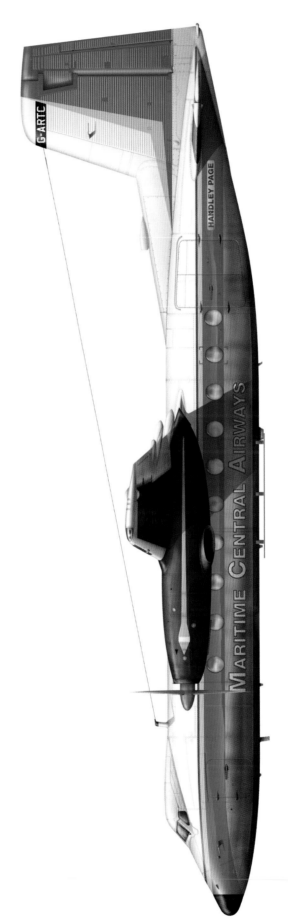

Originally built as the second prototype four piston-engined Herald registered as G-AODF, this aircraft was modified as a twin Dart Herald 100. It later became the Herald 200 prototype and was re-registered as G-ARTC. Although it is illustrated in Maritime Central Airways livery the airline never operated the Herald.

for the RAF Military Transport contract. In the same year it also flew paratroop-dropping trials with the SAS from 34,350 feet. It was withdrawn from use in May 1962 and scrapped at Radlett in 1969.

Data	Herald 200
Length	75 ft 6 in
Wingspan	94 ft 9 in
Height	30 ft
MTOW	43,000 lb
Cruising speed	270 mph
Range	700 mls
Passengers	50

Powerplant:
2 x 2,105 ehp Rolls-Royce Dart 527

Production by type:
HPR 3 Herald: 2 (later HPR 7 Heralds)
HPR7 Herald 100: 4
HPR7 Herald 200: 44

Total built: 50 (8 at Woodley, 42 at Radlett)

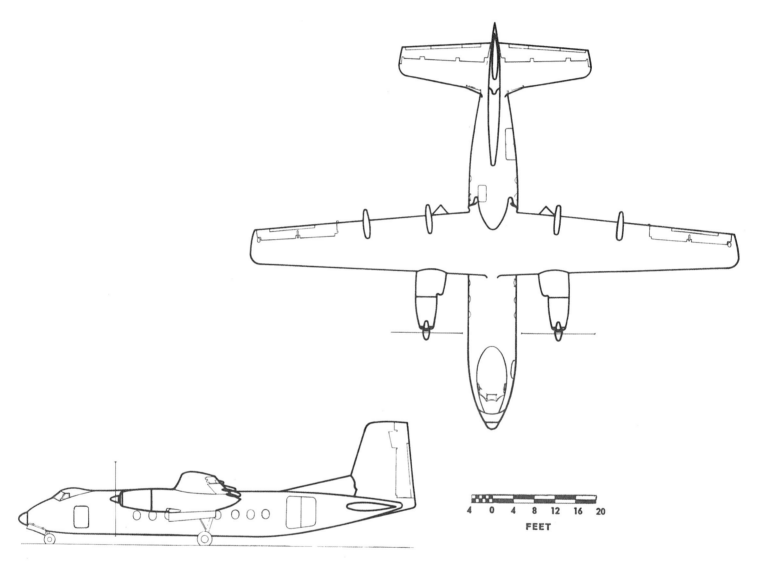

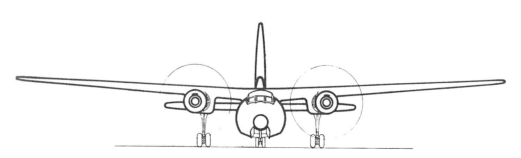

Three-view drawing of the Herald 200 (Author's collection)

Aviation Traders Accountant

G-41-1

ACCOUNTANT

IN international aviation circles there were many attempts to replicate the Douglas DC-3 – in Britain the Handley Page Herald and Avro 748 vied for this category as did another British design, the Aviation Traders ATL90 Accountant.

Whereas Handley Page and Avro were well-established aircraft manufacturers, the Southend-based Aviation Traders was a rather different firm. It had only been formed in 1948 by a man who was to be regarded as one of Britain's great aviation entrepreneurs, Freddie Laker. Initially Aviation Traders dealt with the scrapping of war surplus aircraft; later it moved into modifying aircraft and then entered the aircraft component manufacturing industry.

At the 1953 Farnborough Air Show details were released of the new design powered by Rolls-Royce Dart turboprops and able to accommodate 28 passengers – a simple, rugged aircraft designed to operate from relatively under-developed airfields. To compete with two larger types, the Handley Page Herald and Fokker Friendship, a lengthened 42-passenger version of the Accountant (and an executive variant) was projected. The Aviation Traders' ATL.90 Accountant had a distinct advantage over its rivals as production aircraft would be fitted with a swing-nose to allow straight-in freight loading. To accommodate this feature the fuselage shape (slightly reminiscent of the Constellation) was rather odd and necessitated the aft nosewheel position, giving the aircraft a rather ungainly appearance on the ground.

The prototype flew in July 1957 and appeared at Farnborough in September but only five months later it made its final flight. Although the Indian Air Force and other customers showed interest, no orders were

received; Aviation Traders was at a disadvantage for it was not an established aircraft manufacturer. Freddie Laker could not continue to fund the project and as he had persuaded no other manufacturer to take on the design, production would have been a problem for Aviation Traders as it lacked both the skills and infrastructure. Besides this, the larger Fokker Friendship had just entered service and its early popularity would be hard to beat. Aviation Traders never again designed a completely new aircraft.

Prototype

Aviation Traders Accountant prototype
G-14-1 / G-ATEL

The Accountant's first flight was on 9 July 1957 at Southend, Essex. It had the 'B' Class registration of G-41-1 and was piloted by Leonard Stuart-Smith. During the flight it experienced severe stability problems and as a result did not make its second flight until more than a month later. Having flown the minimum required 15 hours, the Accountant was demonstrated in public at the 1957 Farnborough Air Show registered as G-ATEL.

With the cancellation of the project its last flight (Flight 30) was on 4 January 1958 having flown approximately 200 hours. It was scrapped at Southend in February 1960.

The Accountant's roll-out at Southend bearing 'B' class registration G-14-1. (Brian Burrage)

The Accountant at the SBAC Show at Farnborough in September 1957 with the 'out of sequence' registration of G-ATEL. (ATEL standing for Aviation Traders Ltd.) Such out of sequence registrations are commonplace nowadays but then were most unusual. (Peter Berry)

Data	Accountant
Length	62 ft 1 in
Wingspan	82 ft 6 in
Height	25 ft 3 in
MTOW	28,500 lb
Cruising speed	250 mph
Range	2,088 mls
Passengers	28

Powerplant:
2 x 1,740 hp Rolls-Royce Dart 512

Total built: 1 at Southend

The Accountant in flight registered as G-ATEL. Note the anti-spin parachute housing at the aircraft's tail. (Brian Burrage)

Fairey Rotodyne

THE Fairey Rotodyne was the world's first VTOL airliner. It was based on convertiplane principles and aimed at overcoming the shortcomings of the helicopter by eliminating the tail rotor with its complex transmission. The Rotodyne was remarkably innovative; it could take off vertically like a helicopter from a city centre with all the lift coming from the tip-jet driven rotor and then increase the pitch of its propellers and reduce the power on the rotor, so that eventually all the power from the engines was transferred to the propellers with the rotor autorotating but providing 65 per cent of the lift. The Rotodyne could then cruise at approximately 175 mph to another city where the rotor tip-jet system would be restarted to allow it to land vertically in the city centre.

The Rotodyne was developed from designs which originated at Fairey in 1947 and led to a proposal to the Ministry of Supply in 1949 for 20-seater aircraft with a rotor and twin turboprops. In the following year BEA expressed a requirement for a 30-40 seater aircraft operating from city centres. In July 1953 Fairey was given a contract to build the Rotodyne "Y" as a research prototype powered by Napier Elands.

The prototype XE521 flew in December 1957 but by mid-1958 was able to demonstrate the full transition from vertical take-off, to normal flight and back again. Not only was it larger than helicopters of its day but its performance was superior and a bright future was expected. Both civil and military applications were possible as it had a large, unobstructed fuselage with rear opening doors which would be attractive to military users.

In 1958 Kaman Aircraft Corporation of the USA secured a licensing agreement and Okanagan

Helicopters of Vancouver ordered one while New York Airways signed a letter of intent to buy five Rotodynes with an option on ten more. BEA was still interested but sought a larger machine – which would only be possible if the poorly-performing Napier Elands were replaced with Rolls-Royce Tyne, which potentially had twice the power of the Elands.

This larger Rotodyne "Z" was really a new design for which XE521 had been a "proof of concept" vehicle. The Rotodyne "Z" would have had Rolls-Royce Tyne engines and a larger 69 ft 5 in fuselage able to carry 57-75 passengers. The Government offered to fund 50 per cent of development on condition that BEA also purchased the aircraft.

Sadly, the Rotodyne was overtaken by events. In May 1960 the aviation interests of Fairey were sold to Westland Aircraft which became the sole British Helicopter manufacturer when it also took over Bristol's and Saro's helicopter divisions.

With the Rotodyne now under Westland's control the Government promised continuing support. However, Westland had a large transport helicopter – the privately-funded Westminster – which had grown from a proposal to the Ministry of Supply for licence production of the Sikorsky S-56. Since there had been no support

The prototype Fairey Rotodyne XE521 in flight. When in horizontal flight the main rotor auto-rotated, providing lift. (David Gibbings)

Artist's impression of the proposed Fairey Rotodyne, on the cover of Flight, 16 October 1953. (Author's collection)

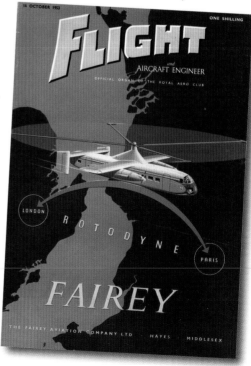

A clear view of the underside of the Rotodyne, showings its stub wings, twin-fin arrangement and the unobstructed rear clam-shell fuselage doors, which allowed ease of loading and unloading. (Westland Helicopters Ltd)

for this, Westland had made an agreement with Sikorsky to employ certain components of the S-56 to produce its own heavy lift helicopter.

Westland had proposed two Westminster variants: a 40-seater to fulfil BEA's proposal for city centre operation; and a version to meet military requirements for a large transport helicopter able to carry heavy field equipment, tactical and nuclear weapon loads and armed troops over stages of 150 miles or more. In March 1956 Westland decided to construct a flying test rig powered by twin Napier Elands which flew in June 1958 and was joined by a second prototype in September 1959.

With two competing projects now to manage, Westland decided to concentrate on the Rotodyne since it was at a more advanced stage of development and showed greater potential than the Westminster. Project work on the Westminster therefore ceased in September 1960 and the two prototypes were dismantled.

However, the future for the Rotodyne was far from assured. The Rotodyne "Z" would be costly to develop and there was still a problem of the extreme noise made by the tip-jets. However, the jets were only run at

full power for a brief period during take-off and landing and when two flights were made over central London, including visits to Battersea Heliport, no complaints were registered.

Since neither military nor BEA orders were forthcoming and, recognising the lack of progress, the North American operators also cancelled their orders. On 26 February 1962 the Government, unwilling to finance the project further, announced its cancellation.

Prototype

Fairey Rotodyne
XE521 (c/n 9429)

Ron Gellatly piloted the unpainted Rotodyne on its first flight (in helicopter mode only) at White Waltham, Berkshire on 6 November 1957. Over the following six months XE521 flew only in this mode before finally making the transition from helicopter to autogyro flight.

In mid-1958 XE521 was painted in an airline style livery and the fixed undercarriage was replaced by retractable units. It made the first of four appearances at the Farnborough Air Show in September that year. On 5 January 1959 it established a World Speed Record for a helicopter of 190.9 mph flying on a circular course between White Waltham and Hungerford, Berkshire. On 16 June 1959 it flew from Heathrow to Le Bourget, Paris to demonstrate at the Paris Air Show. Following the Show it also gave demonstrations in Brussels before returning to Heathrow. On 24 July 1959 the Rotodyne demonstrated its lifting capability at the Mechanical Engineering Experimental Establishment at Christchurch by laying a 100 ft span bridge across a river. To demonstrate that noise was not a problem it paid two visits to Battersea Heliport in early 1960.

Following the takeover of Fairey by Westland in 1960 a central fin was installed. Subsequently the prototype was retitled as the Westland Rotodyne. The project was cancelled on 26 February 1962 and the Rotodyne was scrapped although some parts are now on display at the Helicopter Museum, Weston-super-Mare, Somerset. XE521 had flown approximately 300 hours in 430 flights.

Data	Rotodyne
Length	58 ft 8 in
Wingspan	46 ft 6 in
Height	22 ft 2 in
MTOW	33,000 lb
Cruising speed	185 mph
Range	450 mls
Passengers	30-40

Powerplant:
2 x 2,800 SHP Napier Eland NEL 3

Total built: 1 at White Waltham, Berkshire

Close-up of the Rotodyne's main undercarriage with its oleos depressed. (Brian Burrage)

Another view of this most unorthodox, yet oddly attractive looking aircraft. (David Gibbings)

Besides the obvious benefits of the Rotodyne in an airliner role it also had considerable military potential. In this view it is possible to imagine the Rotodyne sweeping down and opening its large rear doors to deposit troops and equipment and speedily departing. (British Aerospace)

The Rotodyne with an added central fin, taking off from the Battersea Heliport, London and showing its stalky undercarriage in early 1960, with Fulham Power Station in the background. The Rotodyne would have enabled speedy city centre to city centre travel. (David Gibbings)

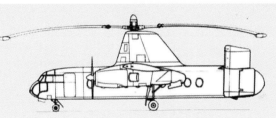

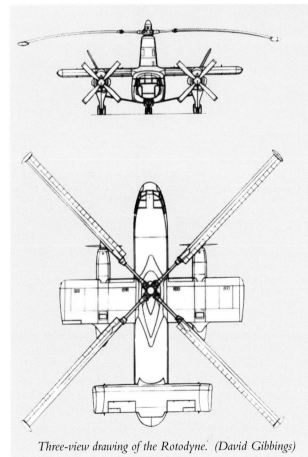

XE521 at the SBAC Show at Farnborough in September 1958. Note that the upper rear tail fins folded down to allow clearance for the rotor during start ups, take offs and landings. (Peter Berry)

Three-view drawing of the Rotodyne. (David Gibbings)

125

Vickers Vanguard

On schedule
VICKERS *VANGUARD*
FOUR ROLLS-ROYCE TYNE JET-PROP ENGINES

The Vanguard prototype G-AOYW on the production line at Vickers-Armstrongs' Weybridge factory. (Author's collection)

Vickers Armstrongs logo.

BAE SYSTEMS

THE Vanguard grew out of a requirement first raised by BEA in 1953 a few days before the Viscount entered service, which called for an airliner faster than the Viscount and with 10 per cent greater economy. Trans-Canada Airlines (TCA), another major Viscount customer, was also interested in this broad specification and Vickers' design teams began to examine options.

Many in the Vickers Project Office were convinced that the airliner should be a jet but BEA's view prevailed that the new aircraft should be propeller driven. Following a lengthy project definition stage the design was finally fixed on the Vickers Type 950 powered by the new Rolls-Royce Tynes, capable of carrying 139 passengers in six-abreast seating together with the capacious under floor cargo provision. BEA's aircraft were classed as Type 951 and TCA's, which operated at higher weights, as 952s. BEA took advantage of these higher weights and fourteen of its order became 953s with the greater payload of the 952.

Sales
When the prototype G-AOYW took to the air for the first time in 1959, 40 were already on order from BEA and TCA but only three more were ever ordered. Even though the Vanguard was very economical, by 1960 both passengers and airlines wanted jets; by this time many European airlines had ordered the Sud Aviation Caravelle twin jet with which the Vanguard had to compete. Unlike the Viscount, which had proved very profitable, Vickers lost £17m (at 1960s prices) with its successor, the Vanguard.

A total of 44 Vanguards were built, all but one entering airline service. The last delivery was of CF-TKW to Trans-Canada Airlines on 3 April 1964. The test programme proved troublesome, with vibration

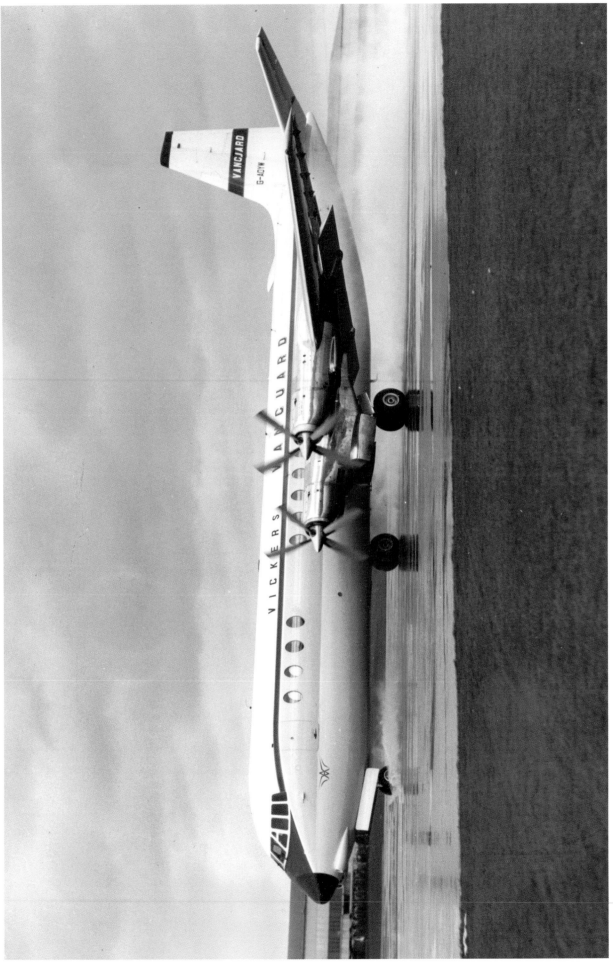

G-AOYW on taxiing trials prior to its maiden flight on 20 January 1959 from the short Weybridge runway to the nearby Wisley Test Centre. It was piloted on this flight by Vickers' Chief Test Pilot, Jock Bryce, and his Deputy, Brian Trubshaw. (BAE SYSTEMS)

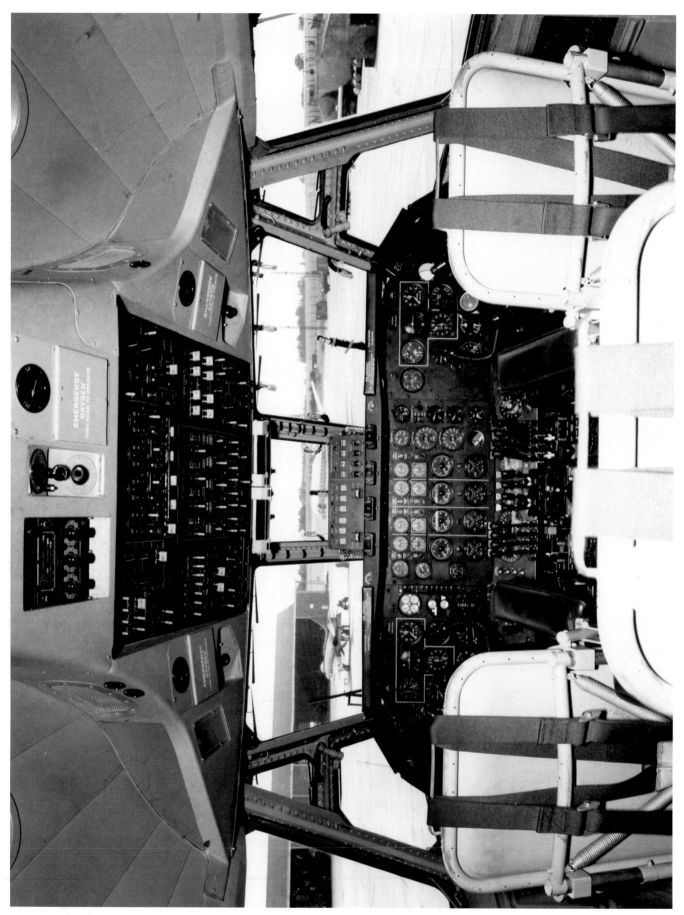

The flight deck of G-AOYW. A Scimitar and Viscount are visible on the Apron at Wisley. (BAE SYSTEMS)

The Vanguard prototype coming in to land at Wisley, Vickers Flight Test Centre. (BAE SYSTEMS)

G-AOYW in its second and final colour scheme. It had a short life and was broken up in October 1964.

and stalling problems and major problems with the Tyne engine, which delayed entry into service by six months.

In service

Both BEA and TCA put these sturdy workhorses to good use but as early as 1966 one of Air Canada's (as TCA became in 1964) aircraft, CF-TKK, was converted to all-freight operation and renamed Cargoliner. BEA improved on this idea by having all the windows removed, a strengthened floor fitted and large forward freight door fitted to G-APEM by Aviation Traders. The same firm versioned G-APEO and the type was named the Merchantman – though BEA crews jokingly called it the 'Guardsvan'. BEA then converted seven more of its Type 953 to become Merchantmen.

Air Canada withdrew its Vanguards from passenger service in October 1971 and the sole Cargoliner in mid-1972, while the last BEA Merchantman flight was flown by G-APEJ on 2 December 1979. All these aircraft now joined the second-hand market but as they were propeller-driven they were not readily marketable. Operations by a number of second-tier carriers took the aircraft to unusual climes with airlines in Iceland, Indonesia, France and Sweden and also with British carriers such as Invicta and Air Bridge. The last Vanguard passenger flight was operated by Merparti Nusantara Airlines of Indonesia in 1987. The valuable Merchantmen remained in service for almost another decade and the final operator, Hunting Cargo Airlines, delivered G-APEP back to its birthplace at Brooklands on 16 October 1996 where it is now preserved.

they were replaced. G-AOYW made an 18-minute first flight in Vickers livery from Weybridge to Vickers' Test Airfield at Wisley on 20 January 1959 piloted by Jock Bryce and Brian Trubshaw. The Vanguard had vibration and stalling problems and Brian Trubshaw wrote that 'OYW carried out more than 2,000 stalls before an acceptable performance was achieved.

In November 1959 'OYW was fitted with a dorsal fin and repainted in modified Vickers livery. In May 1960 the whole test programme, which was virtually complete, was suspended owing to compressor problems with the Tynes. However on 4 July 1960, G-AOYW recommenced flying with modified engines and other Vanguards followed suit, enabling certification to be completed. With the end of the test programme the prototype was stored at Wisley; its registration was cancelled in October 1964 and it was broken up at Wisley.

Powerplant:
Vanguard Type 951 – 4 x 4,985 ehp Rolls-Royce Tyne R.Ty. 506
Vanguard Type 952 – 4 x 5,545 ehp Rolls-Royce Tyne R.Ty. 512

Production by type:
Vanguard 950: 1
Vanguard 951: 6
Vanguard 952: 23
Vanguard 953: 14

Total built: 44 at Weybridge

Prototype

Vickers Vanguard 950 G-AOYW (c/n 703)
G-AOYW was rolled out at Weybridge on 4 December 1958 for ground testing. Following problems with the initial Rolls-Royce Tynes,

Data	Vanguard Type 951	Vanguard Type 952
Length	122 ft 10½ in	122 ft 10½ in
Wingspan	118 ft	118 ft
Height	34 ft 11 in	34 ft 11 in
MTOW	135,000 lb	141,000 lb
Cruising speed	400 mph	400 mph
Range	2,070 mls	2,070 mls
Passengers	126	139

A second view of G-AOYW in her final livery. Wool tufts, used in test flying to indicate the direction of the airflow, are visible below the underside of the starboard tailplane. Two other Vanguards are in the hangars beyond. (BAE SYSTEMS)

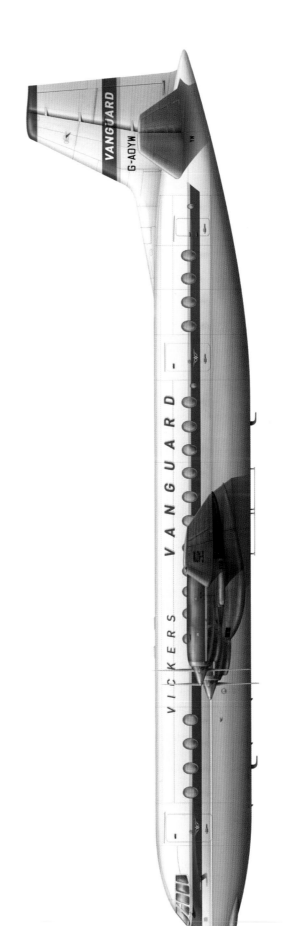

Vickers Vanguard prototype G-AOYW had a short life. It made its first flight on 20 January 1959 and was scrapped in October 1964.

Hawker Siddeley 748 and BAe ATP

The first Avro 748 G-APZV under construction at Avro's Chadderton factory. Immediately behind it is the 748 mock-up. (Brian Burrage)

Hawker Siddeley 748

WHEN the prototype 748 G-APZV took to the air on 24 June 1960 few would have predicted that over the next 26 years the 748 would prove so successful that a total of 380 civil and military versions would be manufactured.

Design

Following its disastrous experience with the Tudor, Avro had stayed out of civil aircraft manufacture for almost a decade, but in January 1959 Avro's Chief Designer, J.R. Evans, proposed a conventional low wing design powered by Rolls-Royce Darts with a capacity for 44 passengers as a Dakota replacement. The Avro Board gave the go-ahead for the construction of two prototypes. As this was a private venture project (i.e. without Government financial support) Avro was gratified to receive a substantial fillip in December 1959 when it negotiated a licence agreement with the Indian Government for the assembly of 748s in India. As a result, 89 were built in India between 1961 and 1984. In March 1960 Aerolineas Argentinas ordered nine aircraft. By then the Avro Board had authorised the establishment of a production line at the Chadderton factory with final assembly at Woodford.

In April 1961 the second prototype G-ARAY made its first flight and was later converted to the prototype 748 Series 2 when it was fitted with higher-powered Darts. These enabled it to fly at higher weights and at higher altitudes which translated into either greater payload or longer range. During testing the decision was also made to extend the 748's wingspan by 3 ft 6 in and this was subsequently applied to both prototype aircraft.

RAF order

For the RAF Military Transport contract, trials were organised to assess rough field performance in competition with the Handley Page Herald on a ploughed-up field at Martlesham Heath Airfield in January 1962. The 748 was the winner of these trials and the RAF ordered 31 of the military freighter variant – which had a longer fuselage and high tail with a ramp that could be opened in flight to allow for straight-in loading, unloading and aerial delivery. To hasten flight testing of this variant the first prototype was re-engineered as the aerodynamic prototype of the military freighter and flew in December 1963.

In Airline service

Meanwhile, the 748 entered airline service with Aerolineas Argentinas in April 1962 and the airliner began to make headway in the very competitive market conditions earning orders from Skyways Coach-Air, BKS, Aden Airways, LAV of Venezuela, Air Ceylon, AVIANCA Leeward Islands Air Transport, Austrian Airways and Channel Airways. The 748s flown by Aerolineas Argentinas were later joined by others in South America, when LAN-Chile and Varig of Brazil purchased examples. On the opposite side of the world Philippines Air Lines followed suit. Air forces as well as the RAF (including the Queen's Flight) also purchased examples as VIP and military transports.

Following the restructuring of the British aircraft manufacturing industry into two major groups in 1960, Avro became fully absorbed into Hawker Siddeley and from 1963 the Avro 748 became the Hawker Siddeley 748.

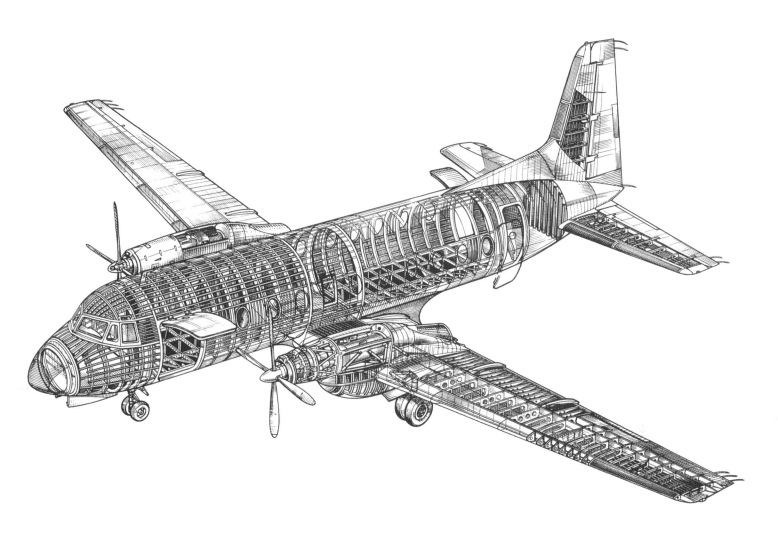

A drawing showing the internal structure of the Avro 748. (Author's collection)

Continuing improvement

In August 1967 G-ARAY was sold and was replaced the following month by the first Series 2A G-AVRR powered by uprated Dart 532 engines with 2,230 shp. To take advantage of the improved performance most of the Series 2 aircraft were later modified to this standard. To capitalise on this increased power and the demand from the military market, a new version of the 2A was offered incorporating a Large Freight Door (LFD) which could be opened in flight on the left rear of the airframe. Production of this development also took place in India under the licence.

Hawker Siddeley sought sales of a maritime surveillance development of the 2A dubbed the 'Coastguarder' and a demonstrator G-BCDZ flew successfully in this role but did not win any orders. This was later superseded by G-BDVH which was branded as the Multi-Role 748 but this too did not win any orders.

Development under BAe

Just as the Avro 748 had become the Hawker Siddeley 748, with the nationalisation (and later privatisation) of British Aerospace in 1977 it was rebranded again as the BAe 748. In a competitive market place development had to continue and the basis for the BAe 748 2B was the uprated Dart 536 with 2,280 shp fitted with 12 ft

propellers. Wingspan was extended to 102 ft 5 in and avionics and soundproofing were upgraded. G-BGJV, the prototype 2B (which was also fitted with a Large Freight Door) first flew on 22 June 1979. Even this development was not this sturdy airliner's last, for in 1983 BAe announced the Super 748 with yet more powerful Darts, together with hush kits, greater fuel efficiency, interior redesign and a more advanced flight deck. When 748 production ended in 1986 a total of 382 had been manufactured.

Prototypes

Hawker Siddeley 748 Series 1 prototype 1
G-APZV (c/n 1534) / G-ARRV (c/n 1548)

The prototype made a 2 hours 41 minutes first flight from the Avro airfield at Woodford on 24 June 1960 piloted by Avro's Chief Test Pilot, Jimmy Harrison. It was immediately put to work on the test programme and was exhibited at the 1960 Farnborough Air Show in September. Its last flight as 748 was on 11 July 1962.

Total time: 841 hours, 857 landings

G-APZV was dismantled at Woodford and returned to the Chadderton Factory on 2 August 1962 for conversion into the aerodynamic prototype of the Hawker Siddeley 748 Military Freighter and received a

AVRO 748
WITH ROLLS ROYCE DART ENGINES

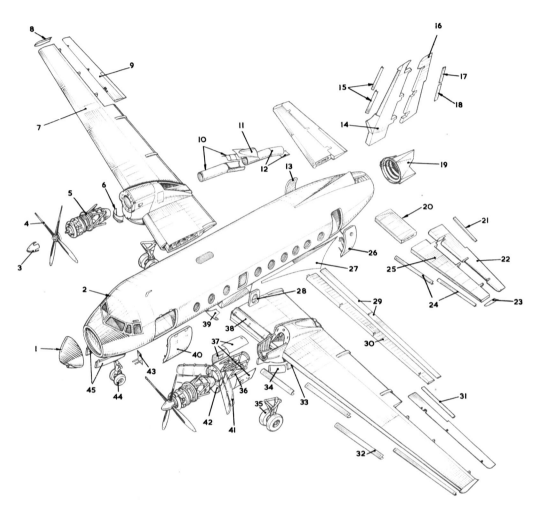

Drawing showing the main structural sub-assemblies, which came together to make the completed aircraft. (Author's collection)

1. NOSE CONE	12. JET PIPE	23. TAIL PLANE TIP	34. MAIN WHEEL DOORS
2. FUSELAGE	13. BAGGAGE DOOR	24. TAIL PLANE LEADING EDGES	35. MAIN UNDERCARRIAGE
3. SPINNER	14. FIN	25. TAIL PLANE	36. POWER PLANT SUB-FRAME
4. PROPELLER	15. FIN LEADING EDGES	26. PASSENGER ENTRANCE DOOR	37. NACELLE ACCESS PANELS
5. POWER PLANT	16. RUDDER	27. WING FILLET	38. WING HINGED LEADING EDGE
6. NACELLE FAIRING	17. RUDDER TRIM TAB	28. ESCAPE HATCH	39. WING LEADING EDGE FILLET
7. WING	18. RUDDER SPRING TAB	29. TAB FLAPS	40. FREIGHT DOOR
8. WING TIP	19. TAIL CONE	30. FLAPS	41. COWLINGS
9. AILERON	20. TAIL PLANE TORSION BOX	31. AILERON TAB	42. NACELLE FIREWALL
10. JET PIPE SHROUD	21. ELEVATOR TRIM TAB	32. WING LEADING EDGES	43. NOSE UNDERCARRIAGE FAIRING DOOR
11. JET PIPE FAIRING	22. ELEVATOR	33. MAIN UNDERCARRIAGE DOORS	44. NOSE UNDERCARRIAGE
			45. NOSE UNDERCARRIAGE DOORS

new construction number and registration: G-ARRV (c/n 1548). In this guise it flew on 21 December 1963 for 2 hours 5 minutes from Woodford, again piloted by Jimmy Harrison. It was on public show at the following year's Farnborough and was demonstrated to the Indian Air Force in April/May 1965. On return from India G-ARRV made its last flight on 27 May 1965 and was

then transferred to the Woodford Apprentice Training School. In 1979 it carried 'Soviet Air Force' livery for a television programme about the Soviet invasion of Czechoslovakia. It was then sent to RAF Benson as an instructional airframe 8669M and scrapped in 1993.

Total time: 490 hours, 824 landings

The first prototype Avro 748, G-APZV undertaking engine runs at Woodford prior to its maiden flight on 24 June 1960 piloted by Avro's Chief Test Pilot, Jimmy Harrison. (Avro Heritage)

G-APZV was converted to become the aerodynamic prototype of the 748 Military Freighter with a high tail and rear-opening doors to allow for air dropping and straight-in loading. It was re-registered G-ARRV and flew in this form on 21 December 1963. It is seen here at the 1964 Farnborough Air Show. (BAE SYSTEMS)

After the end of its flying days the first 748 prototype, the former G-APZV/ G-ARRV, was retired to the Avro Apprentice School. In 1979 it became a television star and carried 'Soviet Air Force' livery for a programme about the Soviet invasion of Czechoslovakia. (Author's collection)

Hawker Siddeley 748 Series 1 prototype 2
G-ARAY (c/n 1535)

The second prototype was damaged during construction at Chadderton when a fire caused the hangar roof to collapse on the fuselage in April 1960. The much delayed first flight took place on 10 April 1961 with Jimmy Harrison at the controls. In July 1961 it flew on tropical trials in Nicosia, Cyprus and Torrejon, Spain and was then upgraded to 748 Series 2 with the installation of Rolls-Royce Dart 531s. It flew with these on 6 November 1961.

On 29 January 1962 the aircraft took part in comparative trials for take-off, landing and taxiing on rough ground for the RAF Military Transport contract against the Handley Page Herald at RAF Martlesham Heath. Avro won this contract and the RAF ordered 31 examples.

G-ARAY was regularly displayed at Air Shows – Paris in 1961 and 1963, Hannover in 1962 and Farnborough in 1964 and 1966. In between these shows it flew on demonstration tours to Africa and the Far East in April 1963, Central and South America from December 1963 to March 1964 and in July 1965 visited Central America again.

G-ARAY initially flew in a red livery with Avro titles and at Farnborough 1964 appeared in quasi-Queen's Flight livery with Hawker Siddeley 748 titling. At the end of 1964 in preparation for its lease to LAV of Venezuela it was painted in the airline's livery. It flew with LAV from February until July 1965 registered as YV-C-AMC and was then returned to the UK for leasing to Skyways Coach-Air. Continuing in its sales role

G-ARAY then flew back across the Atlantic in December 1965 for evaluation by Varig of Brazil against the Fokker F-27. From Brazil it flew to the Leeward Islands Air Transport in the Caribbean for a brief lease as VP-LIO.

During January 1967 the aircraft flew trials with reconfigured engine nacelles and in February 1967 was leased to Philippine Air Lines in Hawker Siddeley colours. During the lease it acquired PAL livery and was registered as PI-C784, returning to Woodford in June 1967.

After almost 1,000 hours of test flying and more than 91,000 miles flying on sales tours and on leases clocking up 30 sales, Hawker Siddeley sold G-ARAY to Falcks Flyvetjeneste in August 1967. With a change in the ownership of Falkair it received Maersk livery in January 1970.

Its final operator was Dan-Air. It was delivered to Lasham, Hampshire as OY-FDV for an overhaul and repaint on 1 May 1971 and made its last passenger flight on 7 October 1989. It was withdrawn from use at Lasham and was broken up in April 1990.

Hawker Siddeley 748 Series 2A prototype
G-AVRR (c/n 1635)

G-AVRR, a 748 Series 2A fitted with the uprated Dart 532, first flew on 5 September 1967 at Woodford. After initial trials at Woodford it left for tropical trials in Ethiopia during January and February 1968.

During 1968 it also demonstrated to Saudi Arabian Airlines in Jeddah and toured the USA, the Far East and Africa. G-AVRR spent a busy year in 1969 with leases to SATA, Skyways and Olympic Airways plus a

The second prototype Avro 748, G-ARAY, shows off its clean form and the distinctive underwing pods which housed the undercarriage. (Avro Heritage)

The second prototype G-ARAY in the air on its first flight on 10 April 1961 piloted by Jimmy Harrison. (Avro Heritage)

G-ARAY demonstrating its sprightly take-off performance at the 1964 Farnborough Air Show. It is wearing Queen's Flight livery but with Hawker Siddeley 748 titling. (Alex Christie)

The second prototype Hawker Siddeley 748 G-ARAY had an active life; testing, demonstrating and on lease to many airlines. It is illustrated here in partial Queen's Flight livery.

demonstration in Romania and tours of Canada and Africa, where it was registered ZS-IGI.

1970 held a similarly busy schedule with a lease to Malaysia - Singapore Airlines, a lease to Zambia Airways as 9J-ABM, South African Airways as ZS-HIS and Merparti of Indonesia. The year was rounded off with a demonstration tour of East Africa and Iran in December.

From October 1971 the aircraft was leased for a year by Trans Gabon Airways as TR-LQJ and in December

was sold to them. Trans Gabon sold it to Eastern Provincial Airways as C-GEPH in March 1976. On 29 December 1981 its brakes failed: it collided with the terminal building at Sydney, Nova Scotia and was written off.

BAe 748 Series 2B prototype
G-BGJV (c/n 1768)
G-BGJV made its first flight on 22 June 1979 from Woodford. After testing it was leased to Deutsche

Second prototype G-ARAY at RAF Martlesham Heath on 29 January 1962 for the RAF Military Transport contract take-off and landing trials. The 748 was competing against the Handley Page Herald and won the RAF contract for 31 aircraft. (Author's collection)

G-AVRR, the 748 Series 2A, at Cape Town Airport in 1970. After trials and sales tours it went into airline service but was written off after colliding with an airport terminal building In Nova Scotia. (Avro Heritage)

*British Airways'
G-BCOE and the
Brazilian Air Force's
C-91 2509 under
construction on the
Woodford production
line in early 1975.
(Author's collection)*

*The 748 Series 2B
prototype G-BGJV
on its maiden flight
on 22 June 1979.
The extended wing
tips and rear freight
door are clearly
visible. (Author's
collection)*

The 748 Series 2B G-BGJV flying over Manchester. It has the unusual and unfortunate distinction that while in service with the Sri Lankan Air Force it was shot down by a SAM missile fired by Tamil separatists.
(Avro Heritage)

Three Avro Chief Test Pilots at Woodford in 1986. (From the left) Robby Robinson who made the first flight of the ATP, Jimmy Orrell who carried out much of the Tudor testing and Jimmy Harrison who made the maiden flight of the 748.
(Avro Heritage)

Luftverkehrs three times during 1981-82 and Marshall Islands Airline as MI-GJV, but returned to BAe in 1982. British Airways then leased it from January 1985 to December 1991. In January 1992 the Sri Lankan Air Force purchased it, but on 29 April 1995 when descending towards Palaly Airfield it was shot down with a SAM missile fired by Tamil separatists.

BAe ATP / Jetstream 61

Following on from the success of the 748, British Aerospace Woodford examined further developments and the Chief Designer Alan Troughton's brief was to produce a larger aircraft with a minimum of changes. As a result of these studies the main Board of British Aerospace agreed to the go-ahead of the ATP (Advanced Turboprop) in March 1984.

The ATP could accommodate 72 rather than its predecessor's 44/52 passengers which was achieved by lengthening the 748's fuselage by 16 ft both fore and aft of the wing, while the wing dimensions remained similar to those of the 748 Mk. 2. As Rolls-Royce was no longer developing turboprops, BAe chose the Pratt & Whitney Canada PW124 with 2,570 shp with six-bladed 13 ft 9 in BAe / Hamilton Standard propellers, a combination which proved remarkably quiet and fuel efficient. In addition to the lengthened fuselage the original 748 nose was sharpened and the vertical tail was swept back.

The initial intention was for the UK Civil Aviation Authority to certify the ATP as a modified 748 but the inclusion of all the new equipment such as EFIS and

FADEC (Fully Automated Digital Engine Control) meant that the aircraft was 85 per cent new and so it had to be certified as a new type.

Maiden flight to schedule

The ATP made its first flight at 10:00 hrs on 6 August 1986 – a date set two years earlier by Charles Masefield, former Test Pilot and the Managing Director of Woodford. The prototype was joined in the test programme by the first two production aircraft (G-BMYM and G-BMYK) and received certification in March 1988. American FAA certification followed in late 1988 and the following year Air Wisconsin ordered 14 with first deliveries in 1989, but ceased operations with the type in 1993. Other operators included British Airways, British Midland, the Azorean operator SATA, and Air Europa of Spain.

At the time of the first flight there were 24 orders but unfortunately the aircraft initially had a troubled time in service with engine, de-icing and undercarriage problems although these were all eventually cured. Claims have also been made that its sales prospects were adversely affected by heavy price discounting by its major competitors, the Fokker 50 and ATR 42/72.

The ATP becomes the Jetstream 61

In January 1993 the management of British Aerospace decided to transfer all aspects of the ATP to Jetstream Aircraft Ltd, its turboprop subsidiary based at Prestwick (the former Scottish Aviation factory). This placed production of the ATP alongside that of the Jetstream 31 and 41 and on 26 April 1993 BAe announced the

The ATP prototype being moved in the final assembly area in the huge Woodford hangars in early 1986. (BAE SYSTEMS)

BAE SYSTEMS

*The prototype ATP
G-MATP on its
first flight on
6 August 1986.
(Avro Heritage)*

*A close up of
G-MATP's nose
and Pratt &
Whitney Canada
PW124 engines.
(Derek Ferguson)*

Following the rebranding of the ATP as the Jetstream 61 and the transfer of final assembly to Prestwick, G-MATP was painted in Jetstream 61 livery and re-registered G-PLXI (LXI = 61). It is seen here at Woodford with Jetstream 41 prototype G-GCJL. (Derek Ferguson)

At the time of writing the ATP prototype is still stored at Woodford in a poor condition. This photograph shows how it appeared in March 2004. (Author)

rebranding of the ATP as the Jetstream 61. The first Jetstream 61 to be assembled at Prestwick was c/n 2064. Modifications incorporated on the Jetstream 61 were a more powerful Pratt & Whitney 127D with 2,750 shp, an improved interior and an increase in operating weights.

The ending of production

In 1995 BAe decided to combine with Aerospatiale of France and Alenia of Italy to form the European regional aircraft consortium AI(R) (Aero International (Regional)), to jointly market their regional aircraft. The decision was then made to end production of the ATP / Jetstream 61 as it would directly compete with the more successful Aerospatiale / Alenia ATR 42/72.

The first Jetstream 61 G-JLXI had made its maiden flight in May 1994 and the second (G11-065) in July 1995 but as a result of this change in strategy these first two aircraft and ten more in various states of completion on the Prestwick production line were scrapped. BAe did not remain long in the AI(R) consortium and left in April 1998.

The first ATP or Prestwick-built Jetstream 61 as it was rebranded was G-JLXI (i.e. J for Jetstream & L+X+I=61 in Roman numerals) which made its maiden flight on May 9, 1994. It was ferried to East Midlands Airport for painting in July and was exhibited at the September 1994 Farnborough Air Show. Following the decision to end development it was scrapped at Prestwick in April 1997. (Avro Heritage)

The ATP Freighter

From a total of 63 ATP completed aircraft, BAE Asset Management owns 40 and identified a new market for the aircraft by converting them into freighters. In 2000 the freighter project was launched offering both bulk 'E' class and Large Freight Door versions with a potential payload in excess of 8 Tonnes.

ATPs are capable of carrying eight LD3 containers or six larger LD4s when fitted with the BAE-designed Large Freight Door. The first of these flew on 10 July 2002 and by the end of 2007, 20 ATPs will have been converted in this manner while 23 ATPs already serve in the bulk freight role. Airlines operating the ATP Freighters are West Air Sweden, International Air Parts, Atlantic Airways and First Flight Couriers.

Prototype

BAe ATP
G-MATP (c/n 2001)

The first ATP made its maiden flight on schedule at Woodford on 6 August 1986 piloted by Chief Test Pilot, 'Robby' Robinson. As a result it was exhibited at the Farnborough Air Show in September 1986 and was also demonstrated to a Chinese delegation at Hatfield on 8 September 1986. G-MATP was also demonstrated at Farnborough 1992 in the livery of United Express. It first flew with more powerful Pratt & Whitney PW127D engines on 21 June 1993.

Following the rebranding of the ATP as the Jetstream 61 it was re-registered on 26 August 1994 as G-PLXI and flew in J61 livery. It was ferried from Woodford to Prestwick on 16 September 1994, returning to Woodford after the end of development on 28 October 1997. At the time of writing it was stored outside at Woodford.

Powerplant:
748 Srs 1 – 2 x 1,740 ehp Rolls-Royce Dart R.Da.6 Mk. 514
748 Srs 2B – 2 x 2,280 ehp Rolls-Royce Dart R.Da.7 Mk. 536-2
ATP – 2 x 2,570 shp Pratt & Whitney Canada PW124

748 Production by type:
748 Series 1: 24
748 Series 2: 192
748 Series 2B & Super: 101
748 C.1: 31

ATP Production by type:
ATP: 63
Jetstream 61: 2

Total number of 748s built: 382 (291 at Woodford, 2 at Chester, 89 by licence production in India)

Total number of ATP / Jetstream 61 built:
65 (63 at Woodford, 2 at Prestwick)

Total number of Avro 748 & ATP / Jetstream 61 built:
447

Data	748 Series 1	748 Series 2B	ATP
Length	67 ft	67 ft	85 ft 4 in
Wingspan	98 ft 6 in	98 ft 6 in	100 ft 6 in
Height	24 ft 10 in	24 ft 10 in	23ft 5 in
MTOW	36,800 lb	46,500 lb	50,550 lb
Cruising speed	257 mph	281 mph	306 mph
Range	630 mls	904 mls	1,134 mls
Passengers	44	44	72

Hawker Siddeley Trident

THE great expectations held out for the Trident were never realised. It was modelled too closely to a specification set by BEA rather than the original intention to build a larger aircraft approximately the same size as the Boeing 727. Had the original design been proceeded with, far more Tridents would have been sold.

Changing specification

In mid-1956 BEA had issued a specification for a 100-seat jet airliner with a range of 1,000 miles. Competition was fierce amongst the British manufacturers and in all six companies vied for this order. In August 1958 BEA decided to order 24 de Havilland 121s and began working with the manufacturer on a 117-seater powered by three Rolls-Royce Medways. But over the next twelve months the design was substantially scaled down as BEA decided that the original aircraft was too large. Accommodation was reduced to only 79 passengers in a mixed-class layout and lower-powered 9,850 lb Rolls-Royce Speys were substituted for the Medways. Seemingly the de Havilland management offered little resistance to this major change of specification.

Trident 1

The first Trident 1C G-ARPA flew at Hatfield on 9 January 1962. Further aircraft destined for BEA joined the lengthy test programme. Although the Trident flew 14 months before its rival, the Boeing 727, it was the American tri-jet that entered service first. However on 11 March 1964 Tridents entered service with BEA and one year later 14 were flying on BEA routes.

Trident 1E

The first development beyond the BEA Trident 1C was the Trident 1E which utilised higher-powered 10,680 lb thrust Speys and wider span wings fitted with leading edge slats. Although the 1E's fuselage was the same length as the 1C, through refinement of the cabin design and the removal of a service door it was capable of accommodating 113 passengers in a single class, six-abreast arrangement. Whereas the 1C was only purchased by BEA, the 1E received orders from three overseas customers: Kuwait Airways, Iraqi Airways and Pakistan International. Each ordered three, though Pakistan International later ordered an additional machine. The first Trident 1E destined for Kuwait Airways flew on 2 November 1964, temporarily registered as G-ASWU for flight testing.

UK-based charter operator, Channel Airways, ordered five 1Es in a special high density seating configuration with accommodation for 139 passengers with seven-abreast in the front cabin. However as financial difficulties curtailed this order to only two, another British airline, BKS, took two while the final 1E was delivered to Air Ceylon. Following the crash of one of Kuwait's aircraft its remaining two Tridents were sold to Cyprus Airways. Most importantly for Hatfield, Pakistan International sold its Tridents to CAAC of China in 1970 which a short time later led to orders for the Trident 2E.

The Trident 2E

BEA had originally taken out an option on twelve Tridents at the time of its initial order and had always envisaged buying developed versions of its chosen type. Eventually the airline agreed with Hawker

The first Trident G-ARPA taking off on its maiden flight on 9 January 1962. (BAE SYSTEMS)

*The first Trident
G-ARPA bearing
the colours of BEA
during its maiden
flight on 9 January
1962 piloted by
Hatfield's CTP,
John Cunningham.
(BAE SYSTEMS)*

Siddeley to order a new version – the Trident 2E, similar to the Trident 1E but with higher thrust 11,930 lb Speys, a fuel tank in the fin to increase its range and Küchemann wingtips which slightly increased the wingspan. BEA ordered fifteen and Cyprus Airways took two; in 1971 CAAC ordered six 2Es, ultimately increased to a total of 33.

The final Trident development – the 3B

In 1966 BEA sought Government approval to order Boeing 727-200s and 737s, which caused considerable dismay within the British aircraft industry. The Government refused to grant approval and insisted that BEA buy British. As a result the Trident 3B and BAC One-Eleven 500 were developed.

The Trident 3B's fuselage was lengthened by 8 ft 5 in forward and 8 ft aft of the wing, providing accommodation for 146 passengers in a mixed-class layout or up to 180 in all economy seating. Wing area was increased and to provide power for this much heavier aircraft the three 11,960 lb thrust Speys were augmented by a booster Rolls-Royce RB162 providing 5,230 lbs thrust for take-off and climb. The first 3B registered G-AWYZ flew on 11 December 1969 and the first services were on 1 March 1971. BEA was not the only customer: CAAC also received two Super 3Bs which had an additional centre fuel tank and could operate at higher weights.

BEA had specified that the Trident should be able to land in zero visibility, fully automatically and the second Trident 1, G-ARPB, was dedicated for more than three years to testing this facility. This ambitious programme

led in May 1972 to approval for landings with operation in visibility of only 150 ft. Autoland was also introduced on BEA's Trident 2s and 3s as they entered service.

Trident production came to an end on 13 September 1978 when the last and 117th Trident was delivered to CAAC. With its Trident 1s, 2s and 3s BEA had for a time a remarkably homogenous fleet. Noise legislation and the impossibility of adequately hush kitting the aircraft spelled its end and the last BEA flight took place on 31 December 1985. On the other side of the globe however, the Chinese Tridents continued in service well into the 1990s.

Prototypes

Strictly speaking there were no prototypes for the Trident but the initial aircraft of each Mark took that role.

Hawker Siddeley Trident 1C first production G-ARPA (c/n 2101)

The first Trident flew piloted by John Cunningham (who first flew all the later marks of Trident) in BEA livery on 9 January 1962. The flight which lasted 1 hour 21 minutes was not without its difficulties as there was a problem with the undercarriage with a mainwheel jamming when retracting against an undercarriage door. Fortunately, by allowing the undercarriage to freefall, the problem was solved.

The initial flight trials included a general handling assessment, take-off and landing trials and use of in-flight reverse thrust. 'RPA appeared in the air at the

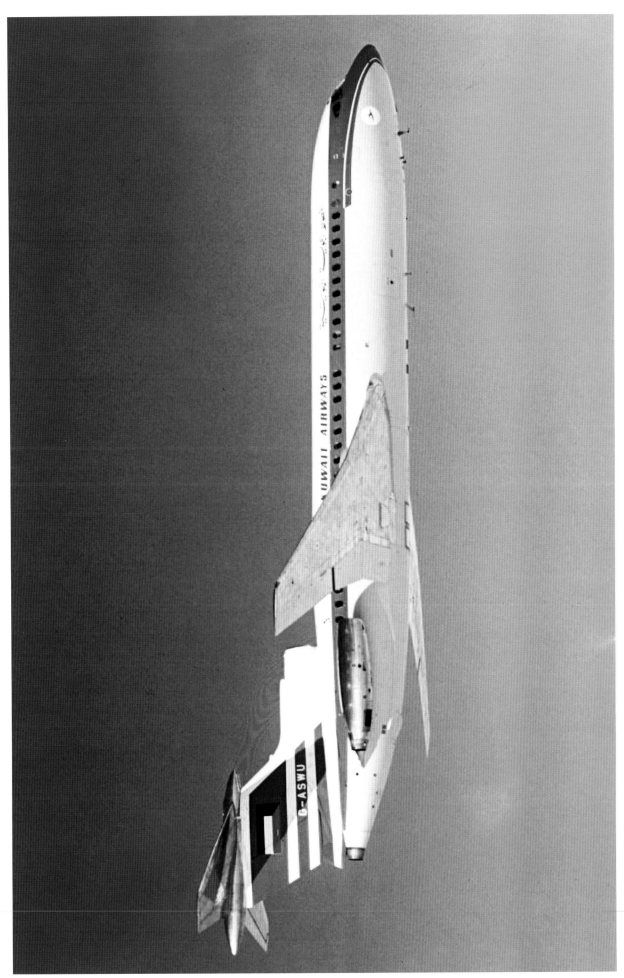

The first Trident 1E registered as G-ASWU for testing was destined for Kuwait Airways and flew in its attractive livery. Following its maiden flight on 2 November 1964 it embarked on a lengthy trials programme and was delivered to Kuwait Airways on 19 March 1966 as 9K-ACF. (BAE SYSTEMS)

Close up photo of the leading edge slats fitted to the Trident 1E G-ASWU (subsequently Kuwait Airways 9K-ACF) which superseded the droop leading edge installed on BEA's Trident 1Cs. The wool tufts on the wing and leading edge are to indicate the air flow during testing. These wool tufts are observed by Flight Test Observers and cameras. (BAE SYSTEMS)

1962 Farnborough Air Show. With the completion of 593 hours testing 'RPA was delivered to the Hawker Siddeley plant at Bitteswell on 17 February 1964 for refurbishment to delivery standard. It was delivered to BEA on 18 August 1965. It served with the airline until 7 February 1975 when it was stored at Prestwick and was broken up in March/April 1976.

Total time: 19,979 hours

Hawker Siddeley Trident 1C second production G-ARPB (c/n 2102)

First flown at Hatfield on 20 May 1962 it appeared at the Farnborough SBAC in September 1962 (and also in 1964). It was employed on tropical trials in Khartoum in November 1962 and in September 1963 in Torrejon and Cairo. 'RPB flew with a mock-up of the repositioned APU (auxiliary power unit) at the base of the fin (previously it was under the fuselage centre-section) on 3 February 1964. G-ARPB made its first Autoland at Bedford on 3 March 1964. On 30 June it was delivered to BEA and leased back for continuing Autoland development. It made its first low-visibility Autoland at Heathrow on 4 November 1965.

Its last test flight was on 31 January 1967 and it was then refurbished to BEA standard, reflown on 3 December and delivered to BEA on 20 December 1967. 'RPB was flown to Prestwick for store on 5 April

1975 and from 1978 was employed by the BAA Prestwick Fire Service for fire/rescue training. It was scrapped at Prestwick by February 1985.

Total time: 16,612 hours

Hawker Siddeley Trident 1E first production G-ASWU (c/n 2114)

Originally destined for BEA as G-ARPN it was reallocated to Kuwait Airways as a Trident 1E. The maiden flight of G-ASWU bearing Kuwait livery was on 2 November 1964.

Following one week's trials in Madrid in March, on 17 April 1965 the aircraft departed on a series of trials in 'hot and high' conditions in Africa, the Middle East and Pakistan lasting 17 days. Following the trials 'SWU was brought up to delivery standard which included its APU being fitted at the base of the fin which was to become standard on Tridents. It was delivered to Kuwait Airways on 19 March 1966 as 9K-ACF.

Following six years of service the aircraft was acquired by BEA in January 1972 and sold to Cyprus Airways as 5B-DAD on 15 March 1973. In July 1974 Cyprus was invaded by the Turkish Army and the Trident received minor damage in the attack. It remained abandoned at Nicosia until May 1977 when it was repainted in quasi British Airways colours, registered as G-ASWU and delivered to Heathrow on

The first six Trident 1s in the Hatfield Flight hangar during the test programme. Clockwise from top left: G-ARPA, B, F, E, C, D. 'RPB was employed on Autoland trials, 'RPE carried out sales demonstrations in the Far East and 'RPD trialled the leading edge slats devised for the Trident 1E. Although Hatfield Airfield is no longer in existence, the Flight Test hangar is preserved. (BAE SYSTEMS)

Kuwait Airways operated 9K-ACF until January 1972 and was sold to Cyprus Airways as 5B-DAD on 12 March 1973. Following the invasion of Cyprus by the Turkish Army in July 1974 the Trident remained at Nicosia Airport. It flew into Heathrow as G-ASWU in May 1977 in a hybrid colour scheme as pictured here. Then in full livery it served with BEA for three years until August 1980. It was withdrawn from use and scrapped in April 1981. (Author's collection)

Three Trident 2s on the Hatfield apron. The nearest is the first Trident 2 G-AVFA which has reference markings used in performance measurement. This view shows the repositioning of the APU below the rudder from under the centre-section (cf. photos above). G-AVFA flew on 27 July 1967 but was held back by the manufacturer for trials and Autoland development and only delivered in December 1969. (BAE SYSTEMS)

The first Trident 2 G-AVYA flew initially in the BEA "Red Square" livery but this is the final livery it wore in service with BEA's successor, British Airways. (Authors collection)

The first 3B G-AWYZ on the Hatfield apron. This final development of the Trident was substantially longer than the earlier Marks and, owing to its heavier weights, required a Rolls-Royce RB.162 booster engine below the rudder to provide adequate take-off and climb performance. (The APU was relocated to the front of the fin.) (BAE SYSTEMS)

12 May. It flew with BEA until 1 August 1980 when it was withdrawn from use at Heathrow and scrapped in May 1981.

Total time: 20,719 hours

Hawker Siddeley Trident 2E first production G-AVFA (c/n 2140)

The first Trident 2E made a 3 hours 30 minutes first flight from Hatfield in BEA livery on 27 July 1967, piloted by John Cunningham. Following initial flight testing 'VFA left Hatfield on 5 November for 'hot and

G-AWYZ in the air over Cyprus. It was first flown on 12 November 1969 and was delivered to BEA on 23 March 1972. It was only in service with BEA / British Airways until 16 October 1983 and was scrapped in June 1984. (BAE SYSTEMS)

high' trials in Nairobi until 6 December. On return to the UK 'VFA was fitted with a nose probe for high speed trials and flew up to a speed of Mach 0.97.

G-AVFA was the penultimate 2E to be delivered to BEA on 23 December 1969 as it took over from G-ARPB on Autoland development, flying 170 hours of trials between June 1968 and May 1969. It was withdrawn from use on 29 March 1983 and scrapped at Heathrow in January 1984.

Hawker Siddeley Trident 3B first production G-AWYZ (c/n 2301)

The final Mark of the Trident, the Trident 3B, made its maiden flight of 2 hours 50 minutes in BEA livery on 12 November 1969. Only a mock-up of Trident's new booster engine was installed for initial flights. The first flight with the booster was on 21 February 1970 and the first boosted take-off was from Bedford on 26 March 1970. From August to September 1970 'WYZ was engaged in tropical trials in Madrid and Dubai.

G-AWYZ was retained by Hawker Siddeley on Autoland trials and was only delivered on 23 March

1972. It was withdrawn from use on 16 October 1983 and scrapped at Heathrow in June 1984.

Total time: 20,511 hours

Powerplant:
Trident 1C – 3 x 9,850 lb Rolls-Royce Spey 505
Trident 1E – 3 x 11,400 lb Rolls-Royce Spey 511
Trident 2E – 3 x 11,930 lb Rolls-Royce Spey 512
Trident 3B – 3 x 11,930 lb Rolls-Royce Spey 512 & 1 x 5,250 Rolls-Royce Rb 162

Production by type:
Trident 1C: 24
Trident 1E: 15
Trident 2E: 50
Trident 3B: 28

Total built: 117 at Hatfield

An evocative view of the brand new Trident 3B G-AWYZ at height over Cyprus. (BAE SYSTEMS)

The powerful "all flying tail" of Trident 3B in the attitude it would assume on full down elevator. The APU was removed from the tail to the forward part of the fin to allow for the booster in the tail. (BAE SYSTEMS)

The Trident 2 production line at Hatfield. The Trident 2 was the most numerous of the Trident versions built owing to the order for 33 placed by the Chinese State Airline, CAAC. (BAE SYSTEMS)

Data	Trident 1C	Trident 1E	Trident 2E	Trident 3B
Length	114 ft 9 in	114 ft 9 in	114 ft 9 in	131 ft 2 in
Wingspan	89 ft 10 in	95ft 0 in	98 ft 0 in	98 ft 0 in
Height	27 ft 0 in	27 ft 0 in	27 ft 0 in	28 ft 3 in
MTOW	117,300 lb	130,000 lb	144,500 lb	150,000 lb
Cruising speed	610 mph	590 mph	590 mph	550 mph
Range	1,300 mls	2,700 mls	2,700 mls	2,235 mls
Passengers	109	115	115	146

Vickers VC10 & Super VC10

The first air-to-air views of the VC10 were taken on 25 August 1962 from an ETPS Meteor. This view shows the leading edge slats taped over during trials. (BAE Systems)

IN 1950 the Ministry of Supply issued a specification for a long-range jet transport for the RAF. Vickers was awarded the contract and began work on the design known as the V1000 or VC7 in its airliner manifestation. It was 146 ft long and powered by Rolls-Royce Conway engines which would provide it with trans-Atlantic range and a capacity for 120 passengers. Unfortunately, in December 1955, it was cancelled by the Government and consequently the prototype, already 80 per cent complete at Vickers-Armstrong's Wisley airfield, was scrapped. The RAF had no need for it and neither did BOAC, which stated that it would be using turboprop Britannias on its Atlantic routes in the years ahead. Yet one of BOAC's major competitors, Pan Am, had already ordered transatlantic jets in the shape of Boeing 707s and Douglas DC-8s and less than a year after the scrapping of the VC7, BOAC followed suit and ordered 707s. Thus at this crucial moment in the development of long-range airliners the British aircraft industry was unable to compete – as Vickers' Sir George Edwards remarked, "A decision we shall regret for many years". Vickers' next foray into the jet airliner market did, however, come to fruition and the VC10 flew in June 1962 entering service with BOAC on African routes in April 1964.

BOAC's requirement

The VC10 grew from a BOAC requirement for a jet airliner to service African and Eastern routes from airfields that might have comparatively short runways. The result was rear-engined design with a 'T' tail with a large unencumbered wing to provide the required runway performance, powered by four Rolls-Royce Conways. In May 1957 BOAC ordered 35 VC10s with options on a further 20 and in June 1960 converted these options to 10 Super VC10s with transatlantic range and capacity for 212 passengers. During 1961 the order was again altered to 12 Standard VC10s and 30 Super VC10s (although these Supers were much reduced in size with capacity for only 174 passengers).

Maiden flight and drag problems

The prototype VC10 embarked on the test programme on 29 June 1962 and was soon joined in the air by production VC10s destined for BOAC. Of these, G-ARVA-C and 'RVE were all involved in flight testing while 'RVF carried out route proving. Vickers soon discovered that the aircraft's drag was greater than calculated and engaged on a programme to alleviate this. The modifications required were alterations to the rear of the engine nacelles and their pitch, the leading edge slats and also the wingtips.

The VC10 entered service with BOAC on 29 April 1964 shortly before the first flight of G-ASGA, the first Super VC10 on 7 May. As the Super was little more than a stretched variant of the Standard it entered service with BOAC's transatlantic routes less than one year later, on 1 April 1965.

BOAC's attempt to cancel its Super VC10 order

Throughout this period BOAC's management showed little evidence of quality decision making, for in 1964 it distinguished itself by endeavouring to cancel the order for Super VC10s and order more Boeing 707s, which the airline stated were cheaper to operate. This information was soon in the public domain and adversely affected possible VC10 sales. On the North Atlantic routes BOAC Super VC10s achieved 71.6 per

The first VC10 G-ARTA at Weybridge on 15 May 1962 undergoing engine runs with silencers in place. The following day one of the silencers was blown off its mounting and landed 150 ft away. Engine runs continued without it. (BAE Systems)

cent load factors when the market average was 52.1 per cent. But BOAC demanded a Government subsidy to operate the VC10 while refusing to reveal its true operating costs. If it had not been for these actions it is likely that more VC10s would have been sold.

Fortunately, Government intervention ensured that BOAC accepted the 12 Standards and 17 of the 30 Supers while the RAF's order for 11 was increased to 14. The RAF's VC10 C1s were hybrids, with a Standard fuselage fitted with a freight door, the Super's fin fuel tank and higher-powered Conway engines.

Other operators

In addition to BOAC and the RAF, other initial VC10 customers were British United, which eventually operated four, Ghana Airways which received two and East African Airways, which ordered five Super VC10s fitted with cargo doors. Later users were Gulf Air which bought five Standard VC10s from BOAC, Middle East Airlines which leased two aircraft and Nigeria Airways and Air Malawi which both flew a single example in airline service. Additionally, the United Arab Emirates and the Sultan of Oman flew single aircraft as VIP transports, and RAE Bedford used one for research.

RAF Tankers

Following the VC10's withdrawal from airline service, the five former Gulf Air VC10s and the four surviving East African Supers were purchased by the RAF in 1977-78 for conversion into three-point flight refuelling tankers with additional tanks in the fuselage. The Standard VC10s became K2s and the Super VC10s were designated as K3s.

In 1991 an additional contract led to the RAF finally making some real use of five of the 15 former BOAC Super VC10s which had been purchased from BOAC ten years earlier. The five (including the first Super G-ASGA) were also converted into three-point flight refuelling tankers (as K4s) but without the additional fuselage fuel tanks. As part of the same contract the RAF's original VC10s were modified into two-point tankers with underwing refuelling pods, becoming C1Ks. At the time of writing it appears that the RAF's 16-strong fleet (ten CIK, four K3 and two K4) will remain in service until 2015, until replaced.

G-ARTA, the VC10 prototype airborne on its first flight from Brooklands on 29 June 1962. It landed at the nearby Wisley Flight Test Centre. The VC10 was crewed by Jock Bryce, Brian Trubshaw and Bill Cairns. (Author's collection)

A beautiful photo of G-ARTA landing at Wisley in the evening sun. On 31 December 1963 the prototype almost came to grief on stalling tests when an elevator bracket broke causing violent flutter. Brian Trubshaw who was captaining the flight thought the VC10 might break up, however a slow, safe return was made to Wisley and the VC10 was repaired. (BAE Systems)

Prototypes

Vickers VC10 prototype
G-ARTA (c/n 803) Type 1100

G-ARTA was rolled out of the Weybridge factory in April 1962 and two months later, on 29 June 1962, piloted by Jock Bryce, it made its maiden flight from the extremely short 3,600 ft runway situated within the former Brooklands racing circuit. As this was not a suitable length of runway for a maiden flight, a large yellow hatched marking about 20 ft deep was painted across the runway to warn pilots that there should just be sufficient runway remaining in which to stop if the aircraft was not lifting off at that point.

G-ARTA made an untroubled take-off in the late afternoon for the brief flight to Wisley, BAC's Flight Test Centre just three miles away which had a much more generous 6,700 ft runway. Unlike later VC10s, 'RTA was fitted with thrust reversers on each engine but the aircraft's landing performance was deemed more than adequate and production VC10s received reversers only on their outer engines. Less than three months after its first flight G-ARTA appeared at the 1962 Farnborough Show where it made a big impression on the crowd.

'RTA's flight test role was to test stability and control, flying controls, flutter, and part of the autopilot trials. Owing to the discovery of higher than calculated cruise drag; G-ARTA flew sorties with the flaps and slats taped over in the closed position to ascertain whether this would reduce drag. The fix decided upon was to fill in the area between the exhausts with the so-called 'beaver tail', realign the leading edge slats and extend the wingtips. These modifications were installed on 'RTA in May 1963.

On 31 December 1963 'RTA took off at 14:16 hrs to engage in stalling tests and was almost lost during this flight. While recovering from one of the stalls an elevator bracket broke causing violent flutter. The aircraft was vibrating so badly that Brian Trubshaw, who was in command, thought it might break up. As the behaviour of the aircraft was so alarming the escape chute door was explosively jettisoned at full cabin differential pressure, around 8 p.s.i. Consequently, the chute and the cabin floor had to withstand this differential pressure instantaneously because the freight bays were not vented. This resulted in the escape chute being crushed and much of it was torn out of the aircraft, making it unusable for the crew. Moreover, some areas of the cabin floor buckled, including the floor beams, which contained the flying control cable runs. Fortunately the aircraft did not break up and made a slow return to Wisley where it landed at 14:54 hrs with all the airfield's fire appliances in attendance. Following repair it was back in the air on 7 February 1964.

Over 2,300 stalls were flown by G-ARTA during stall testing. The prototype remained in its development role for several years but at the end of 1967, after approximately 700 hours flying, it was flown back to Weybridge to be converted to airline standard. Following refurbishment it was leased to Laker Airways, which immediately sub-leased the aircraft to Middle East Airlines as OD-AFA from 30 January 1968 to March 1969 when it was returned to BAC. It was then sold to British United on 1 May 1969 and with the merger of BUA and Caledonian in November 1970, it emerged in British Caledonian colours, named 'Loch Ness'.

In late January 1972 G-ARTA was diverted to Heathrow since its Gatwick base was fogged in.

Following almost six years of trials G-ARTA was refurbished and leased to Middle East Airlines (MEA) as OD-AFA. It is seen here at Wisley just prior to delivery, with G-ASYD One-Eleven 500 prototype just beyond. (BAE Systems)

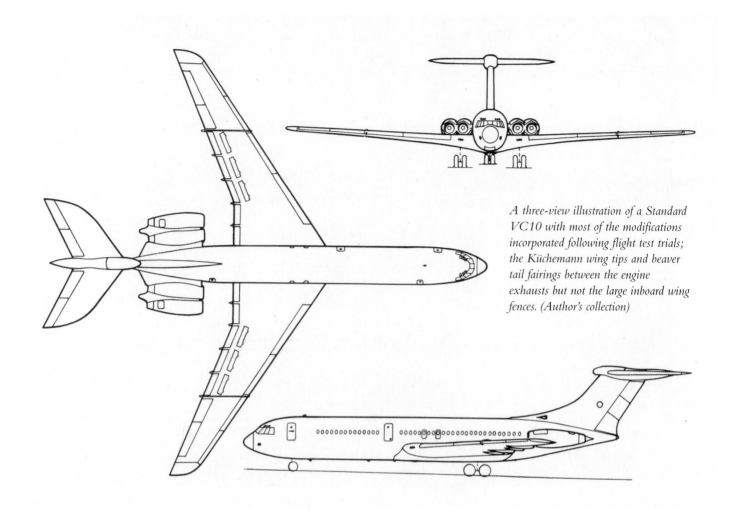

A three-view illustration of a Standard VC10 with most of the modifications incorporated following flight test trials; the Küchemann wing tips and beaver tail fairings between the engine exhausts but not the large inboard wing fences. (Author's collection)

On its return from lease to MEA G-ARTA served with British Caledonian until 28 January 1972 when, following a heavy landing at Gatwick, it was written off. This photograph shows it being cannibalised prior to being broken up. (Paul Robinson)

When the fog lifted on 28 January 1972 a short ferry flight was scheduled to Gatwick. Shortly after selecting spoilers and reverse thrust (after touching down on Gatwick runway 08) the aircraft became airborne again, landed back heavily and bounced twice. The fuselage was creased fore and aft of the wings, one nosewheel tyre burst and one wheel had separated. The aircraft was parked at Gatwick awaiting a decision on whether it was viable for repair, but in the end it was decided not and G-ARTA was broken up in 1975.

One of the two large final assembly hangers built at Weybridge for the VC10s. The first Super VC10 G-ASGA is pictured in primer with three Standard VC10s for BOAC in various stages of completion. (BAE Systems)

The roll out of G-ASGA at Weybridge in BOAC livery. Note the four thrust reversers initially fitted to the Super VC10. Following trials the inboard reversers were removed saving weight and complexity. (BAE Systems)

The first Super VC10 G-ASGA made its first flight in BOAC livery on 7 May 1964. For the September SBAC Show it was repainted in a one-off Super VC10 livery. Note the Lightnings of 92 Squadron in the background. (BAE Systems)

Vickers Super VC10 first production
G-ASGA (c/n 851) Type 1151

The first Super VC10 made its maiden flight from Weybridge in BOAC colours piloted by Brian Trubshaw on 7 May 1964. As it had an important testing role to fulfil, half of the cabin was fitted out with flight test instrumentation. By September 1964 'SGA had flown 140 hours on handling and stability trials and appeared in 'Super VC10' livery at the 1964 Farnborough Air Show. It carried out a full flight test programme

including stalling trials fitted with a tail parachute and tests carrying a spare engine in a nacelle under the right wing.

G-ASGA was delivered to BOAC in the airline's livery on 31 December 1965. It was withdrawn from service in March 1981 and initially was stored at Prestwick. It was then purchased by the RAF on 3 April 1981. The Super VC10 (along with others) was positioned at RAF Abingdon from May 1981 for eventual use by the RAF as ZD230. After almost ten

Following 15 years of service with BOAC / British Airways, G-ASGA was stored at Abingdon for ten years. After a three month refurbishment to basic flying standard it was delivered to BAe Filton for conversion to a VC10 K4 tanker. It is seen here arriving in a rather shabby external condition at Filton. (BAE Systems)

Registered as ZD230 the first Super VC10 flew with the RAF for 13 years as a VC10 K4 Tanker and made its last flight on 16 December 2005 from RAF Brize Norton to St Athan where it was scrapped. (Michael Brazier)

years of external storage, a basic refurbishment was carried out over a three month period to return the aircraft to flying condition. The short ferry flight to BAe Filton on 24 January 1991 was made with undercarriage, flaps and slats locked down.

At Filton the Super VC10 was rebuilt as a Mk. 4 flight refuelling tanker for the RAF and delivered to 101 Squadron coded as 'K' on 15 December 1994. During its

years of military service it took part in many missions including service on the Falkland Islands, and in the Balkan conflict, Afghanistan and Iraq. ZD230 made its last flight from RAF Brize Norton to RAF St Athan on 16 December 2005 where it was scrapped during 2006.

Powerplant:
Standard VC10 – 4 x 21,000 lb Rolls-Royce Conway R.Co. 42
Super VC10 – 4 x 22,500 lb Rolls-Royce Conway R.Co. 43

Production by type:
Standard VC10: 18
Standard VC10 C.1: 14
Super VC10: 22

Total number of VC10s built: 54 at Weybridge

Data	Type 1101 Standard VC10	Type 1151 Super VC10
Length	158 ft 8 in	171 ft 8 in
Wingspan	146 ft 2 in	146 ft 2 in
Height	39 ft 6 in	39 ft 6 in
MTOW	312,000 lb	335,000 lb
Cruising speed	580 mph	580 mph
Range	6,725 mls	7,190 mls
Passengers	135	163

Hawker Siddeley / BAe 125

The first prototype 125 G-ARYA with de Havilland titling. It made its maiden flight from Hatfield on 13 August 1962. Both G-ARYA and G-ARYB were shorter, had less wingspan and narrower doors than the initial production aircraft. (Hawker archive)

FOLLOWING on from the great success of the Dove, the de Havilland Board gave approval for work to proceed on an executive jet replacement in March 1961. This proved a very sound move as in the intervening 45 years more than 1,450 125s have been delivered and it remains in production, albeit in the USA.

The 125 has gone through many name changes since its inception. Originally known as the de Havilland 125, it was renamed the HS 125 when de Havilland was fully integrated into the Hawker Siddeley Group in 1965. When Hawker Siddeley Aircraft merged with BAC to form British Aerospace in 1977, it became the BAe 125 and, with the sale of the 125 programme to the American company Raytheon in 1993, the 125 was renamed the Hawker, (i.e. the BAe 125-800 became the Hawker 800). In March 2007 the Raytheon Aircraft Company was purchased from Raytheon by Beechcraft and the firm is now known as Hawker Beechcraft.

The fuselage, wings and vertical tail are still assembled and partially equipped at Airbus' Broughton plant and are then shipped to Wichita, Kansas in the United States for final assembly. Work was gradually transferred to Wichita and the first US-built Hawker 800 flew on 5 November 1996 although the last UK-built 800 did not fly until 29 April 1997.

First Prototypes and early development

The first of two prototypes flew at Hatfield on 13 August 1962 powered by the Bristol Siddeley Viper turbojet. The two prototypes were not wholly representative as they were shorter and had less wingspan than production models, but they were soon followed into the air by the first 125 Series 1 which was assembled at Broughton, as were all subsequent British-built 125s. After only eight Series 1s the 1A (American version) and 1B were introduced with upgraded engines. Aircraft were completed either as 'A' Series which were delivered 'green' (i.e. unfurnished and unpainted) to North American distributors, while 'B' 125s were furnished and painted at Broughton before delivery.

The RAF was an early customer for the 125 Series 2 (christened the Dominie by the Air Force) which entered service as Navigation Trainers in 1965. But the continuing and largest market for the 125 was in North America and to maintain its competitive edge the manufacturer continued to refine the jet. Even though the dimensions of the Series 3 and Series 400 remained the same as their precursors, they benefited from further product refinement, better interiors, greater range and Vipers with increased power.

Series 600 & 700

There was no Series 500 but the 600 received a 24 in fuselage plug, increasing maximum passenger capacity to 14, aerodynamic improvements and more economical Viper 601s giving a range of up to 1,876 miles. Two 400s already on the production line were versioned to become the 600 Series prototypes. Due to the increase in oil prices and the noise of the Rolls-Royce Vipers the 600 only made 71 sales. This indicated the need to introduce quieter, fuel-efficient turbofan engines, as had already been done by some of the executive jet competition.

The second prototype 600 G-AZHS, re-engined with American Garrett TFE731-3 turbofans and appropriately re-registered as G-BFAN, flew on 28 July 1976. This new version, the 125-700, offered almost double the range while external noise was reduced to acceptable standards. It resulted in a spurt in sales and became the best-selling model with 215 sales until the advent of the 800. On 29 October 1980 Hawker Siddeley celebrated the sale of the 500th 125 which also had the distinction of being the 300th sold in the USA. In the meantime Hawker Siddeley offered owners of earlier airframes the oppurtunity to re-engine their aircraft with turbofan Garretts replacing the Vipers.

Series 800 & 1000

By 1980 the time was ripe for a major re-think over the 125's design. Hatfield's engineers devised the 800 which differed from the 700 with a forward extension of the fin leading edge, greater wingspan and deeper fuselage. The nose, windscreen and canopy were re-profiled while the ventral fin was removed. Among the internal improvements was an EFIS flight deck. The British-built Viper engines were replaced with the American Garrett TFE-731-5R.

Two 700 Series airframes were set aside at Broughton for conversion to become the 800 Series prototypes. Following a successful test programme the 800 sold well in executive markets and also made inroads into a specialist military market with purchases by the USAF and the Japanese Self-Defence Force.

BAe decided to exploit the 800 further and by introducing a 33 in stretch to the fuselage married to the Pratt & Whitney PW305 engine, produced the BAe 1000 which flew on 16 June 1990. It is identifiable from the 800 by an additional cabin window on each side and the improved fairing between the wing and the fuselage which offered greater tankage and therefore greater range. In contrast to the popularity of the 800, only 52 BAe 1000s were built. Final assembly was not transferred to the USA and the final Hawker 1000 flew at Broughton on 18 March 1997.

Raytheon

From 1993, with the change in ownership, development of the 125 was in the hands of Raytheon, an American firm. Raytheon introduced the Hawker 800XP (Extended Performance), essentially an 800 with the wing of the 1000, Garrett TFE731-5R turbofans, new systems and interior, and increased fuel capacity thrust reversers as standard. Subsequently the 800XP has been developed by Raytheon into the 850XP with winglets and further models have come in the form of the Hawker 750 and 900XP, which flew in late 2007.

Hawkers (and 125s) continue in service with many international corporate customers, air forces and Governments. As total production approaches 1,500 this is a tribute to the quality of the original design and the implementation of a series of refinements in response to market needs.

Prototypes

Hawker Siddeley 125 prototype 1
G-ARYA (c/n 25001)

Although built at de Havilland's Broughton factory, 'RYA was assembled at Hatfield. It was built with a narrower door, shorter fuselage and wingspan than standard.

The second prototype G-ARYB, flew from Hatfield on 12 December 1962. The first two 125s were the only ones assembled at Hatfield. (Hawker archive)

1963 for Viper engine development. After a wheels-up landing at Filton on 11 December 1964 it was returned to Broughton for repair. G-ARYC was used for Viper development and communications flying until it was withdrawn from use on 7 September 1973 and taken by road to Hatfield in March 1976. It was delivered to the de Havilland Aircraft Heritage Centre, London Colney, Hertfordshire in May 1979.

Total time: 4,566 hours

Hawker Siddeley 125 Series 600 prototype 1
G-AYBH (c/n 25256)

G-AYBH was first flown unpainted by Mike Goodfellow from Broughton to Hatfield on 21 January 1971. 'YBH left Hatfield on 24 August 1971 for tropical trials in Spain. Between November 1972 and June 1974 it carried out sales tours of the Far East, Australasia and the Americas and was exhibited at the Paris Air Show.

On 15 June 1974 it was delivered as RP-C111 to Philippines Air Lines. Registered as G-5-13 it returned to BAe in April 1978. It was then delivered to the Irish Air Corps as 236 on 18 May 1979. Following a birdstrike on take-off it crashed on 27 November 1979 at Dublin-Baldonnel. The 125 was damaged beyond repair but there were no injuries. The fuselage was returned to Broughton for use as a sales mock-up.

Hawker Siddeley 125 Series 600 prototype 2 / Series 700 prototype
G-AZHS / G-BFAN (c/n 25258)

G-AZHS was completed in February 1971 but due to Rolls-Royce's bankruptcy, no engines were available and it did not fly until 25 November 1971. It was delivered to Hatfield for trials in December and in September 1972 was demonstrated at the Farnborough Air Show. During 1973 it tested a mock-up photo survey camera pod and in 1974 flew with drag reduction modifications.

Returned to Broughton to become the Series 700 prototype, it first flew at Broughton on 28 June 1976 as G-BFAN with TFE731-3 turbofan engines. In September 1976 it was exhibited at Farnborough and in November 1976 there were tropical trials at Nairobi, followed by noise trials in Granada in February 1977. G-BFAN returned to Broughton on 15 July 1977 for refurbishment to F600 standard for flight deck modifications. More tropical trials followed in February 1978 in Nairobi and on 20 February 1978 it was rebranded as a BAe 125-F600. (i.e. a 600 Series with Fan engines.)

G-BFAN was stored at Woodford from May 1993 to April 1995 when it was registered to May Ventures,

At the end of its trials programme G-ARYB was delivered to the HSA Apprentice Training School at Astwick Manor, Hatfield. Following the closure of Hatfield it was acquired by the Midland Air Museum at Coventry Airport. (Author)

Piloted by Chris Capper, it made its maiden flight on 13 August 1962 and appeared at the Farnborough Air Show one month later.

G-ARYA was at Broughton from November 1962 to April 1963 for an increase to its wingspan and the fitting of Viper 520s instead of 511s. The prototype carried out tropical trials at Nairobi and Khartoum in January - February 1964. It was later used for 125 Series 3 tests with a mock-up long-range tank and undercarriage doors. G-ARYA's final flight was on 11 January 1966. It was stored at Hatfield from January 1966 to April 1968, when it was sent to Broughton. It was transferred to Flintshire College, near Chester in 1971 but its nose is now stored at the de Havilland Aircraft Heritage Centre, London Colney, Hertfordshire.

Total time: 714 hours

Hawker Siddeley 125 prototype 2
G-ARYB (c/n 25002)

Built to the same smaller dimensions as 'RYA, G-ARYB was also built at de Havilland's Broughton factory but was assembled at Hatfield. It first flew piloted by Chris Capper on 12 December 1962. Its wingspan was later extended to the production dimensions. It flew its last flight on 22 January 1965. 'RYB was stored at Hatfield from 1965 and in June 1968 was passed to the HSA Apprentice Training School at Astwick Manor, Hatfield. In December 1993 it was acquired by the Midland Air Museum at Coventry Airport.

Total time: 478 hours

Hawker Siddeley 125 Series 1 first production
G-ARYC (c/n 25003)

G-ARYC was the first 125 assembled at Broughton. Unlike the first two aircraft, it was built to production dimensions. Its first flight from Broughton to Hatfield was on 12 February 1963. Following trials at Hatfield it was delivered to Bristol Siddeley at Filton on 24 July

The first 125 Series 1 G-ARYC was the third 125 built and the first one assembled at Broughton. Following trials with the manufacturer it flew with Bristol Siddeley Engines (later Rolls-Royce) on Viper development and communications work. (BAE SYSTEMS)

G-ARYC was withdrawn from use by Rolls-Royce on 7 September 1973 and roaded to Hatfield in March 1976. It was delivered to the DH Aircraft Heritage Centre, London Colney, Hertfordshire in May 1979 and has recently been restored. (Author)

which sold it the following year to Crystal Trading as VR-CJP. In April 1996 it was registered as VP-CJP and re-registered as G-OJPB in September 1997. In July 1998 it was purchased by Gold Air International. It was last reported at Faro, Portugal in July 2004 as 9Q-CBC owned by Scibe Trading.

BAe 125 Series 800 prototype
G-5-11 / G-BKTF (c/n 258001)

The Series 800 prototype had an anonymous first flight unpainted as G-5-11 and piloted by Mike Goodfellow on 26 May 1983 from Broughton. In contrast, a week later on 1 June, for its public debut, there was a ceremonial roll-out and demonstration flight fully painted as N800BA. Then registered as G-BKTF it carried out the bulk of the 125-800's nine months test programme from

Hatfield, which included the fitting of special equipment such as a tail parachute for stall protection.

It then flew in primer on digital avionics development and then, after a four months refurbishment at Broughton, flew as G-5-522 before appearing at Farnborough in September 1986 registered as G-UWWB. Briefly G-5-557, it was sold to Wilson Neil Ltd as ZK-TCB on 26 June 1987. In May 1989 it was purchased by Continental Aviation as N785CA. It flew in Hungary as OH-JOT from April 1990 to August 1992, returning to the USA as N801CR with Central Romania Corp. in September 1992. Romeo Mike Aviation purchased it in April 2003 as N800RM.

The first 125-600 G-AYBH was first flown unpainted by Mike Goodfellow from Broughton to Hatfield on 21 January 1971. It is pictured here by the Hatfield flight shed with the control tower above. The 125-600 was 2 ft longer and also had a more pointed nose than the previous 125s. (Hawker archive)

The 125 production line at Broughton on 9 March 1977. In addition to the 125s, Airbus wings are being constructed on the left of the photo. (Author's collection)

BAe 125 Series 1000 prototype 1
G-EXLR (c/n 258151)

G-EXLR's first flight was on 16 June 1990 followed by a ceremonial 'first flight' from Broughton to the BAe Flight Test Centre at Woodford on 28 June. G-EXLR was exhibited at the 1990 Farnborough Show and it then carried out noise trials at Stockton, California during May 1991. Its final flight was Woodford - Broughton on 10 July 1992. First stored, it was then dismantled and shipped to Wichita, USA on 28 October 1995. It is now used as a training aid.

BAe 125 Series 1000 prototype 2
G-OPFC (c/n 258159)

G-OPFC made a 2 hours 40 minutes maiden flight on 26 November 1990 in primer from Broughton, piloted by Tom Miller, during which it reached 43,000 ft. G-OPFC was delivered to BAe's Woodford Flight Test Centre for flight testing on 30 November. Registered as G-OPFC, the PFC is in honour of Peter Cedervall who was the 125's Chief Designer for 20 years. It was employed on icing trials in Iceland during March 1991, performance trials at Roswell, New Mexico from June - August 1991 and Almeria, Spain in March 1992. It was delivered to Raytheon, Wichita in September 1995 and was registered N10855 in February 1996. It was used as an engineering instructional airframe and scrapped by 2005.*

Powerplant:

DH 125 prototype – 2 x 2,500 lb Bristol Siddeley Viper 511
HS 125-600 – 2 x 3,750 lb Rolls-Royce Viper 601
BAe 125-800 – 2 x 4,300 lb Garrett TFE-731-5R
BAe 125-800 – 2 x 5,225 lb Pratt & Whitney PWC305B

Production sites:

Hatfield 2, Broughton 871, Wichita approximately 594

Production by type:

Series 1-400: 288
Series 600: 72
Series 700: 215
Series 800 and variants: approximately 840
Series 1000: 52
Total: Approximately 1,467 (at the time of writing)

* Author's note: subsequent prototype development by Raytheon falls outside this survey of British prototypes.

G-AZHS flying over the QE2. This photograph shows it in its original configuration as the Viper-powered second prototype 125-600 Series. It was re-engined with Garrett TFE731-3 turbofan engines and first flew at Broughton on 28 June 1976 as the Series 700 prototype with the new registration of G-BFAN. (Hawker archive)

G-BFAN (formerly G-AZHS) flying with Garrett turbofan engines as the 125-700 prototype. (Hawker archive)

Data	DH 125 prototype	DH 125 Series 1	HS 125-600	BAe 125-800	BAe 125-1000
Length	43 ft 6 in	47 ft 5 in	50 ft 6 in	51 ft 2 in	53 ft 11 in
Wingspan	44 ft	47 ft	47 ft	51 ft 5 in	51 ft 5 in
Height	14 ft	16 ft 6 in	17 ft 3 in	17 ft 7 in	17 ft 1 in
MTOW	19,000 lbs	20,000 lbs	25,000 lbs	27,400 lbs	31,000 lbs
Cruising speed	n.k.	485 mph	526 mph	510 mph	521 mph
Range	900 mls	1,005 mls	1,570 mls	2,450 mls	3,044 mls
Passengers	n.a.	Max. 10	Max. 12	Max. 14	Max. 15

Ceremonial roll-out of the first 125-800 as N800BA at Broughton on 1 June 1983. It had made an anonymous first flight unpainted as G-5-11 piloted by Mike Goodfellow on 26 May 1983. (BAE SYSTEMS)

Three view illustration of the BAe 125-800. (BAE SYSTEMS)

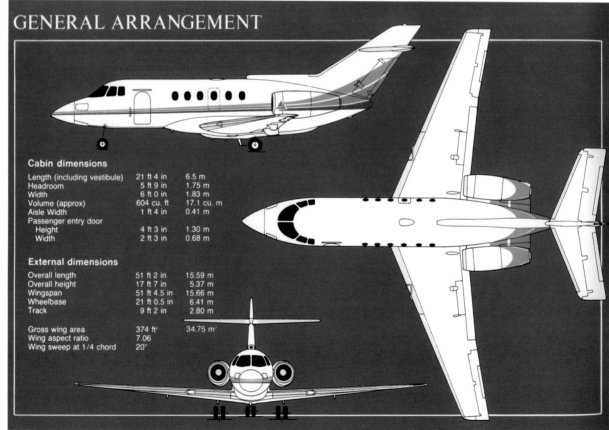

GENERAL ARRANGEMENT

Cabin dimensions

Length (including vestibule)	21 ft 4 in	6.5 m
Headroom	5 ft 9 in	1.75 m
Width	6 ft 0 in	1.83 m
Volume (approx)	604 cu. ft	17.1 cu. m
Aisle Width	1 ft 4 in	0.41 m
Passenger entry door		
Height	4 ft 3 in	1.30 m
Width	2 ft 3 in	0.68 m

External dimensions

Overall length	51 ft 2 in	15.59 m
Overall height	17 ft 7 in	5.37 m
Wingspan	51 ft 4.5 in	15.66 m
Wheelbase	21 ft 0.5 in	6.41 m
Track	9 ft 2 in	2.80 m
Gross wing area	374 ft^2	34.75 m^2
Wing aspect ratio	7.06	
Wing sweep at 1/4 chord	20°	

The 125-800 prototype G-BKTF (formerly G-5-11 and N800BA) with nose probe and stall recovery parachute fitted for flight testing. This view clearly shows the revised windscreen of the 800 Series. (Hawker archive)

G-EXLR arriving at Woodford on 28 June 1990. This BAe 125-1000 had a short life, flying for only two years before being scrapped at Wichita. (Derek Ferguson)

The first three BAe 125-1000s at BAe's Woodford Flight Test Centre in August 1991 during the test programme. Furthest from the camera is the first prototype G-EXLR, then the second, G-OPFC, in primer with large camera tracking marker and, closest, the third 1000, G-ELRA. G-ELRA is currently flying in the USA as N261PA. (BAE SYSTEMS)

Shorts Skyvan, Shorts SD 330 and Shorts SD 360

Shorts Skyvan

A Vauxhall estate being loaded into the rear of the first Skyvan prototype G-ASCN's hold. The internal dimensions of the freight hold were 16 ft x 6 ft 6 in x 6 ft 6 in. (Brian Burrage)

Shorts logo

THE Shorts SC.7 Skyvan concept was influenced by the Miles Aerovan utility aircraft which first flew in 1945. An Aerovan was modified in 1957 to incorporate an experimental 75 ft span Hurel-Dubois wing and Miles approached Shorts to propose joint development of this model. Although Shorts purchased the concept, the resulting Shorts Skyvan was a more conventional machine and built without Miles' involvement.

Shorts built a comparatively low-cost aircraft of functional construction – a twin piston-engined design with a braced high-wing configuration which did not impinge on the square unpressurised fuselage, a beaver tail and twin fins allowing for rear-loading, and a fixed undercarriage. The sloping rear panel of the underside was hinged at the bottom to serve as the loading door, enabling direct loading of freight.

Construction of the prototype began to a tightly controlled budget in 1960 and it did not fly until January 1963. It had been recognised in 1962 that it would be underpowered with the Continental piston engines and these were replaced with turboprop Turbomeca Astazou 2s in October 1963. In 1964 substantial alterations were made – lowering the tail assembly and installing higher-powered Astazous 10s. The slow pace of the programme continued and the

second Skyvan, designated as a Skyvan 2, did not fly until October 1965. It incorporated these changes as standard plus a more pointed nose, a shorter ramp to increase the available fuselage load space and a simplified undercarriage. A further refinement introduced to increase range was to expand the hump over the wing and incorporate this as a fuel tank.

The first Skyvan delivery was to AerAlpi in Italy in 1966 and others soon followed to Emerald Airways, Ansett-MAL, Papuan Air Transport and Northern Consolidated of Alaska. However, as the Astazou proved a disappointment in 'hot and high' conditions, consideration was given to abandoning the project, but it was decided to continue so the 715 shp Garrett TPE-331 engine was offered as an alternative and G-ASZJ flew with Garretts in December 1967. The improvement provided by these engines was soon evident and they became standard on the Skyvan 3, while seven Series 2s were converted to Mk. 3s. Shorts' agents in North America promoted this version strongly and announced sales of 50 Skyvan 3s during 1967.

The design was further exploited into the multi-role STOL 19-seat Skyvan 3M Military transport aircraft which proved very popular, achieving 60 sales to the armed forces in 17 countries.

Although the majority of Skyvan sales were for military or utility use, there was also a special de luxe all-passenger version developed during 1969-70 called

The first prototype G-ASCN carrying out engine runs at Sydenham, Belfast. It made its maiden flight on 17 January 1963 in its original form with Continental piston engines which left it severely underpowered. These piston engines were soon replaced and it flew with Turbomeca Astazou turboprops on 2 October 1963. Bombardier)

the Skyliner with a more luxurious cabin interior – twelve of these were produced. Overall the Skyvan was sold to civil operators in 25 countries. It may not have won plaudits for its looks but the concept was successful and when production ended in 1985 a total of 154 had been manufactured.

Prototypes

Shorts Skyvan 1 / 1A / 2 prototype
G-ASCN (SH.1828)

The prototype Skyvan 1 powered by twin 390 hp Continental GTSIO-520 piston engines flew from Sydenham, Belfast for the first time on 17 January 1963, piloted by Denis Taylor. Only shortly into the test programme on 29 May 1963 the aircraft made an emergency landing at Newtownards Airfield, Northern Ireland and had to be returned by road to the factory, where it was re-engined with Astazou engines. It then flew again as a Skyvan 1A on 2 October 1963. Intensive testing continued, including trials with skis, followed by public display at the Hannover and Farnborough Air Shows in 1964, and the Paris Air Show in 1965. In November 1964 the aircraft returned to the factory to have its tailplane lowered, single piece rudders fitted and higher-powered Astazous 10s installed. It flew again on 15 March 1965 in near production-standard in AerAlpi livery. Trials continued until its last flight on 15 August 1966, when it was retired to the Apprentice Training School. It was scrapped in November 1976.

Shorts Skyvan 2 prototype
G-ASCO (SH.1829)

The second Skyvan had a short life – first flying on 29 October 1965, initially with Astazou 10s which were replaced in 1966 by Astazou 12s. It flew at the 1966 Farnborough Air Show in full Ansett-MAL livery and later bore Eastern Airlines colours. Its last flight was in May 1968 and it became an instructional airframe. It was broken up at Shorts in 1972.

Shorts Skyvan 2 pre-production 1 / Skyvan 3 prototype 1
G-ASZI (SH.1830)

The first pre-production Skyvan 2, furnished with all the modifications applied to G-ASCO, first flew on 28 January 1966. It was leased to Aeralpi from February to June 1966 for crew training and route proving. It was then returned to the production line to become the prototype Series 3 with Garrett TPE-331 turboprops. It first flew in this form on 15 December 1967 and was employed on Series 3 test flying. Landing at Sydenham on 30 December 1968 the right undercarriage collapsed, causing significant damage. Following this accident the aircraft never flew again and was used for trial installations. It was withdrawn from use in 1972 and scrapped.

'The van that flies' – Shorts' slogan for the Skyvan, G-ASZI first flew as a Skyvan 2 on 28 January 1966 with Astazous but was converted to become the prototype Series 3 with Garrett TPE-331 turboprops flying on 15 December 1967. (Bombardier)

Shorts Skyvan 2 pre-production 2 / Shorts Skyvan 3 Prototype 2
G-ASZJ (SH.1831)

G-ASZJ (the second pre-production machine) was completed as a Series 2 and flew on 3 March 1966 but was almost immediately converted to a Series 3 to expedite certification and flew on 20 January 1968. In the summer of 1968 it flew on a sales tour of the USA (which included demonstrations to the US Army) and Mexico. It was employed as a demonstrator/trials aircraft and in January 1970 was converted into the all-passenger Skyliner prototype and exhibited at

Farnborough 1970 in British Air Services livery. Following evaluation by British Air Services in November 1970 it was converted to the full Skyliner specification and was exhibited at the 1971 Paris Air Show in Interstol colours. In 1973 it appeared in BEA colours and in 1975 in British Airways livery although it was still Shorts' demonstrator. It was leased to McAlpine Aviation in October 1986, and then purchased by Trygon Ltd in January 1999. It was briefly on the Burundian register and then sold to Gallovents Ten Ltd of South Africa in 2000 as ZS-ORN.

The fourth Skyvan prototype G-ASZJ on show at the 1970 Farnborough Air Show in British Air Services livery. (Author)

The second Skyvan 3 prototype G-ASZJ on the island of Barra, Outer Hebrides in November 1970 during a two day evaluation of its suitability to replace BEA's Herons. The result was an order for two Skyliners, the all-passenger version of the Skyvan. (Bombardier)

Skyliners, which were luxury passenger versions of the Skyvan, in production for BEA on the production line at Belfast. (Author's collection)

The first of two SD 330 prototypes, G-BSBH, flew from Sydenham, Belfast on 22 August 1974. These photographs clearly shows its Skyvan lineage. (Jack Wood)

Shorts SD 330

Following the success of the Skyvan, Shorts considered a commuter airliner development of the Skyvan more suitable to the passenger market, with a greater capacity to improve the company's financial viability and offering a passenger cabin with comfort levels of an airliner, albeit without pressurization. Eventually Shorts opted for a 30-seater – originally designated as the Shorts SD3-30 (and later the 330), which received the go-ahead in May 1973. It retained the same fuselage cross-section of the Skyvan but was increased in length and fitted with a 12 ft wider wing with a new centre-section, a retractable wider track undercarriage and a new elongated nose and tail incorporating freight compartments. The manufacturer determined to avoid a repetition of the problems that the powerplant had caused the Skyvan and chose the Pratt & Whitney Canada PT6A-45A.

The prototype G-BSHB flew for the first time on 22 August 1974, having gained its first order from Command Airways of New York just eight days previously. However, as the second prototype only joined the test programme eleven months later, British certification was not awarded until February 1976 and the CAA equivalent in June. Flight trials indicated that the standard Skyvan tail was not quite sufficient for the much extended 330 and 1 ft was added to the height of each fin.

The Shorts 330 became popular as a passenger aircraft for short commuter flights serving throughout the world although generally orders were only in small numbers. As a result of this and the very competitive nature of this market Shorts had to build aircraft 'on spec' so that deliveries could follow very closely after an order.

As the aircraft developed, higher power engines were introduced which allowed for higher weights and greater payload to be carried. At the time of the launch of the Shorts 360 in June 1980 the 330-200 model was also announced with even better payload (and available in a mixed-traffic layout) with better PT6A-45R engines installed.

Mindful of the sales made by the military Skyvan, Shorts promoted a low-cost development designated as the 330-UTT (Utility Tactical Transport). This received the 45R engine, a reinforced floor to carry freight, plus rear passenger doors modified to allow paratroop dropping. This version made modest sales but the Shorts Sherpa, a further and more substantial development available for the military or civilian light freighter role, proved more successful. The Sherpa had its rear door reconfigured to hinge out from the bottom of the fuselage incorporating a roller floor enabling the transport of containers or vehicles such as a Land Rover. A prototype Sherpa flew at the end of 1982 and was demonstrated to the USAF which ordered 18 designated as the C-23A for its European Distribution role. In 1988 when the Sherpa had clearly demonstrated its usefulness, the US Air National Guard followed suit and ordered ten C-23Bs (later increased to

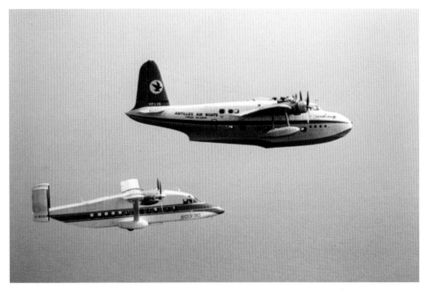

16) but these differed from the earlier Sherpas in that they retained the windows of the airliner, were powered by the PT6A-65AR as fitted to the Shorts 360-200 and had a rear ramp which could be opened in flight.

From 1981 production of the 330 in Shorts' huge Assembly Hall at Sydenham, Belfast continued alongside the new 360 (originally launched as the SD3-60) with the last 330 flying in 1992.

Prototypes

Shorts SD 330 first prototype
G-BSBH c/n SH.3000

The appropriately registered prototype (SBH = Shorts Brothers and Harland) flew for the first time from Sydenham, Belfast on 22 August 1974 on a two hours flight, piloted by Don Wright. On 29 August it flew to Farnborough to appear in the biennial Air Show. Following an undercarriage malfunction on 3 October the prototype made a wheels-up landing at Aldergrove Airport, Belfast but the damage was slight and it was flown back to Sydenham a few days later.

In May 1975 G-BSBH spent 12 days at Istres, France on performance trials. Continuing its busy schedule it was based at Farmington in New Mexico and Yuma, Arizona from September to October 1975 for high temperature and high and low altitude tests respectively. While in the USA it was also demonstrated to customers and potential customers. It returned to Belfast on 20 October. Its Certificate of Airworthiness expired on 13 April 1981 and it was stored at Sydenham and scrapped in 1999.

Shorts SD 330 second prototype
G-BDBS c/n SH.3001

The second prototype first flew on 8 July 1975 and joined in the test programme with the first prototype. It was demonstrated at Farnborough in 1978. During October and November 1978 G-BDBS demonstrated in the Middle East, Far East and Australia, making 67 flights. Just over two years later, in January 1981, it left on a ten week sales tour of south-east Asia,

Two Shorts aircraft together - the second prototype SD 330 G-BDBS built at Belfast and Sandringham VP-LVE built at Rochester flying together over Northern Ireland in 1977. The Sandringham is currently displayed in the Solent Sky Museum in Southampton. The Sandringham was built 1943 as a Sunderland III and served with the RAF but was converted to a Sandringham and operated by TEAL of New Zealand and later, Ansett Flying Boat Services and finally Antilles Air Boat. (Jack Wood)

*The second
prototype SD 330
G-BDBS at
Maningrida Airport,
Northern Territory,
Australia, on its
sales tour of the
Middle East, Far
East and Australia
in October and
November 1978.
(Bombardier)*

*Bombardier (which
had bought Shorts
in 1989) donated
G-BDBS to the
Ulster Aviation
Society and it was
delivered minus
outer wings or tail
by RAF Chinook
to Langford Lodge
Airfield, County
Antrim on 7 April
1993. (Jack Wood)*

G-ROOM prototype 360 made its first flight on 1 June 1981 in the livery of Allegheny Commuter, the first customer for the 360. This aircraft was written off following terrorist bombing at Shorts' factory airfield at Sydenham, Belfast on 28 November 1989. (Jack Wood)

the Pacific Basin, Australia and New Zealand, returning to Northern Ireland in April 1980.

The aircraft was subsequently used for research into noise reduction in conjunction with RAE Farnborough through comparative trials on three different types of propeller for the Shorts 360. It made its first flight as the Utility Tactical Transport prototype on 10 September 1982 and carried out a long series of flight trials including supply and paratroop dropping. Following the conclusion of these tests it was employed as a company communications aircraft until 1992 and withdrawn from use on 1 July 1993. G-BDBS was donated to the Ulster Aviation Society and was delivered without outer wings or tail by RAF Chinook to Langford Lodge Airfield, County Antrim on 7 April 1993. In January 2006 it was moved to Lisburn, County Antrim.

Shorts SD360

On 1 June 1981 the prototype Shorts 360 G-ROOM made its maiden flight more than six months ahead of schedule. This Shorts 360, announced a year earlier, represented rather more than a 'stretched' version of the Shorts 330 to accommodate an extra six passengers. The 360 differed from the 330 by the replacement of its twin fins and rudders by a new single swept tail fin. A 3 ft fuselage plug was inserted forward of the wings, and the changed lines of the aft fuselage to accept the new tail unit increased the internal length of the cabin by 5 ft 1 in. The opportunity was taken simultaneously to introduce more economical and powerful engines (Pratt & Whitney Canada PT6A-45R) with quieter propellers; however this model, like its predecessors, remained unpressurised.

The second 360 G-WIDE did not fly until August 1982 but was soon delivered to Suburban Airlines in the USA as N3605A. The 360 received its CAA certification in September and the FAA equivalent in November 1982. As with the smaller 330, the average fleet size of the 360 was small but even so the 360 sold particularly well in the USA. To capitalise on this success, from the 81st aircraft onwards the design was refined by the introduction of the uprated PT6A-65AR engines and branded as the Shorts 360 Advanced, though later it was redesignated as the 360-200. The first 360-200 was delivered to Thai Airways in November 1985. Further developments in the powerplant naturally led to the 360-300 with more powerful PT6A-67R engines driving six blade propellers, providing a higher cruise speed and improved performance.

Although production of the Shorts 360 ceased in 1991 the original C-23 Sherpa (based on the SD 330) had proved so successful with the United States Army that, to fulfil additional demand, 28 second-hand SD-360s were purchased by Shorts for conversion into Sherpas. This involved a costly and substantial modification programme which was carried out at Bridgeport, West Virginia between 1994 and 1998, from which Shorts made a financial loss. The programme involved shortening the fuselage, and removing the 360's single tail and replacing it with a new 330 twin tail and loading door manufactured by de Havilland Canada. These aircraft, incorporating the higher rated powerplant of the 360, were designated as the C-23B+ and provided the US Army with the aircraft it desired.

Prototype

Shorts SD 360 prototype
G-ROOM c/n SH.3600

The Shorts 360 prototype was first flown in the livery of Allegheny Commuter on 1 June 1981, six months ahead of schedule. This was partly because the prototype employed the fuselage of Shorts 330 (SH.3041) N844SA of Suburban Airlines which had been damaged beyond repair in a tornado in Allentown, Pennsylvania in June 1980 and returned to Belfast.

On only its fourth flight the prototype landed at Paris for the Air Show. It flew with PT6A-45R engines as the airframe was ahead of the powerplant's development; the designated PT6A-65Rs were only installed in January 1982. G-ROOM appeared in the static display at Farnborough 1982 in Shorts' livery. The 360 prototype was unfortunately the victim of a terrorist bomb while parked at Sydenham, Belfast on 28 November 1989 and was written off and scrapped.

Powerplant:
Skyvan 1 – 2 x 390 shp Continental GTSIO-520
Skyvan 2 – 2 x 730 shp Turbomeca Astazou 12
Skyvan 3 – 2 x 715 shp Garrett AiResearch TPE-331-201 Turboprops
SD 330-100 – 2 x 1,173 shp Pratt & Whitney PT6A- 45A
SD 360 – 2 x 1,327 shp Pratt & Whitney PT6A-65Rs

Production by type:
Skyvan 1: 1
Skyvan 2: 13 (7 converted to Mk. 3s)
Skyvan 3: 83
Skyvan 3M: 52
Total number of Skyvans built:
149 at Sydenham, Belfast

SD 330-100: 28
SD 330-200: 70
SD 330 UTT: 8
C-23 Sherpa: 34
Total number of SD 330 and C-23 Sherpas built:
140 at Sydenham, Belfast

SD 360-100: 80
SD 360-200: 38
SD 360-300: 47
Total number of SD 360 built:
165 at Sydenham, Belfast

Total number of Skyvans, SD 330s and SD 330s built: 454

The prototype SD360 G-ROOM parked in the static display at Farnborough 1982. (Tim Rees)

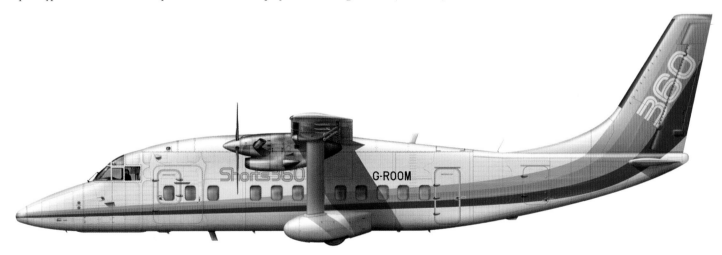

G-ROOM was the sole Short SD 360 prototype which flew on 1 June 1981, and had the unusual distinction of being destroyed by terrorist action at Sydenham, Belfast on 28 November 1989.

Data	Skyvan 3	SD 330 100	SD 360
Length	40 ft 1 in	58 ft ½ in	70 ft 10 in
Wingspan	64 ft 11 in	74 ft 8 in	74 ft 10 in
Height	15 ft 1 in	16 ft 3 in	23 ft 8 in
MTOW	12,5000 lb	22,900 lbs	26,543 lbs
Cruising speed	210 mph	218 mph	245 mph
Range	440 mls	1,055 mls	1,055 mls
Passengers	19	30	36

BAC One-Eleven

The prototype One-Eleven G-ASHG being prepared for its first flight on 20 August 1963. Although painted in British United colours, 'SHG could be distinguished from the early BUA aircraft by the additional wording BAC on the tail and the registration almost hidden from view under the engine nacelles. (BAE SYSTEMS)

ON 20 August 1963 the BAC (British Aircraft Corporation) One-Eleven made its maiden flight. Success looked certain with 60 orders from major airlines such as British United and American Airlines, whereas the sole competitor, the Douglas DC-9, was only in the early stages of development. Over the next 21 years 235 One-Elevens were built in the UK and between 1982 and 1989 nine more were assembled in Romania, making a grand total of 244.

The first flight crew with the BAC One-Eleven prototype G-ASHG (c/n 004) at its roll-out at Hurn on 28 July 1963. Left to right: Mike Lithgow, Deputy Chief Test Pilot, Vickers, Tony Neve, Dick Wright, Flight Test Observers, Jock Bryce, Chief Test Pilot, BAC. Both Mike Lithgow and Dick Wright lost their lives in the crash of the prototype on 22 October 1963. (BAE SYSTEMS)

The One-Eleven was the first project for the newly formed British Aircraft Corporation, created in January 1960 when Vickers-Armstrongs, English Electric and Bristol Aircraft merged. In May 1960 the new Corporation purchased Hunting Aircraft, inheriting the Hunting 107, a 60-seater airliner project with two Bristol Siddeley BS75 engines of 7,000 lb thrust, a 500 mph cruising speed, a range of 600 miles and a 'T' tail. BAC carried out extensive market surveys of potential customers with some 60 airlines indicating interest, which led to increased design weights, the need for additional fuel and the decision to use Rolls-Royce Spey engines.

The launch of the One-Eleven

On 9 May 1961 BAC publicly launched the BAC One-Eleven and announced its first order for ten One-Eleven 200s from British United Airways. Although this order was from a British airline, the One-Eleven was not designed for a single customer, unlike the Trident and VC10 which were tailored to BEA and BOAC needs respectively. As a result, this new jet had a far wider appeal from the outset. A few months later the first American orders were received from Braniff and Mohawk, followed by American Airlines which placed an initial order for 15 aircraft (later increased to 30) in July 1963.

In preparation for the American Airlines order, in May 1963 BAC had announced the 300 and 400 Series, which could carry heavier payloads over longer range and were higher-powered with 11,400 lb thrust Spey 25 Mk. 511-14 engines instead of the 10,410 lb of the 200 Series. The 400 was designed for the American market with its '80,000 lb rule' – above which any aircraft

G-ASHG taking off from runway 26 at 7:44 pm at Hurn Airport for a 24 minute maiden flight on Tuesday, August 20, 1963. (BAE SYSTEMS)

needed three crew. The 300 was destined for all other markets where there was no such limit. Fortunately the FAA's 80,000 lb rule was abolished in 1966 at which point the 300 Series was dropped and only the 400 Series classification used.

The improved 400 Series opened up a new market for BAC in Central America, the Philippines, Germany, Argentina, Brazil, and started the association with Tarom of Romania. The 400 also earned orders from British independent airlines such as Laker, British Eagle Channel Airways and Autair.

Flight testing the One-Eleven

The prototype G-ASHG, a 200 Series, made a successful maiden flight from Hurn on 20 August 1963 but disaster struck on 22 October 1963 when the machine failed to recover while engaged on stall tests and crashed, killing all the crew. Stunned, the manufacturers sought to reassure the customers and rectify the problems. Unfortunately in February 1964 matters were exacerbated by the landing crash and write-off of the second production G-ASJB owing to pilot error. A further delay affected the project when the fourth production aircraft G-ASJD, specially configured for stalling trials, was crash-landed on Salisbury Plain after the pilot mistakenly believed that it was in a stable stall. But despite these tribulations the One-Eleven was certified on 5 April 1965.

The stretched 500 Series

BAC realised by the mid-1960s that demands for a

The tragic scene at Cratt Hill, Chicklade where the prototype One-Eleven, G-ASHG crashed on 22 October 1963 killing all seven crew after entering a deep stall from which recovery was not possible. It had descended at 10,000 ft per minute in a flat attitude and on impact moved forward only 70 ft. (The Times)

The One-Eleven 400 Series prototype G-ASYD taking off from Wisley in a quasi-American Airlines livery with BAC One-Eleven 400S titling. It had made its maiden flight as G-ASYD from Hurn on 13 July 1965 in bare polished metal with red titling 'British Aircraft Corporation' on the front fuselage. (BAE SYSTEMS)

Stretching in progress at Hurn. G-ASYD, previously the 400 Series development aircraft, cut into three and ready to be extended to become the 500 Series prototype with fuselage plugs both forward and aft of the wing. (BAE SYSTEMS)

stretched version of the One-Eleven were intensifying. BEA was also interested and as a result, the Rolls-Royce Spey 512 with 12,000 lb thrust was launched, providing an increase in power, which allowed the basic airframe to be stretched by 8 ft 4 in forward of the wing and 5 ft 2 in aft. This allowed for 4 extra seat rows, increasing normal capacity from 79 to 99 passengers, although 500s sometimes carried as many as 119 passengers.

The 500 Series was launched on 27 January 1967 with an order for 18 from BEA. BAC later refined the specification to produce a developed 500 Series with modified flap tracks fairings, wing leading edge and brakes and higher power 12,550 lb thrust Speys. These were ordered by BUA, Caledonian, Autair (which later became Court), Paninternational, Bahamasair, Court Line, Philippines Air Lines, Bavaria Flug and Tarom, among others.

The hot rod – the One-Eleven 475 and 670

Owing to the Spey's thrust limitations BAC was unable to stretch the One-Eleven beyond the 500 Series and in January 1970 it announced the 475 Series, using the body of the 400 but retaining the extended wing, leading edge and powerplant of the 500 Series, with a larger main wheel undercarriage to give rough field performance. This provided an aircraft of 80-seat capacity, able to operate from 4,000 ft strips and ideal for 'hot and high' operations.

These capabilities allowed the aircraft to be considered for an entirely new market segment, mainly in countries where many of the airfields were in remote locations and of poor quality, perhaps unpaved dirt strips. This variant sold to Peru, the Pacific Islands, Central Africa and the Middle East but sadly, the 1973 Oil Crisis curtailed interest in an aircraft of this size and

capability for many years. BAC made great efforts to sell the 475 into Japan and further versioned the Series to create the 670 Series for this market, but without success.

In 1978, with the decision of the newly formed British Aerospace to launch the BAe 146, there was no possibility of further development of the One-Eleven. Licence production was arranged with Romania and nine aircraft were manufactured there, the last flying in 1989.

The One-Eleven did not go down without a fight, however, and Dee Howard Corporation in the USA re-engined two aircraft with Rolls-Royce Tays which gave greatly improved performance and met noise regulations. However, the company had insufficient resources and BAe's support was never full and so the project stalled. One-Elevens continued widely to fly around the world, gradually retreating from first rank operators and finally being forced from widespread operation by the imposition of new noise regulations in 2002.

The One-Eleven had great potential and should have been re-engined when it was clear that the Spey would never grow to provide the necessary power; this would have given it the possibility of competing fairly against the DC-9 and 737. Had this occurred the One-Eleven would have won far more sales and remained in production for far longer.

Prototypes

BAC One-Eleven 200 prototype
G-ASHG (c/n 004)

The prototype, G-ASHG, was painted in British United's blue and white colours and rolled out at Hurn on 28 July 1963. Captained by BAC Chief Test Pilot,

Corporation' on the front fuselage. The first engines 'SYD flew with were Spey Mk. 510-14, soon exchanged for the Spey 511-14 and it flew with these on the performance trials at Torrejon, near Madrid which started on 11 September 1965, continuing until late October while undergoing FAA certification. In 1966 the aircraft made its first appearance at the SBAC Show at Farnborough.

Conversion of G-ASYD to the 500 Series prototype

On 4 February 1967, G-ASYD flew Wisley to Hurn in order to be versioned as the aerodynamic prototype of the 500 Series. It was cut into three and a 100 in extension fitted fore with a 62 in extension fitted aft of the wing, together with extended wingtips. Six weeks ahead of schedule on 30 June 1967 piloted by Brian Trubshaw, with Roy Radford as co-pilot, 'SYD took off on its 'second' first flight.

It flew to Torrejon for one month in February 1968 for runway trials, accelerated stops and noise tests. Later that year it was engaged in testing for the developed 500 Series with modified flap tracks fairings, leading edge and brakes. For a publicity film in September 1968 'SYD briefly carried BUA's new blue and sand livery on the left side with the more sober BAC red, white and blue colours on the right side.

Conversion of G-ASYD to the 475 Series prototype

The aircraft's 1,000[th] flight involved wet runway tests when the Wisley fire engines sprayed 67,000 gallons of water over the runway. A week later, there were gravel runway tests in preparation for the 475 landing on basic unpaved airstrips. On 8 May 1970 'SYD flew into Hurn for conversion into the 475 prototype. This involved removal of the fuselage plugs which had been inserted when it was extended to the 500 Series length. The mainwheel bay was reconfigured to accommodate larger wheels and tyres, giving a noticeable bulge. One month ahead of schedule, on 27 August 1970, Roy Radford took 'SYD into the air from Hurn for a 'third' first flight as the 475 Series prototype and a few weeks later demonstrated it at the Farnborough Air Show.

Rough field trials followed on a 1,500 ft test strip on a disused runway at Waterbeach in Cambridgeshire between 25 May and 4 June 1971. In all, 'SYD made 25 landings in conditions of pouring rain, hot sunshine and in high crosswinds and tailwinds up to 20 knots, simulating 'hot and high' airfields. Certification for this type of operation was achieved in September 1971. In 1973 BAC and Rolls-Royce developed a hush kit to reduce the noise of the Spey and in September 1974 'SYD appeared at Farnborough sporting this.

G-ASYD as the One-Eleven 500 prototype at Hurn. It flew as a 500 Series for three years and was then 'downsized' to become the 475 prototype. (BAE SYSTEMS)

Jock Bryce, with Project Pilot Mike Lithgow, it lifted off on the evening of 20 August 1963 at 19:42 hrs after a 20 minute maiden flight. After four flights 'SHG transferred to Wisley. The test programme set off at a cracking pace with G-ASHG making 53 flights of 81 hours in 63 days. On 22 October 1963, G-ASHG took off from Wisley at 10:17 hrs piloted by Mike Lithgow. At 10:40 hrs it crashed and exploded at Cratt Hill, Chicklade in Wiltshire, killing all seven crew after entering a deep stall from which recovery was impossible.

BAC One-Eleven 400 Development aircraft 1 & 500/475/670 prototype
G-ASYD (c/n 053)
Piloted by Brian Trubshaw and Peter Baker, G-ASYD took to the air from Hurn on 13 July 1965 in bare polished metal with red titling 'British Aircraft

Stalling was a critical matter for the One-Eleven following the loss of G-ASHG and as a result any stalling trials required a large anti-stall parachute and emergency escape hatches to be available for the crew. The anti-stall parachute installation on the One-Eleven was very large and fitted far back in order to provide a sufficient nose-down pitching moment and not to become entangled with the tail. It is shown here on 'SYD at Hurn following a practise deployment. (BAE SYSTEMS)

G-ASYD as the Series 670 development aircraft making its 'fourth' first flight. The 670 was a specialised development of the 475 for the Japanese market. It was fitted with an anti-stall parachute, visible at the rear of the aircraft on this flight, and immediately embarked on a stalling trials programme. (BAE SYSTEMS)

G-ASYD's final first flight – as the 670 Series prototype

In an effort to win an order from the Japanese domestic airlines, the One-Eleven was demonstrated daily at the 1976 Japanese International Air Show in Iruma simulating airline route flying into small airfields. Still in pursuit of this Japanese order 'SYD entered the Hurn hangars in March, 1977 for its last metamorphosis. A small triangular cuff was fitted between the wing leading edge and the wing fence which increased the lift coefficient by up to 20 per cent and reduced the approach speed by 6 to 8 knots and take-off speed by up to 12 knots.

On 13 September 1977, Roy Radford and John Cochrane made the first flight of 'SYD as the 670 prototype from Hurn to Filton where flight test was based. 'SYD immediately engaged on a full test programme. As part of the same programme in April 1978 there were wet runway trials on Hurn's main runway. G-ASYD made its fourth and final Farnborough appearance in 1978.

Although One-Eleven development was at an end, 'SYD still had 15 years of useful life ahead on trials and communications work for BAe. In 1980 nine flights were flown investigating relaxed stability, manoeuvre and gust alleviation. The final role in this long and distinguished career was testing Lucas Industries' light activated spoilers and ailerons. To herald this, the fuselage was painted with the titling 'Fly by Light Control Technology' above the windows. 'Yankee Delta' was retired in October 1993 but fortunately saved from the scrap heap and generously donated to the Brooklands Museum by BAe Airbus. Piloted by John Faucett, Filton's Chief Test Pilot, 'SYD took off from Filton on its last flight on 14 July 1994, safely landing on the 1,800 ft remaining of the Brooklands' runway.

BAC One-Eleven 400 development aircraft 2 G-ASYE (c/n 054)

On 16 September 1965, G-ASYE made its maiden flight

from Hurn. After shake-down trials it was delivered to Marshall of Cambridge in November for the fitting of an executive interior in the front cabin and airline seating in the back in preparation for the three sales tours. From November 1965 to May 1966 G-ASYE travelled 160,000 miles, making 334 separate flights – on average two flights a day – and visiting to nearly 70 airlines and 40 business corporations, hosting 4,600 guests and all at the comparatively low cost of £250,000.

Such concentrated efforts brought results, with orders valued at £10m for five aircraft from TACA, LACSA, LANICA, and Victor Comptometers. Soon after returning home in May 1966 G-ASYE was reconfigured as a 410 Series executive jet for Victor Comptometers and delivered as N3939V on 8 September 1966.

The Chesapeake & Ohio Railroad acquired the One-Eleven on 16 October 1972 as N77CS. Having served for just over four years, it was re-registered as N77QS in 1977 and sold for $5 million in March 1979 to Sheikh Abdul Maksoud Khota. Registered in Saudi Arabia as HZ-AMK, the jet became one of several One-Elevens used as personal aircraft by the Saudi royal family. It returned to the United States in 1985, first as N77QS.

After an eventful and testing life 'SYD's last landing was a short one on the 1,800 feet remaining of the Brooklands runway on 14 July 1994. This prototype is now on view at the Brooklands Museum, Surrey. (Cliff Knox)

On the second part of G-ASYE's World Sales Tour during early 1966 it was demonstrated throughout South-East Asia and Australasia. In the Philippines its tail was temporarily repainted in Philippines Air Lines (PAL) livery and a vestige of this remained on its engine nacelle proclaiming "PAL JET ONE-ELEVEN" for the remainder of the Tour. (BAE SYSTEMS)

On its world sales tours G-ASYE displayed the logos of all the One-Eleven customers at that time: (from the top left) British United, Braniff, Mohawk, Kuwait Airways, Central African Airways, Aer Lingus, American Airlines, Philippines Airlines, Aloha, British Eagle, British Midland and TACA. (BAE SYSTEMS)

It then went through a succession of three different US registrations and four owners over the ensuing decade, finally emerging as N17MK with Executive Air Leasing in July 1990. From January 2001 the former 'SYE, reconfigured with 79 conventional seats, was under the ownership of Go Jet, in Tulsa, Oklahoma. Stored from March 2002, it was broken up for spares in 2005.

Powerplant:
One-Eleven 200 – 2 x 10,410 lb Rolls-Royce Spey 506
One-Eleven 400 – 2 x 11,400 lb Rolls-Royce Spey 511
One-Eleven 500 – 2 x 12,550 lb Rolls-Royce Spey 512
One-Eleven 475 – 2 x 12,550 lb Rolls-Royce Spey 512

Production by type:
One-Eleven 200: 58
One-Eleven 300/400: 79
One-Eleven 500: 95
One-Eleven 475: 12

Total built: 244 (222 at Hurn, 13 at Weybridge, 9 at Baneasa, Romania)

Data	One-Eleven 200	One-Eleven 400	One-Eleven 500	One-Eleven 475
Length	93 ft 6 in	93 ft 6 in	107 ft 0 in	93 ft 6 in
Wingspan	88 ft 6 in	88 ft 6 in	93 ft 6 in	93 ft 6 in
Height	24 ft 6in	24 ft 6 in	24 ft 6 in	24 ft 6 in
MTOW	79,00 0 lb	88,500 lb	104,500 lb	98,500 lb
Cruising speed	548 mph	548 mph	541 mph	541 mph
Range	2,130 mls	2,250 mls	2,165 mls	2,300 mls
Passengers	89	89	119	89

Britten-Norman Islander and Trislander

IN more than 40 years of production, with three interruptions caused by bankruptcy and four changes of ownership, Britten-Norman has at the time of writing built 1,238 Islanders and Trislanders

The Islander was the brainchild of two de Havilland-trained aeronautical engineers, John Britten and Desmond Norman, who commenced design in 1963 of a 10-seat STOL aircraft to replace the de Havilland Dragon Rapide. They decided to keep the design as simple as possible by using a virtually square fuselage, high-wing and fixed undercarriage. To maximise space they cleverly designed the aircraft so that doors opened on both sides to provide access, obviating the need for a gangway. Although initially a private venture, when Britten-Norman needed assistance the Ministry of Aviation provided 50 per cent of the launch costs repaid by a levy on sales.

First flight and production
On 13 June 1965 the BN-2 Prototype G-ATCT made its first flight. Following initial flight trials the 210 hp Continental engines were replaced by Lycoming 260 hp units and the wingspan was increased by 4 ft. The BN-2 type was named the 'Islander' in August 1966. In August 1967 the Islander received UK CAA certification and in December US FAA certification.

During 1968, as demand grew, production was expanded with the assistance of BHC at Cowes on the Isle of Wight and the signing of a Romanian production agreement which led to the first Romanian-built BN-2A Islander G-AXHY flying in May 1969. In September that year the 100th BN-2 was delivered to Aerial Tours, Papua New Guinea.

Detail refinement resulted in the BN-2A Islander which flew on 20 June 1968 and further improvements in performance and comfort ten years later led to the BN-2B. The current BN-2B Piston Islander incorporates many hundreds of modifications that have been developed to meet customer needs since the Islander's maiden flight in 1965.

Trislander
Buoyed up by the success of the twin-engined Islander, the company sought means to offer a larger version with 18 seats by extending the fuselage with two 30 in plugs fore and aft of the wing. The necessary additional power was found by unconventionally fitting a third engine to the vertical tail fin.

The second Islander, G-ATWU, was chosen as the prototype and was rebuilt at Bembridge, Isle of Wight, flying on 11 September 1970. During trials it was found necessary to add an extension to the fin above the rudder. In January 1971 the aircraft was named the Trislander and the first delivery was to Aurigny Air Services in June 1971. Trislanders have served in airline service with other operators such as Blue Islands, Loganair, Lydd Air and Great Barrier Airlines. Production continued until September 1984 when the last Belgian-built Trislander was delivered to Botswana.

Defender
In June 1971 Britten-Norman decided to build on the success of those Islanders sold to police forces and launched the BN-2A Defender at the Paris Air Show. This had a strengthened airframe and four underwing hard points suitable for target towing, parachuting and military surveillance.

The first two Islander prototypes in flight. G-ATCT, the first prototype, flew on 13 June 1965 from Bembridge on the Isle of Wight, piloted by its designers Desmond Norman and John Britten. It crashed in Holland on 9 November 1966. G-ATWU, the second Islander, joined it in the air on 28 August 1966. It had a longer life, later becoming the Trislander prototype. (BN Historians Collection)

*G-ATWU's
surprise appearance
at Farnborough on
12 September
1970. It had made
its maiden flight as
the BN 2 Mk. 3
(later named
Trislander) only
the previous day.
(Author)*

Continuing demand led to the launch of the BN-2T-4S Defender 4000 at the 1994 Farnborough Air Show. The prototype Turbine Defender had a 30 in fuselage plug (unlike the Trislander's two) plus a 53 ft wingspan. The Defender can be used in urban and maritime surveillance and counter-terrorism operations.

Changes in the ownership of Britten-Norman

In October 1971 Britten-Norman Limited went into receivership but was reformed in August 1972 when Fairey of Belgium bought the firm, moving main production to Gosselies in Belgium, although completion work continued at Bembridge. Fairey also went into receivership in 1978 and the company was purchased by the Swiss aircraft company, Pilatus, which switched production back to Romania. Pilatus sold its stake to Biofarm in 1998 and after a somewhat insecure period a rescue operation resulted in the purchase of the company by Omani interests to form BN Group in May 2000.

Britten-Norman now concentrates on the defence market but continues to support its existing airframes. Constant refinement has ensured that the Islander family of aircraft continues to excel in modern day roles including passenger transport, environmental protection, air ambulance, fisheries protection, photo surveillance, policing and parachuting. The designers, both now dead, would be proud of their legacy. Indeed, the Islander and its developments are the best-selling British transport aircraft.

Prototypes

Britten-Norman BN-2 Islander prototype 1
G-ATCT (c/n 001)

On 13 June 1965 the unpainted BN-2 prototype G-ATCT

made its first flight of 27 minutes duration at Bembridge piloted by Desmond Norman and John Britten. Only four days later it made its first public appearance at the Paris Air Show and on 26 June 1965 carried out its first flying demonstration at the Exeter Air Day. It flew with its wingspan extended by 4 ft and its Lycoming 0-540 engines replaced by Continentals on 17 December 1965. It was demonstrated at Farnborough 1966 but because of heavy icing on 9 November 1966, G-ATCT crashed at Sneek, Holland killing the Test Pilot, Peter Hillwood.

Britten-Norman BN-2 Islander prototype 2 & Trislander prototype
G-ATWU (c/n 002)

G-ATWU first flew on 28 August 1966 at Bembridge and became the development prototype, appearing at Farnborough that year. In 1968 it was stretched by 33 in to become the sole BN-2 Super. It was further modified and first flew as a BN 2 Mk. 3 (later named Trislander) on 11 September 1970. The following day it made a surprise appearance at the Farnborough Show and was put on display in the static park. Although withdrawn from use on 30 October 1970, it was only scrapped in 1979.

Britten-Norman BN-2A-41 Turbo Islander prototype
G-BDPR (c/n 504)

The Turbo Islander flew on 6 April 1977 with Lycoming LTP-101 engines but the type did not go into production. Withdrawn from use in 1979 it was rebuilt as a piston-engined BN-2A-27LN in 1993. Currently it serves as VQ-TDA with InterIsland Airways in the Turks and Caicos Islands.

G-ATWU as the Trislander prototype following painting and the addition of a fin above the rear engine.
(BN Historians Collection)

The Turbo Islander G-BDPR flew on 6 April 1977 with Lycoming LTP-101 engines. This choice of engine did not prove satisfactory and it was rebuilt as a piston-engined BN-2A in 1993.
(BN Historians Collection)

Following the decision not to proceed with the Turbo Islander, Britten-Norman trialled the Rolls-Royce Allison 250 in G-BPBN. This installation proved successful and led to production as the Turbine Islander. (BN Historians Collection)

Britten-Norman BN-2T Turbine Islander
G-BPBN (c/n 419)

The Turbine Islander G-BPBN first flew on 2 August 1980. It was a conversion of a BN-2A-21 which had originally flown in 1974. It was sold to a private owner in 1983 and scrapped in 1999.

Data	BN-2 prototype	BN-2B-26 Islander	BN-2T Turbine Islander	BN-2A-3 Trislander
Length	35 ft 3 in	35 ft 8 in	35 ft 8 in	43 ft 9 in
Wingspan	45 ft	49 ft	49 ft	53 ft
Height	13 ft 8 in	14 ft 6 in	14 ft 6 in	13 ft 4 in
MTOW	4,750 lb	6,600 lb	7,000 lb	10,000 lb
Cruising speed	156 mph	143 mph	170 mph	185 mph
Range	950 mls	735 mls	837 mls	400 mls
Passengers	10	10	10	18

Powerplant:
BN-2 – 2 x 210 hp Continental IO-360-A
BN2B-26 – 2 x 260 hp Lycoming 0-540-E4C5
BN2T – 2 x 420 hp Rolls-Royce Allison 250-B17C
BN2A-3 – 3 × 260 hp Lycoming O-540-E4C

Total built:
1,155 Islanders and 83 Trislanders
1,238 of all models built at the time of writing

Handley Page Jetstream/ British Aerospace Jetstream 31 and Jetstream 41

THE Handley Page Aircraft Company, formed in 1909, was a well known manufacturer of large military and civil aircraft. Following the restructuring of the British Aircraft industry into two major groups in 1960, neither of which included Handley Page, the firm had no prospect of Government contracts. However Handley Page was determined to remain in aircraft manufacturing.

Thanks to legacy programmes the company had time to examine projects that would not stretch its financial resources. A proposal came from an American, Jack Riley, to re-engine and possibly pressurise the de Havilland Dove. Handley Page recognised this compromise as far from ideal and went ahead to design a new pressurised, low wing aircraft powered by twin turboprops capable of transporting 18 passengers in a three-abreast layout. This was launched in January 1966 as the HP137 Jetstream, tailored to fill a gap in the feeder-liner market aimed primarily at the United States. With early estimates of development and production of the prototypes estimated at £2.6m, Handley Page was surprised and gratified to receive launch aid from the Ministry of Aviation of £1.5m.

First flight

As there was no suitable British engine in the required power range, the French Turboméca Astazou 14 of 840 hp was chosen for the Jetstream production aircraft. The prototype, G-ATXH, flew from Radlett for the first time in August 1967. In order to keep to the very tight development programme it was decided to base two of the Jetstream prototypes at Turboméca's base at Pau in Southern France for several months to provide close

proximity to the engine manufacturer, since engine performance was temperamental and below specification. Although commonplace with new designs the aircraft was overweight, and drag was higher than calculated. These problems all led to a delay in certification and an increase in costs far greater than the original estimate of £3m, which Handley Page could ill afford.

While endeavouring to certify the Astazou Jetstream, Handley Page was also engaged in work for a large USAF order and had received a contract to produce eleven Jetstream 3Ms powered by the American Garrett AiResearch TPE-331. To hasten development of the USAF version the fifth aircraft flew with the Garrett engines and was later joined by the second prototype G-ATXI. Consequently the test programme for the Astazou version had to be handled by just three machines.

18 August 1967 and the first Jetstream prototype takes to the air on an eventful first flight from Handley Page's airfield at Radlett, Hertfordshire. During the flight the nosewheel initially refused to lower and one of the brakes jammed on landing. (Handley Page Association)

The flight crew for the Jetstream's third flight: (from the left), Spud Murphy (Dep CTP), Ray Funnell (FTO) Johnny Allam (CTP), Charles Joy (Technical Director) and John Collar (Chief FTO). (Handley Page Association)

*Three of the four
Jetstream prototypes
on the Radlett
apron. G-ATXJ,
'TXH and 'TXI.
(Handley Page
Association)*

The first prototype Handley Page Jetstream G-ATXH flew on 18 August 1967 and was used on trials until
February 1970 when it was grounded following the demise of Handley Page.

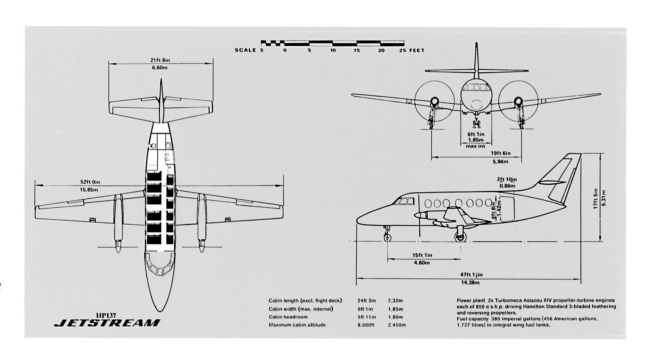

*Three-view drawing
of the Jetstream 1
(Handley Page
Association)*

Handley Page into receivership

Owing to the deficiencies of the Astazou 14 and its effect on the aircraft's performance, the firm developed the Jetstream 200 with the more powerful Astazou 16. Loss of trading confidence brought about a downturn in the company's fortunes and on 8 August 1969 Handley Page went into receivership. However there were grounds for optimism when four months later the newly formed Handley Page Aircraft rose from the ashes. With this apparent security three aircraft were re-engined with the more powerful Astazou 16 and another aircraft left on a demonstration tour of Australia – but then the USAF cancelled its order and on 27 February 1970 the backers of Handley Page Aircraft withdrew their support and the newly formed company went out of business.

Jetstream Aircraft

Fortunately the Jetstream was kept alive by interested parties who formed a company called Jetstream Aircraft. Three completed Jetstreams, 21 engineless airframes and a large quantity of spares and design authority were purchased from Handley Page's receivers. This nascent firm used Jetstream 200 G-AXFV to achieve certification for this development and kept the project alive.

Jetstream Aircraft proposed a version of the Jetstream 200 for the RAF as a training aircraft. Against stiff American competition the Government awarded a contract for 26 but insisted that the production contract should be managed by Scottish Aviation at Prestwick (to whom Handley Page had originally subcontracted the building of the wings). Scottish Aviation was able to furnish the contract using aircraft stored at Sywell, Northamptonshire and six new-build aircraft. The first of these, XX483, flew on 13 April 1973.

British Aerospace and the Jetstream 31

On 5 December 1978 the newly formed and state-owned British Aerospace decided to relaunch a new version – the Jetstream 31, based on the Jetstream 200 fuselage and powered by the Garrett TPE-331 as originally flown in the USAF version designed by Handley Page, albeit in a different configuration. Building on the experience gained with the RAF contract, the Jetstream 31 was produced at BAe's Prestwick plant (the former Scottish Aviation factory). A Radlett-built Jetstream was purchased and modified to become a development aircraft and flew in 1980 as G-JSSD.

The Jetstream 31 offered airline seating for 19 or an 8-12 passenger corporate layout. It proved very successful, with large orders in the United States and at the height of its popularity wore the liveries of United, American, Northwest, TWA and USAir. To maintain market position the Jetstream Super 31 (Jetstream 32) was announced at the 1987 Paris Air Show with uprated engines, higher operating weights and double the range. When production of the Jetstream 31 ceased in early 1997 after delivery of 383 aircraft, more than 200 had been delivered to US Airlines.

Prototypes

Handley Page Jetstream 1 prototype 1 & Jetstream 200 prototype 1
G-ATXH (c/n198)

Its maiden flight was at Radlett on 18 August 1967 piloted by Chief Test Pilot, John Allam. There were problems during the 110 minute first flight: the nosewheel initially refused to lower and had to be shaken down while on landing a jammed brake required the application of reverse thrust on the right to keep the aircraft straight on the runway. During the next few days there were 13 more flights and then the prototype was laid up from 29 August until 29 November for the Astazou 12s to be replaced with Astazou 14s. From 4 December 1967 to 20 March 1968 'TXH was based at Turboméca airfield in Pau, France to expedite flight testing. Later that year it was demonstrated at the Farnborough Air Show and re-flown with Astazou 16s.

It first flew as the reconfigured 200 Series prototype on 18 September 1969. It was based at Rolls-Royce Filton for engine development, flying in January 1970, but was grounded in February 1970 following Handley Page's demise. G-ATXH was dismantled in October 1972 when the fuselage went to Scottish Aviation at Prestwick. Other parts were scrapped in 1976.

Total time: 1,004 hours, 973 landings

Handley Page Jetstream 1 prototype 2
G-ATXI (c/n199)

Following use for resonance testing, G-ATXI made its first flight powered by Astazou 16s on 8 March 1968 at Radlett. It was transferred to the Mark 3M test programme for the USAF order and first flew on 7 May 1969 with Garrett AiResearch TPE-331 engines replacing the Astazous. It exhibited at the Paris Air Show in June 1969 and was based at Marrakesh in August 1969 for performance trials. Its last flight was on 21 September 1969. Following the cancellation of the USAF contract it was stored and then dismantled at Radlett 1970 following the demise of Handley Page.

Total time: 262 hours, 186 landings

Handley Page Jetstream 1 prototype 3
G-ATXJ (c/n 200)

The third prototype made its first flight powered by Astazou 14s on 28 December 1967 at Radlett and almost immediately left for Pau, where it remained for flight testing until 20 March 1968. Unfortunately it was damaged following a heavy landing at Hatfield during short landing trials on 4 September 1968. The aircraft was taken by road the short distance to Radlett on 16 September and was back in the air on 8 December 1968. It returned to Pau on 13 December for ten days. G-ATXJ was in Khartoum from 20 January to 31 January 1969 on 'hot and high' trials. More hot trials followed in Entebbe, Khartoum and Dubai from June to July 1969.

A rather unhappy G-ATXJ after it had made a heavy landing at Hatfield during short landing trials on 4 September 1968. Fortunately the damage was not too great and it was returned by road to Radlett and was back in the air on 8 December 1968. (Handley Page Association)

Total time: 636:25 hours, 616 landings

Handley Page Jetstream 1 prototype 4
G-ATXK (c/n 201)

The final Jetstream 1 prototype made its first flight at Radlett on 8 April 1968. As a fully furnished demonstrator it appeared at the Hannover Air Show in April/May 1968 followed by demonstration flights in Europe. On 28 May 1970 it left on a tour of North America and was transferred to the ownership of International Jetstream Corporation as a demonstrator. On 12 December 1968 it lost a passenger door in flight. It was withdrawn from use in 1970 and stored at St. Louis, Minnesota. It was purchased by Riley Jetstream in August 1975 and sold on as N2958F and was used in the ground scenes for the James Bond 007 film 'Moonraker' in 1978. It was finally stored engineless at Santa Barbara, California in 1980.

As part of the Jetstream 200 programme it was re-engined with Astazou 16s and flew on 16 December 1969. It carried out hot fuel tests at Hatfield on 3 January 1970 and on 10 February left for Cyprus for low-level trials and then to Fort Lamy in Chad for tropical trials, arriving on 21 February 1970. When Handley Page collapsed the aircraft returned to Luton on 8 March 1970 and was impounded by UK Customs where it was dismantled and shipped to the USA.

In 1981 it was shipped to Hurn for re-work to become the Jetstream 31 mobile cabin mock-up. It was rebuilt as Jetstream 41 customer interior mock-up in 1991 and delivered to the Customer Centre at Hatfield. Following the closure of Hatfield it went to the Wales Aircraft Museum in 1995 and then to the Cardiff Airport Fire Service in February 1996.

Handley Page Jetstream 200 prototype 2
G-8-8 / G-AXFV (c/n 211)

This aircraft first flew as G-8-8 on 24 April 1969 at Radlett. A month later it became G-AXFV and, following installation of Astazou 16s and systems modifications, flew as the second Jetstream 200 prototype on 17 February 1970. After Handley Page's collapse it was sold by the receiver to the Cranfield Institute of Technology where it was delivered on 3 September 1970.

Following the collapse of Handley Page interested parties formed Jetstream Aircraft and kept the Jetstream project alive. G-AXFV was used to complete certification of the Jetstream 200, for which an order was received from the RAF. Eventually G-AXFV was sold to an operator in Zaire but was later purchased by BAe and converted to a Jetstream T.2 for the Royal Navy as ZA111. (Handley Page Association)

G-JSSD, the prototype Jetstream 31 was actually a conversion of a Handley Page-built Jetstream. The original Astazou engines were replaced and Garrett AiResearch TPE-331 engines. It first flew at Prestwick as a Jetstream 31 on 28 March 1980. (Handley Page Association)

Terravia (later Jetstream Aircraft) reached agreement to continue Series 200 certification trials in December 1970 and exchanged a Jetstream 1 for 'XFV which completed the trials and was also exhibited at the Paris Air Show that month.

RAF evaluation trials followed from 9 August to 2 September 1971 at the A&AEE Boscombe Down with the Jetstream in competition against the Turbo Commander. The aircraft then set off on tropical trials in Teheran and Dubai during September 1971. Terravia sold 'XFV to Gecamines of Tanzania as 9Q-CTC in January 1974. BAe purchased it on 31 January 1977 and converted it to a Jetstream T.2 at Prestwick. It flew as ZA111 on 23 December 1981 and was delivered to the Royal Navy on 18 June 1982 as ZA111.

BAe Jetstream 31 prototype
G-JSSD Jetstream 31 (c/n 227)

This was the 27th production Jetstream 1 and was registered respectively as N510F, N12227 and G-AXJZ. On 26 December 1978 it was ferried from Natchez, USA to Prestwick for conversion to become the prototype Jetstream 31. The major aspect of the conversion was the removal of the Astazou engines and their replacement with Garret TPE331, as had originally been intended for the Jetstream for the USAF; however the actual installation was inverted in contrast to the original.

Its first flight as a Jetstream 31 of 1 hour 22 minutes piloted by Len Houston and Angus McVitie, was at Prestwick on 28 March 1980 and it was exhibited at the Farnborough Air Show in September 1980. Since April 1996 it has been on display at the Scottish Museum of Flight, East Fortune.

BAE SYSTEMS

British Aerospace Jetstream 41

Encouraged by the success of the Jetstream 31, BAe decided to develop the design further and launched the Jetstream 41 in 1989. The fuselage was lengthened with an 8 ft 3 in plug forward of the wing and a 7 ft 9 in aft increasing its length to 63 ft 2 in to accommodate 29 passengers. This re-proportioning allowed the cabin door to be moved to the front of the fuselage.

The Jetstream 41 proved a major alteration to the original design with more powerful AlliedSignal TPE331 turboprops in new nacelles, EFIS glass displays, a re-profiled cockpit window layout and a lowered, increased span wing to remove the protrusion of the wing main spar into the cabin aisle. As a result, the Jetstream 41 was certified as a new aircraft.

Sales were subject to the vagaries of the North American airline market. For example, in 1993 there were almost no orders from the USA but the following year there were 53. Unfortunately, following this flood of orders there was famine once again and the company decided to cease production in May 1997. In December 1998 BAe delivered its last Jetstream 41 to the Hong Kong Government Flying Service.

BAe Jetstream 41 prototype 1
G-GCJL Jetstream 41 (c/n 41001)

The first J41 made a 2 hours 45 minutes first flight at Prestwick on 25 September 1991 and was delivered to the Woodford Flight Test Centre on 19 November 1991. It was initially employed on general handling trials and later on icing and cold weather systems trials. In 1998 J41s carried out trials for the Hong Kong Government Flying Service fitted with a dummy Satellite Communications antenna and search radome

respectively above and below the fuselage. It made its final flight on 27 August 1998 and was stored at BAe Woodford. Following acquisition by Eastern Airways for training purposes on 7 August 2004 it was taken by road to Humberside Airport and dismantled.

Total time: 1,521 hours, 1,344 landings

BAe Jetstream 41 prototype 2
G-PJRT (c/n 41002)

The second prototype made its first flight on 6 February 1992 and underwent 'hot and high' trials in Arizona, testing the take-off and landing performance and ventilator and generator cooling systems. It was exhibited at the 1992 Farnborough Air Show. The last flight was on 26 February 1996. It was scrapped at Prestwick on 1 November 1997 and its nose went to the BAe Flying College.

Total time: 1,016 hours 1,619 landings

BAe Jetstream 41 prototype 3
G-OXLI (c/n 41003)

It first flew at Prestwick on 27 March 1992 and was then engaged in EFIS and autopilot trials at Phoenix, Arizona. After a short flying career it was withdrawn from use in April 1997. In June 1997 the fuselage was sent to FR Aviation, Bournemouth for test-rig use for the Hong Kong Government Flying Service Jetstreams. It was scrapped in 1999.

Total time: 794 hours, 596 landings

The first J41 prototype, G-GCJL, flew from Prestwick on 25 September 1991. Although bearing the 'snowman' logo for its icing trials, it appears to be in a rather warmer environment. Note the wided tail fin fitted as the result of flight trials. (Avro Heritage)

G-GCJL derelict at Humberside Airport in September 2004 for use as spares for Eastern Airways. (Steve Mills)

BAe Jetstream 41 prototype 4
G-JMAC (c/n 41004)

Following its maiden flight on 8 July 1992 at Prestwick it was heavily involved in testing and was exhibited at the 1993 Paris Air Show and the 1994 Farnborough Air Show. It was employed on steep approach certification trials into London City Airport on 1 June 1999. Its last flight was on 15 July 1999 and it was stored at BAe Woodford. On 27/28 January 2003 it was dismantled and delivered by road to Liverpool Speke Airport's Marriott Hotel (the former Airport terminal building) for display on 29 January 2003.

Total time: 2,128 hours, 3,043 landings

Powerplant:

Jetstream 1 – 2 x 850 hp Astazou 14
Jetstream 31 – 2 x 940 shp) Garret TPE331
Jetstream 41 – 2×1500 shp AlliedSignal TPE33114

Production by type:

Handley Page / Scottish Aviation Jetstream
    1/2/3/200/T.1: 67
BAe Jetstream 31/Super 31: 386
BAe Jetstream 41: 104

Total number of Jetstreams built:

557. 67 Jetstream 1/2/3 (including 26 Jetstream T.1. RAF primarily built at Radlett). The RAF aircraft were assembled at Prestwick by Scottish Aviation using 20 fuselages built by Handley Page and six newly constructed at Prestwick. The wings had all been built at Prestwick.
    Jetstream 31 / Super 31 and Jetstream 41 all built at Prestwick.

Data	Jetstream 1	Jetstream 31	Jetstream 41
Length	47 ft 2 in	47 ft 2 in	63 ft 5 in
Wingspan	52 ft 0 in	52 ft 0 in	60ft 0 in
Height	17 ft 6 in	17 ft 6 in	18ft 10 in
MTOW	12,500 lb	15,322 lb	24,000 lb
Cruising speed	298 mph	300 mph	340 mph
Range	745 mls	730 mls	891 mls
Passengers	18	19	29-30

The considerable differences between the Jetstream 41 and 31 are indicated in this illustration. (BAE SYSTEMS)

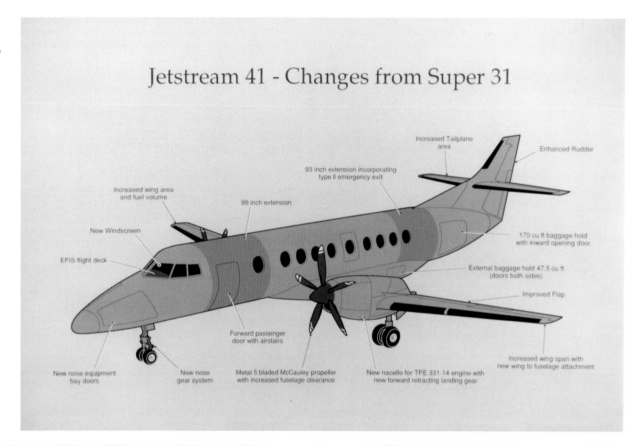

Jetstream 41 - Changes from Super 31

Increased Tailplane area

Enhanced Rudder

93 inch extension incorporating type II emergency exit

Increased wing area and fuel volume

99 inch extension

New Windscreen

170 cu ft baggage hold with inward opening door

EFIS flight deck

External baggage hold 47.5 cu ft (doors both sides)

Improved Flap

Forward passenger door with airstairs

New nose equipment bay doors

New nose gear system

Metal 5 bladed McCauley propeller with increased fuselage clearance

New nacelle for TPE 331-14 engine with new forward retracting landing gear

Increased wing span with new wing to fuselage attachment

G-PJRT during hot and high trials in Arizona with its "Hot and high" logo. Note the widened tail fin, fitted as a result of the trials. (Avro Heritage)

The final Jetstream 41 prototype, G-JMAC, landing at Farnborough during the 1994 Air Show. This J41 is now preserved at Liverpool Airport. (Kev Colbran)

BAC / Aérospatiale Concorde

The first two British Concorde prototypes at the British Aircraft Corporation's Flight Test Centre at Fairford. (From the left) G-AXDN (01) and G-BSST (002). Visible on 002 is the solid visor for supersonic flying (as on French 001), which was superseded on G-AXDN and later aircraft by an attractive, glazed visor.
(BAE SYSTEMS)

IN a BBC poll undertaken in 2006 Concorde was chosen as the greatest design icon of the 20th century. It entered service in 1976 amid controversy over its cost and warnings over its possible environmental impact, but became the acme of prestige trans-Atlantic travel. Even though it is no longer in the air it remains exceedingly popular as a museum exhibit.

With the development of regular services by subsonic jet airliners in the 1950s aeronautical engineers began to consider the idea of a supersonic airliner. Where military aircraft might only need to exceed Mach 1 for a short dash, a supersonic airliner would need to maintain supersonic speeds for several hours, presenting a series of technical challenges to engineers and designers.

Development
The Supersonic Transport Aircraft Committee, with representation from both industry and the Government, was formed in Britain in November 1956, promoting research into supersonic airliners. From this research the Bristol Aircraft Company produced several designs which by 1960 had evolved into the Type 223, a 100-seater slender delta concept recognisable as a progenitor of Concorde. In the meantime, Sud Aviation in France was also investigating a short-range 70/80 seat Mach 2 SST to replace the Caravelle, similar to the Bristol Type 223.

Britain and France agreed to co-operate on the supersonic airliner and an agreement was signed in November 1962 with funding shared equally between the two Governments. British Aircraft Corporation (incorporating Bristol) and Sud Aviation (later

Aérospatiale) would build the airframe and Bristol Siddeley (later Rolls-Royce) and SNECMA of France would manufacture the engines. France was granted a larger amount of airframe work as Britain had a greater share of the work on the Olympus engines. Two production lines were established: at Filton, Bristol and Toulouse in France, requiring a substantial infrastructure to support the production effort and the transport of airframe sections between sites.

Technically, Concorde possesses a great many advanced engineering features which required thousands of hours of ground and flight testing. Concorde was the first commercial aircraft to employ 'fly by wire' control technology which has now become the norm with contemporary airliners. The slender delta wing with an ogival leading edge was the result of a huge amount of wind tunnel testing. This configuration resulted in Concorde adopting a very high angle of approach on landing and the nose of the aircraft had to be hinged down 12½° to improve the view of the pilot while landing. Most of the fuel was stored in the wings, where it acted as a heat sink for the wing skin during prolonged supersonic flight. Fuel was pumped into trim tanks in the rear fuselage during acceleration and forward again during deceleration to subsonic speed to counteract the rearward shift in the centre of lift as the aircraft went supersonic. Computer-controlled variable-area air intakes ensured that each engine received an optimum air flow under all flight conditions.

Maiden flights
The first French prototype F-WTSS flew on 2 March with the first British aircraft G-BSST one month later on 9 April 1969 and so the extensive flight test programme

commenced. The first two Concordes were very different from the final aircraft; for example they were each fitted with a metal visor over the front cockpit windows for supersonic flying but this was superseded by a much improved visor design, with far bigger cockpit windows, for the subsequent aircraft. The third Concorde G-AXDN which had the improved visor and an 8 ft 6 in longer forward fuselage followed the first two prototypes into the air in December 1971. The next pre-production aircraft, F-WTSA, was even longer as it had an extended tail common to the production aircraft. As the pre-production aircraft varied considerably from the prototypes, much of the flight testing had to be repeated.

These first four Concordes were intended solely for flight testing and carried approximately 12 tons of electronic test instrumentation which could record 3,000 different parameters on magnetic tape in the aircraft for later analysis on the ground. In addition, basic flight information was continuously telemetered to a ground monitoring centre.

Sales

In 1967 prospects for Concorde were buoyant since it had received 74 options from 16 airlines with the potential for substantial sales. The options were totally

refundable and could only become firm contracts when guaranteed performance figures had been established by the flight test programme. British Airways and Air France placed orders for five and four aircraft respectively in July 1972. But in the event these were the only two airlines ever to operate Concorde, although there were interchange operations with Braniff International and Singapore Airlines. In 1973 the severe oil price rise caused by the 'Yom Kippur' War meant that Concorde ceased to be viable. Eventually BA and Air France received seven aircraft each and as no further orders were received, production ceased after 20 aircraft.

British Concorde first prototype G-BSST (002) just airborne on its maiden flight from Filton to Fairford on 9 April 1969. On 4 March 1976 it made its final flight from Fairford to Yeovilton for preservation. (Author)

The first (and final) flight pilots of G-BSST. British Aircraft Corporation CTP Brian Trubshaw (left) and John Cochrane on the flight deck of G-BSST. (BAE SYSTEMS)

G-BSST demonstrates Concorde's remarkable wing planform. (BAE SYSTEMS)

from Paris to Rio de Janeiro via Dakar. These rather unlikely destinations were chosen as at that time Concorde was unable to fly into the United States owing to noise protests. Once these objections were overcome, regular services from both London and Paris began to Washington DC in May 1976. When noise measurements were taken at John F. Kennedy Airport, New York and Concorde proved to be within the legal limits, services also opened in November 1977 and this great metropolis soon became the favoured destination for Concorde passengers.

As with other aircraft, Concorde testing did not cease after entry into service. The maximum take-off weight was raised to 408,000 lb and to reduce drag a number of aerodynamic refinements were introduced. This combination gave significant reductions in drag and fuel consumption.

Concorde proved to be very reliable in regular service and load factors remained high. British Airways took over support of Concorde from the British Government in 1984 and through very successful marketing, assisted by much cheaper fuel prices, began to make substantial profits.

Into service
After a flight test programme of almost seven years' duration including 1,000 hours of route proving, Concorde was certified at the end of 1975. The first services began on 21 January 1976 with British Airways flying non-stop to Bahrain while Air France flew a route

Crash
On 25 July 2000, while taking off from Paris-Charles de Gaulle Airport, Air France Concorde F-BTSC ran over a long strip of metal dropped on the runway by a previous airliner. This metal strip cut into one of the mainwheel tyres which immediately exploded, sending large chunks of rubber into the underside of the wing, causing a fuel tank to rupture. The venting fuel ignited, one engine lost all power and another began behaving erratically. The pilot could not stop in the runway length remaining and as the landing gear would not retract, the aircraft could not gain airspeed. The aircraft stalled and crashed less than three minutes after take-off, killing all 113 people on board.

As it appeared that a single tyre burst had caused the crash, all Concordes were grounded. Following a thorough investigation and the view of many journalists that Concorde would never fly again, engineers determined to disprove them and devised a solution to the problem. Michelin developed a new tyre which would not explode when punctured, and Kevlar linings were fitted in each vunerable fuel tank to reduce the rate of fuel leakage in the event of damage to the wing. The main landing gear hydraulics were also given additional protection and potential sources for sparks eliminated.

Briefly back in the skies
Regular services began again on 7 November 2001 with the first Concorde receiving an ecstatic welcome at JFK Airport, New York. With plenty of life remaining in the fleet the initial expectation was that Concorde would fly for many more years. However, due to the fall in transatlantic air travel following the terrorist attacks in New York on '9/11', the aircraft was apparently not making a profit. On 10 April 2003, to the dismay of

Three Flight Test Observers on Concorde, G-BSST, wearing pressure helmets and suits, life jackets and parachutes in the event of the need to escape through the emergency escape hatch at altitude. Note the amount of test equipment fitted in the cabin. (BAE SYSTEMS)

The first British
Concorde G-BSST
at night. Note the
camera tracking
marker on the
fuselage side.
(BAE SYSTEMS)

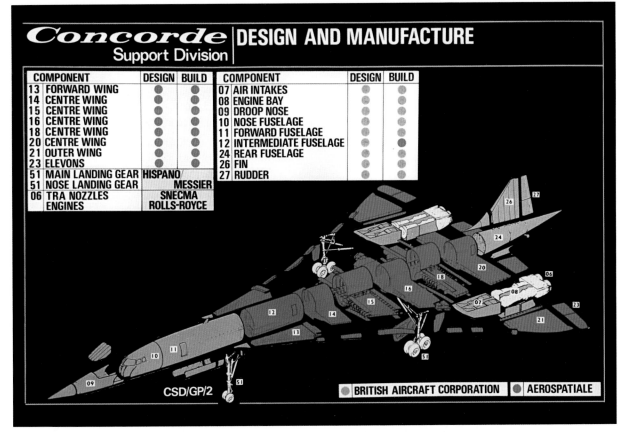

Concorde | DESIGN AND MANUFACTURE
Support Division

COMPONENT	DESIGN	BUILD	COMPONENT	DESIGN	BUILD
13 FORWARD WING	●	●	07 AIR INTAKES	●	●
14 CENTRE WING	●	●	08 ENGINE BAY	●	●
15 CENTRE WING	●	●	09 DROOP NOSE	●	●
16 CENTRE WING	●	●	10 NOSE FUSELAGE	●	●
18 CENTRE WING	●	●	11 FORWARD FUSELAGE	●	●
20 CENTRE WING	●	●	12 INTERMEDIATE FUSELAGE	●	●
21 OUTER WING	●	●	24 REAR FUSELAGE	●	●
23 ELEVONS	●	●	26 FIN	●	●
51 MAIN LANDING GEAR	HISPANO/		27 RUDDER	●	●
51 NOSE LANDING GEAR	MESSIER				
06 TRA NOZZLES	SNECMA				
ENGINES	ROLLS-ROYCE				

CSD/GP/2

| ● BRITISH AIRCRAFT CORPORATION | ● AEROSPATIALE |

Concorde
manufacturing was
shared between
British Aircraft
Corporation, Rolls-
Royce, SNECMA
and Aérospatiale
factories. As Britain
had a greater share
of the engine work,
the French factories
had a proportionally
greater share of the
airframe build.
(BAE SYSTEMS)

many, British Airways and Air France simultaneously announced that they would be withdrawing Concorde from service.

The final Air France service was on 31 May 2003 but British Airways 'stole the show' by celebrating the end of Concorde operations with three aircraft landing one after another at Heathrow in front of a huge crowd on 24 October 2003. The final Concorde flight was on 26 November 2003, when G-BOAF, the last aircraft off the production line, flew back into its birthplace at Filton for preservation.

Following the end of commercial supersonic airliner operations the world returned to the humdrum reality of subsonic aircraft, most of which appear to be clones of each other. Concorde remains a great engineering achievement and an inspiring icon. "Soon there will be only two kinds of airliner: Concorde, and all the rest" was an advertising slogan before Concorde entered service – now there are only the rest.

British Concorde prototypes

(The French prototypes were 001 F-WTSS, 02 F-WTSA, 201 F-WTSB)

BAC / Aérospatiale Concorde prototype 2
G-BSST c/n 002 (Bristol c/n 13520)

The first British-assembled Concorde with a special out-of-sequence registration G-BSST (SST = Supersonic Transport) was rolled out on 19 September 1968 and was then engaged in almost seven months of ground testing. Watched by huge crowds it was airborne for the first time on 9 April 1969 from Filton piloted by Brian Trubshaw and John Cochrane. G-BSST landed at the Concorde Test Centre at Fairford. On approach to Fairford both radio altimeters failed, but Trubshaw made a safe landing. Only two months after its first flight it appeared in the air together with F-WTSS at the Paris Air Show. A few days later it made Concorde's first fly-over of Buckingham Palace as part of the Queen's Birthday celebrations.

G-BSST flew at Mach 1 for the first time on 25 March 1970 and on 12 November reached Mach 2. In September 1970 it had appeared at the SBAC show at Farnborough but on the last day of the Show was unable to return to Fairford because of bad weather and had to land at London Heathrow – its first visit. On 4 November 1970 002 was scheduled to fly at Mach 2 just ahead of F-WTSS on that same day, but at Mach 1.35 a fire warning was indicated and it returned to Fairford. Thus the French prototype was the first to fly at Mach 2. With 001 engaged in high-speed testing,

002 was mainly concerned with low-speed handling. Regular lengthy groundings occurred from the first flight onwards for installation of updated engines, intakes and control systems.

In April 1972 002 was exhibited at the Hannover Air Show. On 2 June G-BSST left Fairford on a 45,000 miles sales tour of the Far East and Australia, returning to London Heathrow on 1 July. Later that year it also appeared daily in the flying display at the September SBAC Farnborough Show. Following three weeks in Johannesburg for 'hot and high' trials, in January 1973 there was a change of temperature for de-icing trials, flying behind Boscombe Down's Canberra WV787 in the UK.

On 24 February 1973 G-BSST returned from a month's 'hot and high' airfield performance trials and demonstrations in South Africa. Similar trials were embarked upon in July at Torrejon, near Madrid and on return from Spain there were water ingestion taxiing trials. As its scheduled test programme was now complete, it was used for some ad hoc trials including searching (unsuccessfully) for high altitude natural icing, demonstrations and stratospheric research.

While demonstrating at the Weston-super-Mare Air Show on 26 August 1975 there was a failure in the left main undercarriage as the locking stay had become disconnected. G-BSST returned to Fairford where a gentle landing piloted by John Cochrane ensured a safe arrival. The landing gear leg was replaced and on 4 March 1976 G-BSST made its final flight to the Fleet Air Arm Museum at the RN Air Station, Yeovilton with the same flight deck crew in command as on its first flight.

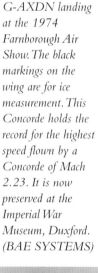

Concorde 01, G-AXDN landing at the 1974 Farnborough Air Show. The black markings on the wing are for ice measurement. This Concorde holds the record for the highest speed flown by a Concorde of Mach 2.23. It is now preserved at the Imperial War Museum, Duxford. (BAE SYSTEMS)

The second British Concorde G-AXDN filmed during icing trials from Boscombe Down's Canberra WV787 on 13 September 1974. The Canberra was specially modified to spray fine particles of water to produce icing and the amount of ice accretion on Concorde could then be measured. (Crown Copyright)

BAC / Aérospatiale Concorde pre-production prototype 1

G-AXDN c/n 101 (Bristol c/n 13522)

G-AXDN was rolled out at Filton on 20 September 1971 for the start of ground testing. Its maiden flight from Filton to Fairford was on 17 December 1971 with Brain Trubshaw as pilot and John Cochrane as co-pilot. Initially fitted with fixed engine intakes, 101 was only able to fly up to Mach 1.5 and engaged in a flutter test programme due to its fuselage being longer than the two prototypes. From August 1972 to March 1973 it was at Filton for installation of new digitally controlled variable-geometry engine air intakes, Olympus 593 Mk. 602 production standard engines together with new wing leading edges to improve performance.

In both January and March 1974 'XDN carried out engine intake performance trials at Tangier. During these tests the aircraft reached the maximum speed ever reached by a Concorde of Mach 2.23 (1,480mph) at a then record height of 63,700 ft. 101 spent time in June 1974 at Toulouse taxiing through water troughs at differing speeds to trial designs of water deflectors to ensure that the engine intakes did not ingest water.

In September 1974 01 was displayed at the Farnborough Air Show. On 7 November it flew from Fairford to Moses Lake in Washington State to check out the de-icing installation and returned on 13 December. The first leg to Bangor, Maine, USA, was flown in 2 hours 56 minutes – the fastest ever east-west crossing of the North Atlantic by a commercial airliner. The second leg to Moses Lake took 4 hours 43 minutes,

which was another record, this time for the fastest east-west crossing of the USA. The aircraft was fitted with an external camera and large areas of black markings on the left wing (still visible on it at Duxford) to indicate ice accretion. Icing trials also took place in the UK with 'XDN trailing Boscombe Down's Canberra tanker and from 26 February to 12 March 1975 it was based at Nairobi for tropical icing trials.

With the completion of G-AXDN's development flying it was used for the training of BAC pilots in preparation for their training of British Airways' pilots. G-AXDN was put into storage at Fairford on 15 May 1975 and on 21 January 1977 returned to Filton for further storage following closure of the Fairford Flight Test Centre. On 18 August it carried out tests at Filton to check its ability to land safely within the confines of Duxford's 6,000 ft runway.

G-AXDN's final flight was on 20 August 1977 when Brian Trubshaw and John Cochrane, the pilots who had made its initial flight, flew it from Filton to the Imperial War Museum, Duxford for preservation and public display.

BAC / Aérospatiale Concorde production prototype 2

G-BBDG c/n 202 (Bristol c/n 13523)

On 13 February 1974 Concorde 202 made its maiden flight of 1 hour 45 minutes duration from Filton to Fairford piloted by Brian Trubshaw and reaching a top speed of Mach 1.4. Just over two weeks later on 28 February, on its fifth flight, it visited Toulouse and on

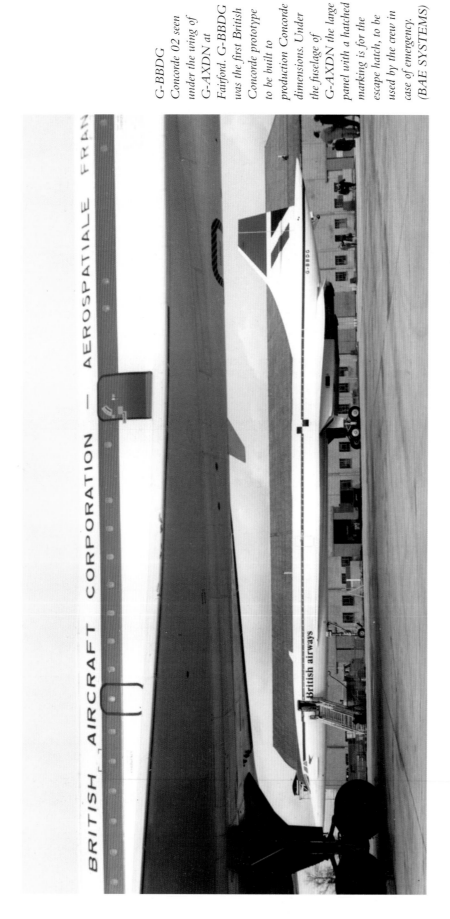

G-BBDG
Concorde 02 seen
under the wing of
G-AXDN at
Fairford. G-BBDG
was the first British
Concorde prototype
to be built to
production Concorde
dimensions. Under
the fuselage of
G-AXDN the large
panel with a hatched
marking is for the
escape hatch, to be
used by the crew in
case of emergency.
(BAE SYSTEMS)

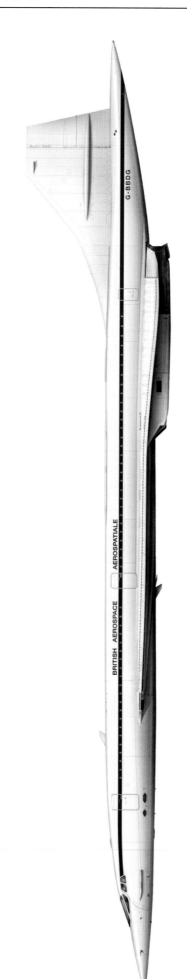

Near the end of the flight trials programme the British production prototype G-BBDG was painted in simplified
livery as illustrated here. G-BBDG is now at the Brooklands Museum.

its fifteenth flight flew at Mach 2.

It then embarked on intensive systems tests, calibration and handling throughout the entire flight envelope. In May - June production specification engines were installed. On 19 July 1974 202 flew Filton to Casablanca return to test the engines and intakes at speeds up to Mach 2.03 ahead of its Middle and Far Eastern tour.

On 7 August 1974 G-BBDG departed Heathrow for Teheran and then on to Bahrain for a sales tour, which also included performance trials. On 17 August it became the first aircraft to carry 100 passengers at Mach 2. It departed Bahrain on 3 September for several days of runway trials in Singapore, returning to Fairford on 13 September.

From 28 October to 18 December 1974 Concorde 202 was based at Casablanca, for certification trials. In March 1975 there were further measured take-off and landing tests at Madrid. Its 200th flight was on 2 April 1975 and later that month 'DG again visited Casablanca to confirm engine surge margins and other performance measurements. On 19 June 1975 the 250th flight coincided with the commencement of flight crew training for British Airways at RAF Brize Norton, which continued until the year's end. During March 1976, following the installation of improved production standard engines, 'hot and high' performance and Autoland trials took place at Capetown.

Following the run down of the Test Programme and the closure of the British Aircraft Corporation's Concorde test base at Fairford, 'DG returned to Filton on 30 November 1976, which became the base for any further testing. In both July 1977 and April - May the following year G-BBDG was at Casablanca for intake and aerodynamic tests to check several modifications: thinning of the intake lips, extending the control surfaces and fitting a sharper fin leading edge which improved the aircraft's performance and payload.

During 1979 the British Airways tail livery was removed and 'DG became white overall with a dark blue cheatline and British Aerospace-Aérospatiale titles. Its final flight was on 24 December 1981 captained by BAe CTP Roy Radford. Initially it was kept in readiness for flight but in late 1982 it was stored outside the Brabazon hangar.

The final phase of 'DG's career began in April 1984 when it was purchased by British Airways for use as a major source of spare parts. During May 1988, with its tail fin removed, 'DG was moved into a purpose-built hangar at Filton. Following damage to G-BOAF's nose 'DG's was put in its place. In November/December 2002 it was temporarily positioned in the Brabazon hangar to

allow fitting and testing of a strengthened cockpit door as required for the Concorde fleets in the aftermath of the 11 September 2001 terrorist attacks.

With Concorde's withdrawal from service on 30 October 2003, British Airways offered G-BBDG to the Brooklands Museum. It was dismantled during March - May 2004 and transported to Brooklands where it was reassembled. Painted in British Airways' 1970s livery it was opened to the public in July 2006. G-BBDG made 633 flights and flew 1282 hours 9 minutes.

Powerplant:
Concorde 002 G-BSST initial installation –
    4 x 34,370 lb st Rolls-Royce Olympus 593-3B
Concorde 01 G-AXDN initial installation –
    4 x 35,080 lb st Rolls-Royce Olympus 593-4
Concorde 202 G-BBDG initial installation –
    4 x 38,050 lb st Rolls-Royce Olympus 602

Production by type:
Prototypes: 2
Pre-production prototypes: 2
Production: 16

Total built: 20 (10 at Filton, Bristol, 10 at Toulouse, France)

G-BBDG taking off. Following seven years of intensive test flying from 1974 to 1981 G-BBDG was stored at Filton and used for spares by British Airways. In 2004 it was dismantled and reassembled at the Brooklands Museum, opening to the public in 2006. (BAE SYSTEMS)

Data	Concorde 002	Concorde 01	Concorde 202
Length	184 ft 6 in	193 ft 0 in	203 ft 9 in
Wingspan	83 ft 10 in	83 ft 10 in	83 ft 10 in
Height	37 ft 5 in	37 ft 5 in	37 ft 5 in
MTOW	326,000 lb	358,000 lb	408,000 lb
Cruising speed	Mach 2.02	Mach 2.02	Mach 2.04
Range	3,390 mls	3,390 mls	3,870 mls
Passengers	n.a.	n.a	100 (first class)

BAe 146 / Avro RJ and Avro RJX

On 3 September 1981, G-SSSH the BAe 146-100 prototype takes off from Hatfield on its first flight. (BAE SYSTEMS)

THE BAe 146 was the product of design studies by de Havilland for a Dakota replacement which began in 1959. These studies were eventually finalised as the high-wing Hawker Siddeley 146 – powered by four Avco Lycoming ALF502s and launched in August 1973 with funding provided equally by the manufacturer and the Government. Within a year, however, costs had spiralled and Hawker Siddeley cancelled the 146 but Government intervention kept the project alive until nationalisation of the industry in April 1977. Just over a year later the 146 was resuscitated as the British Aerospace 146 –available as the 70-88-seater 146-100 and larger 82-102-seater 146-200.

On 20 May 1981, the day of the 146's roll-out, a breakthrough was achieved with a launch order from US regional Air Wisconsin for four 146-200s. This order was significant for the stretched 200 Series, which was to prove the best-selling version of the type. Air Wisconsin's boldness stimulated other American carriers, for example Pacific Southwest Airlines (PSA), to follow suit. Consequently BAe concentrated its marketing effort on the 200 Series rather than the somewhat limited 100 Series.

Maiden flight

The first flight of the prototype 146-100 took place on 3 September 1981 and G-SSSH bore the brunt of the test programme required for certification but was soon joined by the second and third aircraft. To hasten certification of the stretched version, the prototype 146-200 G-WISC was the fourth aircraft to join the test programme following its maiden flight on 1 August 1982.

Even before certification the 146 had flown, on a sales tour of India and the Far East, into many small airfields which previously had never been frequented by jetliners. Comparative trials also demonstrated that it was the world's quietest airliner, beating the Douglas DC-9, Boeing 727 and 737 and others by a very substantial margin.

The BAe 146 received its CAA certification on 4 February 1983 after 1,500 hours of test flying. The first service was in May 1983 with a Dan-Air service from Gatwick to Dublin. A month later Air Wisconsin operated the first 146 revenue service in the USA and was later joined by other US operators and airlines in Canada, Australia, New Zealand and the Far East.

146-300

In 1984 the 146-300 was announced. This development was achieved by stretching the 146-100 fuselage by 15 ft 9 in, but employing the standard engine and wing of the earlier series without seriously degrading airfield performance. Initially envisaged as a six-abreast 120-seater, by the time the prototype 146-300 took to the air it was configured in a 100-seat five-abreast layout. This was chiefly due to the fact that British Aerospace had refocused the 146 Series for the regional airline market – particularly in the USA, where the five-abreast layout on the type was already popular.

Punctually at noon on 1 May 1987 in front of 5,000 guests and employees, G-LUXE took off on a problem-free first flight. On that day Air Wisconsin announced a launch order for five 300s to join the ten 200s it already had in service. Certification of the 300 Series was announced at the 1988 Farnborough Air Show.

Quiet trading

Having identified a market niche, BAe converted a 146 to a freighter (branded as a QT or Quiet Trader) to promote its capabilities. The 146 has many features which make it a good freighter: capacious fuselage, low to the ground and above all it is quiet – so important for air freighting, which often takes place at night.

This freighter was trialled by TNT which recognised the QT's versatility for night operation out of noise-sensitive airfields, and eventually operated 21 aircraft. The QT was available from either the 200 and 300 Series and five 200s were built as QC (Quiet Convertible) aircraft. Additionally, the former 146-100 STA (Sideloading Tactical Airlifter) military demonstrator later became a civil freighter, making 29 conversions in all.

In and out of the City

The first 146 demonstration at London City Airport in July 1988 proved a great success as the aircraft was able to fly the 5½° approach required and its quietness defied any opposition. Not only has the 146 been instrumental in the development of London City, but it is also used at similar city centre airports, such as Stockholm-Bromma, which have difficult approaches and noise restrictions.

In 1996 the Managing Director of London City said, "The 146 would not have achieved the market it has without the Airport, and it is equally doubtful whether the Airport could have achieved its growth without the aircraft. We both needed each other." The 146/RJ is still the predominant jet airliner operating from London City.

Launch of the RJ family

By 1990, with some 202 aircraft ordered and 157 delivered, British Aerospace could feel satisfied that the 146 had proved a success against the competition – such as the Fokker 100. To maintain this position, in 1990 BAe announced a number of major improvements to the 146 family. The aircraft would continue to be available in the three existing fuselage sizes but the most important change to this new version of the 146 was the introduction of digital avionics and the LF507 engine. This change was intended to lower engine maintenance costs, which had deterred some potential orders.

To emphasise the improvements, the new aircraft were rebranded as Regional Jets; each model would be identified by its passenger capacity with five-abreast seating: RJ70 (former 146-100), RJ85 (former 146-200), RJ100 (former 146-300).

RJ test programme

The three RJ development aircraft for the three RJ versions made their maiden flights in quick succession and embarked on a test programme at Woodford. Joint Airworthiness Authorities and Federal Aviation Administration certification was granted to the trio between March and September 1993 with the same type rating for 146 and RJ variants – therefore pilots could fly any of them.

The RJ soon acquired a reputable order book and British Aerospace was justifiably proud of the fact that RJs were ordered in the colours of 'blue chip' operators such as Lufthansa Cityline, Swissair, THY, Sabena, British Airways and Northwest Mesaba Airlines.

The first 146-200 on its maiden flight on 1 August 1982. It was registered G-WISC and painted in the livery of Air Wisconsin – the 146-200's first and loyal operator, which continued operations with the type for almost 23 years. (BAE SYSTEMS)

Stretching in progress at Hatfield. The 100 Series prototype, G-SSSH, cut into three and awaiting the insertion of two fuselage sections, one forward and one aft, to become the 300 Series prototype, with the new registration of G-LUXE. (BAE SYSTEMS)

G-LUXE at Topeka, Kansas in 1995 during 'Rollback' icing trials with jettisonable emergency doors installed, cameras, additional probes, the later LF507 engines and displaying BAe, AI(R) (i.e. Aero International (Regional)) and Avro Test logos. (Derek Ferguson)

RJX – a short-lived development

By 2000 the RJ was in need of further development as it had been in existence for eight years and new Bombardier and Embraer Regional Jets were both gathering large orders. Thus in March 2000 BAE Systems launched the Avro RJX, revamped around an improved powerplant – the Honeywell AS977. In April 2000 Druk Air became the launch customer when it ordered a pair of RJX85s to replace its two BAe 146-

100s and in March 2001, British European, an established 146 operator, ordered twelve RJX100s.

Although the new engine and installation caused problems, the first flight of the Avro RJX85 prototype took place on 28 April 2001. The flight test programme then moved into full swing and the RJX100 prototype, G-IRJX, flew five months later. The aircraft had a noticeably better performance than the RJ, especially at high altitude.

However, BAE SYSTEMS had long held doubts about the economic viability of civil aircraft programmes and had never made money from the 146/RJ programme. On 27 November 2001 BAe made a surprise announcement, closing the Regional Jet programme and 146/RJ/RJX production ended with a total of 394 having flown.

Prototypes and development aircraft

BAe 146-100 & 146-300 prototype
G-SSSH (c/n E1001) / G-LUXE (c/n E3001)

The first prototype was rolled out on 20 May 1981, but the first flight did not take place until 3 September when Hatfield CTP, Mike Goodfellow, took G-SSSH up from Hatfield for a 95 minute flight. G-SSSH shouldered

G-LUXE in its current manifestation as an Atmospheric Research Aircraft equipped with a multitude of sensors and the capability to carry a test crew of scientists. (BAE SYSTEMS)

the greater part of the test programme with general handling, stalling, flutter and autopilot tests.

Its last flight as a 146-100 was on 7 August 1986, having flown 1,239 hours. The aircraft was cut into three and two fuselage plugs inserted to lengthen the aircraft. It was rolled out registered as G-5-300 with the new sections still in primer on 8 March 1987 but for its first flight was repainted and re-registered as G-LUXE. (Its construction number now became E3001 as its fuselage length had increased from a 100 to a 300 Series.)

Maiden flight as the prototype 146-300

At noon on 1 May 1987 in front of 5,000 guests and BAe employees, G-LUXE took off on a problem-free first flight from Hatfield piloted by Peter Sedgwick. The following year it flew at Farnborough and from August 1989 was based at BAe's Civil Flight Test Centre at Woodford.

During the 1990s it carried out tests on icing, flap settings, handling, stalling and certification at higher take-off weights. Prior to the go-ahead of the RJ and its new LF507 engines, G-LUXE flew with a LF507 engine installed in March 1991 and left the following month for performance trials at Roswell in the USA, returning four months later.

A major activity for G-LUXE was in solving the 'Rollback' phenomenon, which affected the 146's ALF502 engines where icing caused a decay to sub-idle speed. The aircraft was based at Panama City in October - November 1992 for trials in thunderstorm clouds with a modified engine and enabled BAe to devise a modification programme to eliminate the problem entirely.

Final transformation

On 6 June 2000 after 1,008 flights as a 146-300, G-LUXE was put into store at Woodford having flown 2,915 hours. Work began in July 2001 to convert it into an Atmospheric Research Aircraft (ARA) on a ten year lease from BAE SYSTEMS. Conversion took over two years as it was decided to zero-life the aircraft, fit 7,000 lb thrust LF507-1H engines and install additional fuel tanks to increase range. External additions were wing pylons carrying sensors, a large pod on the front left forward fuselage and four external TV cameras. Internally the aircraft is full of test equipment and has positions for nineteen scientific crew.

It was rolled out in August 2003 and made a one hour 43 minutes third 'maiden' flight unpainted on 1 October. It then embarked on a 57 flight test programme. Certified as a BAE 146-301, G-LUXE was delivered to its new base in Cranfield, Bedfordshire on 10 May 2004 where it is operated by Direct Flight for the Facility for Airborne Atmospheric Measurements (FAAM). It is now heavily employed on worldwide meteorological research activities.

BAe 146-200 prototype
G-WISC (c/n E2008)

On 1 August 1982 Mike Goodfellow made the 2 hours 45 minutes first flight from Hatfield of the 146-200 prototype which was painted in Air Wisconsin livery. It appeared at Farnborough in September 1982 and was employed on FAA (Federal Aviation Authority) certification and noise trials in Casablanca in November 1982. In mid-August 1984 it was painted in Air W.A. (Western Australia) colours registered as G-5-146 and at the end of the month was re-registered as G-WAUS,

The first Avro RJ development of the BAe 146 to fly was RJ85 G-ISEE. It made its maiden flight in primer on 23 March 1992. It was the last of 8,468 aircraft built at Hatfield, from the beginning of De Havilland's operations in 1934.

The trio of development RJs in September 1992. RJ70 G-BUFI, RJ85 G-ISEE and RJ100 G-OIII all of which later entered airline service. All of the RJs have cameras fitted at the top of the fin (in the red bulge) used for measuring landing performance. (BAE SYSTEMS)

appearing at the Paris Air Show in June 1985 in Ansett W.A. livery. It was repainted in BAe livery and re-registered as G-BMYE in August 1986.

BAe Test Pilot, Dan Gurney, demonstrated G-BMYE at London City Airport on 24 July 1988. The success of this led to the end of local resistance and the 146 was certified to operate from there. From September 1988 the 146-200 prototype was stored at Filton, where it was broken up seven years later.

Total time: 1,869 hours

Avro RJ85 development aircraft
G-ISEE (c/n E2208)

G-ISEE, the last of 8,468 aircraft built at Hatfield from the beginning of de Havilland's operations in 1934, made its first flight in primer on 23 March 1992, piloted by Dan Gurney. A week later it was delivered to Woodford. It was painted in a green RJ85 livery and made its last development flight on 23 July 1993. Following storage at Woodford in April 1997 it was delivered as N501XJ to Northwest Mesaba. It was withdrawn from service and has been stored at Marana, Arizona since November 2005.

Avro RJ100 development aircraft
G-OIII (c/n E3221)

The first RJ100 flew on 13 May 1992 from Woodford piloted by Dan Gurney and at the end of the month was painted in a red RJ100 livery at Hurn. It appeared at the Berlin and Farnborough Air Shows and, following the end of the test programme, was stored at Woodford. In December 1994 it was delivered to SAM of Colombia as N504MM, returning five years later to Woodford. In August 2001 it was delivered to Malmö Aviation as

SE-DSO and in 2006 was operated in Skyways colours by Transwede.

Avro RJ70 development aircraft
G-BUFI (c/n E1229)

The first RJ70 (G-BUFI) flew unbranded on 23 July 1992 from Woodford, piloted by Dan Gurney. Four days later it flew to Hurn and was painted in an attractive RJ70 livery, demonstrating at Farnborough in September that year. It was used on avionics trials and was later delivered to THY as TC-THI in July 1996 but was returned to BAE SYSTEMS in 2005 and stored at Kemble as G-BUFI. It was delivered to MDLR Airlines of India on 1 February 2007 as VT-MDL.

Avro RJX85 prototype
G-ORJX (c/n E2376)

The first RJX G-ORJX lifted off from Woodford Airfield on 28 April 2001 at 12:16 hrs and remained airborne for 2 hours 54 minutes. It completed the planned tests and reached a height of 20,000 ft and a speed of 250 knots, piloted by Avro RJX Test Pilots Alan Foster and Mark Robinson.

The new aircraft's first and only public appearance was at the 'RJX Celebration' at the Imperial War Museum's airfield at Duxford, on 21 - 22 May 2001 where it carried British European titles on the right side and performed a number of demonstration flights.

G-ORJX departed Woodford on 25 August for Williams Gateway Airport in Mesa, Arizona for 'hot and high' trials and then on to Toluca. To the puzzlement of the test crew, they were ordered to return home (because of the impending cancellation of the programme), even though they had not completed the tests – and arrived at Woodford on 22 November 2001.

RJX, it was involved in limited testing from November 2001 to January 2002 and then stored at Woodford. Its last flight was from Woodford to Manchester Aviation Heritage at Manchester Airport on 6 February 2003 where it is now on public display in the Aviation Viewing Park.

Total hours:198

Powerplant:
146-100 & 146-200 – 4 x 6,700 Avco Lycoming ALF502
146-300 – 4 x 7,000 Avco Lycoming ALF502
RJ (all marks) – 4 x 7,000 Textron Lycoming LF507

The final development of the BAe 146 / AvroRJ was the Avro RJX with improved engines and other refinements which was to be developed in two versions – the RJX85 and RJX100. Two prototypes flew, which were to be the last British Airliner prototypes. The first was the RJX85 G-ORJX and the second the RJX100 G-IRJX. This view shows the two RJX prototypes in the air with G-ORJX the nearer. (BAE SYSTEMS)

The last flight was on 9 January 2002 and the aircraft is now stored furnished but engineless at the Customer Training School at Woodford.

Total hours: 322

Avro RJX100 prototype G-IRJX (c/n E3378)
The first Avro RJX100 G-IRJX flew on 23 September 2001 piloted by Bill Ovel and Pete Lofts. On 5 November 2001 G-IRJX visited London City Airport to demonstrate compatibility with the 5½° steep approach on the 3,900 ft runway. Following cancellation of the

Production by type:

146-100:	35	RJ70:	12
146-200:	116	RJ85:	87
146-300:	71	RJ100:	71
		RJX85:	1
		RJX100:	2

Total number of 146 / RJ / RJX built:
394 (165 at Hatfield, 229 at Woodford)

Following the end of the RJX programme and BAE SYSTEMS' decision to withdraw from the civil airliner market, G-IRJX, the last British Airliner prototype, was presented to the Manchester Aviation Heritage Exhibition at Manchester Airport while G-ORJX, the RJX85 prototype (seen here), remains at Woodford minus its engines. (Author)

Data	146-100	146-200	146-300	RJ70	RJ85	RJ100
Length	85 ft 10 in	93 ft 8 in	101 ft 8 in	85 ft 10 in	93 ft 8 in	101 ft 8 in
Wingspan	86 ft 5 in	86 ft 5 in	86 ft 5 in	86 ft 5 in	86 ft 5 in	86 ft 5 in
Height	28 ft 3 in	28ft 3 in	28 ft 3 in	28 ft 3 in	28 ft 3 in	28 ft 3 in
MTOW	84,000 lb	93,000 lb	97,500 lb	95,000 lb	97,000 lb	101,500 lb
Cruising speed	476 mph	476 mph	476 mph	474 mph	474 mph	474 mph
Range	1,000 mls.	1,300 mls	1,200 mls	1,660 mls	1,320 mls	1,320 mls
Passengers	70-82	85-100	100-112	70-82	85-100	100-112

Appendix I

British Airliners from 1945

First flight		Aircraft	Number built
1945	June 14	Avro Tudor	33
	June 22	Vickers Viking	163
	September 5	De Havilland Dove	542
	December 2	Bristol Freighter/Superfreighter	214
	December 2	Handley Page Hermes	29
1946	May 19	Miles Marathon	2
	December 1	Short Solent	23
1947	May 9	Percival Merganser	1
	May 19	Cunliffe-Owen Concordia	2
	July 10	Airspeed Ambassador	23
1948	May 13	Percival Prince	75
	July 16	Vickers Viscount	444
1949	April 10	Armstrong Whitworth Apollo	2
	July 27	De Havilland Comet	113
	September 4	Bristol Brabazon	1
1950	May 10	De Havilland Heron	149
1952	Aug 16	Bristol Britannia	85
	August 22	Saunders Roe Princess	1
1955	June 25	Scottish Aviation Twin Pioneer	87
	August 25	Handley Page Herald	50
1957	July 9	Aviation Traders Accountant	1
	November 6	Fairey Rotodyne	1
1959	January 20	Vickers Vanguard	44
1960	June 24	Hawker Siddeley 748	382
1962	Jan 9	Hawker Siddeley Trident	117
	June 29	Vickers VC10/Super VC10	54
	August 13	Hawker Siddeley 125	1,467*
1963	Jan 17	Short Skyvan	149
	August 20	BAC One-Eleven	244
1965	June 13	Britten-Norman Islander	1,155*
1967	August 18	Handley Page Jetstream	67
1969	April 9	BAC / Sud Aviation Concorde	20
1970	September 11	Britten-Norman Trislander	83
1974	August 22	Shorts SD 330	140
1980	March 28	BAe Jetstream 31	386
1981	June 1	Shorts SD 360	165
	September 3	BAe 146/Avro RJ/Avro RJX	394
1986	August 6	BAe ATP/Jetstream 61	65
1991	September 25	BAe Jetstream 41	104

* At the time of writing

Appendix 2

British Airliner prototypes featured still in existence

de Havilland Heron 1 prototype
G-ALZL dismantled at RAAF Association Aviation Heritage Museum of Western Australia at Bull Creek, Perth.

de Havilland Comet 4C first production
G-AOVU preserved at Seattle Museum of Flight, Paine Field, Everett, Washington USA

Bristol Britannia 101 second prototype
G-ALRX nose at Bristol Aero Collection Kemble, Gloucestershire

Fairey Rotodyne prototype
XE521 parts at the Helicopter Museum, Weston-super-Mare, Somerset.

Hawker Siddeley / BAe 125 prototypes & first production
G-ARYA HS 125 prototype nose stored DH Museum Aircraft Heritage Centre, London Colney, Hertfordshire
G-ARYB HS 125 prototype preserved partly complete Midland Air Museum, Coventry Airport, Warwickshire.
G-ARYC HS 125 first production - preserved DH Museum Aircraft Heritage Centre, London Colney, Hertfordshire
9Q-CBC (fomer G-BFAN) BAe 125-700 prototype in service Scibe Trading
N800RM (fomer G-BKTF) BAe 125-800 prototype in service Romeo Mike Aviation.
G-EXLR BAe 125-1000 prototype training aid Wichita, Kansas, USA.

BAC One-Eleven 475 prototype
G-ASYD preserved at Brooklands Museum, Weybridge, Surrey.

BAe Jetstream 31 prototype
G-JSSD preserved at National Museum of Scotland – East Fortune.

BAC / Aérospatiale Concorde - British prototypes
G-BSST Concorde 002 preserved Fleet Air Arm Museum, Yeovilton, Somerset.
G-AXDN Concorde 01 preserved Imperial War Museum, Duxford, Cambridgeshire.
G-BBDG Concorde 202 preserved Brooklands Museum, Weybridge, Surrey.

Short SD 330 prototype 2
G-BDBS preserved at Ulster Aviation Heritage, stored Lisburn, County Antrim.

BAe 146 / Avro RJ & Avro RJX prototypes & development aircraft
G-LUXE BAe 146-300 prototype in service Atmospheric Research Aircraft, Cranfield, Bedfordshire.
N501XJ (former G-ISEE) Avro RJ85 development aircraft stored Marana, Arizona, USA.
SE-DSO (former G-OIII) Avro RJ100 development aircraft in service with Transwede, Sweden.
VT-MDL (former G-BUFI) Avro RJ70 development aircraft in service with MDLR Airlines, India.
G-ORJX Avro RJX85 prototype stored BAE SYSTEMS Woodford, Greater Manchester.
G-IRJX Avro RJX100 prototype preserved Manchester Aviation Heritage, Manchester Airport.

BAe ATP prototype
G-PLXI (former G-MATP) derelict BAE SYSTEMS Woodford, Greater Manchester.

BAe Jetstream 41 prototypes
G-GCJL derelict Humberside Airport, Lincolnshire.
G-JMAC preserved Liverpool Airport, Merseyside.

Books

Avro since 1908 *A J Jackson* Putnam 1990
Avro *Harry Holmes* Airlife 1994
Avro 748 *Harry Holmes* Tempus 2000
Avro 748 *Richard Church* Air Britain 1986
BAC Three-Eleven *Graziano Freschi* Tempus 2006
BAe 146/Avro RJ Production List *Ken Haynes* 2007
BOAC *Charles Woodley* Tempus 2004
Bristol Aircraft since 1910 *C H Barnes* Putnam 1970
Bristol Britannia *David Littlefield* Halsgrove Press 1992
British Civil Aircraft Vols 1-3 *A J Jackson* Putnam 1987
British Flying Boats *Peter London* Sutton 2003
Britten Norman *George Marsh* Tempus 2000
Comet and Nimrod *Ray Williams* Tempus 2000
Concorde *Brian Trubshaw* Sutton 2002
De Havilland Aircraft *A J Jackson* Putnam 1978
De Havilland Comet *Philip Birtles* Ian Allan 1990
De Havilland Comet *Malcolm Painter* Air Britain 2002
Fairey since 1915 *H A Taylor* Putnam 1984
The Fairey Rotodyne *David Gibbings* RAeS Cierva
    Lecture 2003
Flight Testing to Win *Tony Blackman* Blackman
    Associates 2005
40 years at Farnborough *John Blake & Mike Hooks*
    Haynes 1990
From Bouncing Bomb to Concorde *Richard Gardner*
    Sutton 2006
The Handbook of the Vickers Viscount *St John Turner*
    Ian Allan 1968
Handley Page *Alan Dowsett* Tempus 1999
Handley Page Aircraft since 1907 *C H Barnes* Putnam
    1987
Handley Page Hastings and Hermes *Victor Brinham*
    GMS 1968
Handley Page Herald *G Cowell* Janes 1980
Hawker : The Story of the 125 *Bill Gunston* Airworthy
    Publications 1996
Hawker Siddeley Trident *Max Kingsley-Jones*
    Ian Allan 1993
Hendon to Farnborough SBAC Displays 1932-72
    Mike Hooks Tempus 1996
A History of the Short SC-7 Skyvan Merseyside Aviation
Society & Ulster Aviation Society 1975
Jet Airliners Production List TAHS 2004
Lion Rampant and Winged *Alan Robertson*
    Barassie 1986
Miles Aircraft since 1925 *Don Brown* Putnam 1970
Miles Aircraft *Rod Simpson* Tempus 1998
Percival & Hunting Aircraft *John Silvester*
    Nelson & Saunders1987
Pioneer of the Skies *Michael Done* Nicholson & Bass
    1987
Piston Airliners Production List TAHS 1996
Project Cancelled *Derek Wood* Tri-Armour Press 1990
The Quiet Test Pilot: the Story of Jimmy Orrell
    Peter Clegg Greater Manchester Museum of Science
    & Industry 1989

Saunders & Saro Aircraft *Peter London* Putnam 1988
Saro Princess Flying Boat Project *Bob Wealthy*
    Solent Maritime Enterprises 2003
Sent Flying *Bill Pegg* MacDonald 1959
Shorts Aircraft since 1900 *C H Barnes* Putnam 1989
Shorts - The Foreman Years *Guy Warner* Ulster Aviation
    Society 2008
Stuck on the Drawing Board *Richard Payne*
    Tempus 2004
Test Pilot *Brian Trubshaw* Sutton 2002
Triplane to Typhoon *J Longworth* Lancashire County
    Developments 2005
Turboprop airliners production list TAHS 2004
Vickers Aircraft since 1908 *CF Andrews & Eric Morgan*
    Putnam 1995
Westland Aircraft since 1915 *Derek James* Putnam 1991
Wrecks and Relics 14–20 *Ken Ellis* Midland Counties
    Publications

Brochures

Avro Tudor
Avro 748
BAC One-Eleven
BAe 125
BAe 146 / Avro RJ
BAe Jetstream 31/41
BAe ATP
Bristol Brabazon
Handley Page Bulletins
Handley Page Jetstream
Hawker Siddeley Bulletins
Hawker Siddeley 125
Shorts Skyvan, SD-330
Vickers Viscount
Vickers VC10

Magazines

Aeroplane
Aircraft Engineering
Air International
Air Pictorial
Flight International
Interavia

Index